MW01621084

CUBA

1959

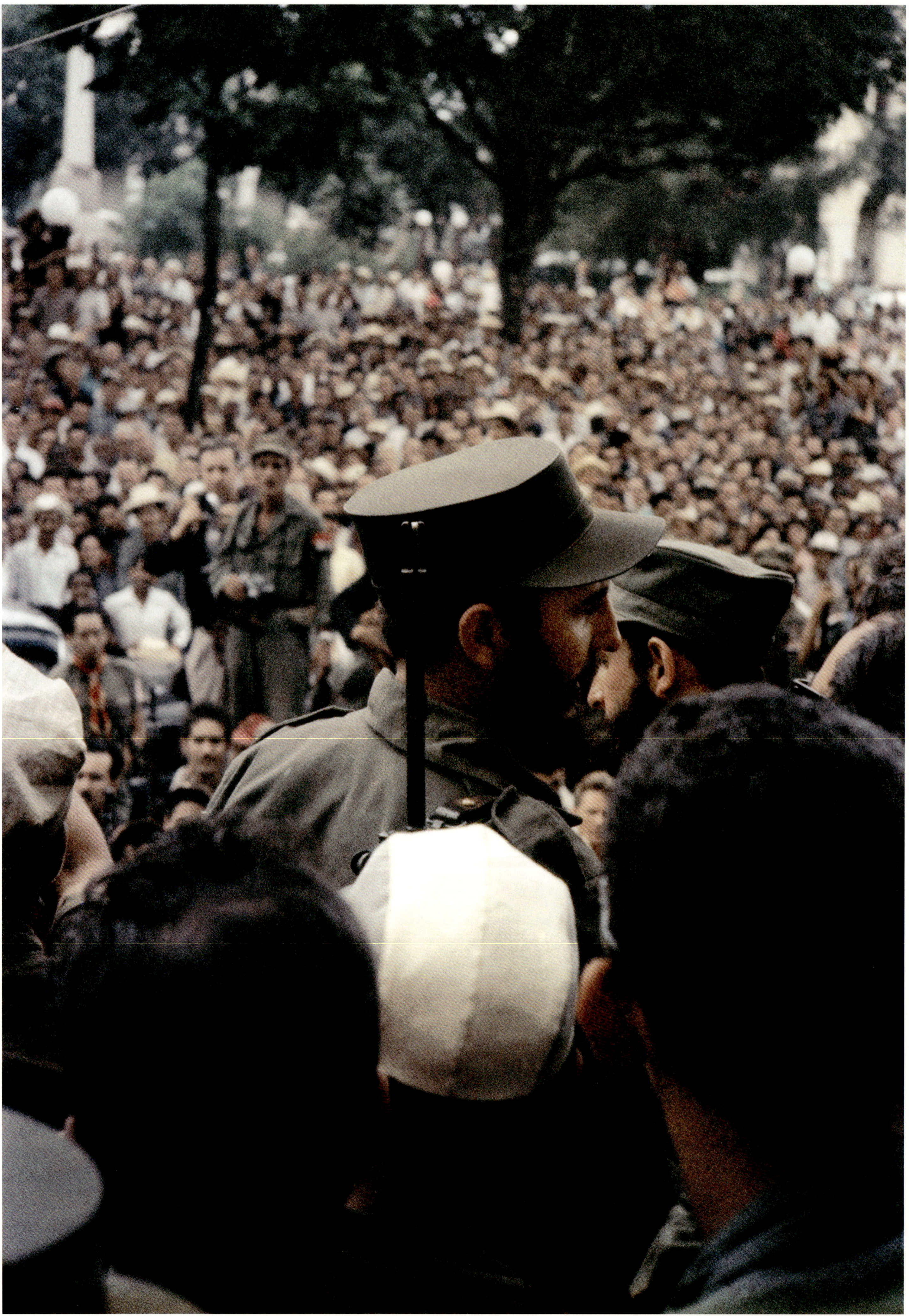

CUBA
1959

Burt Glinn

RAP

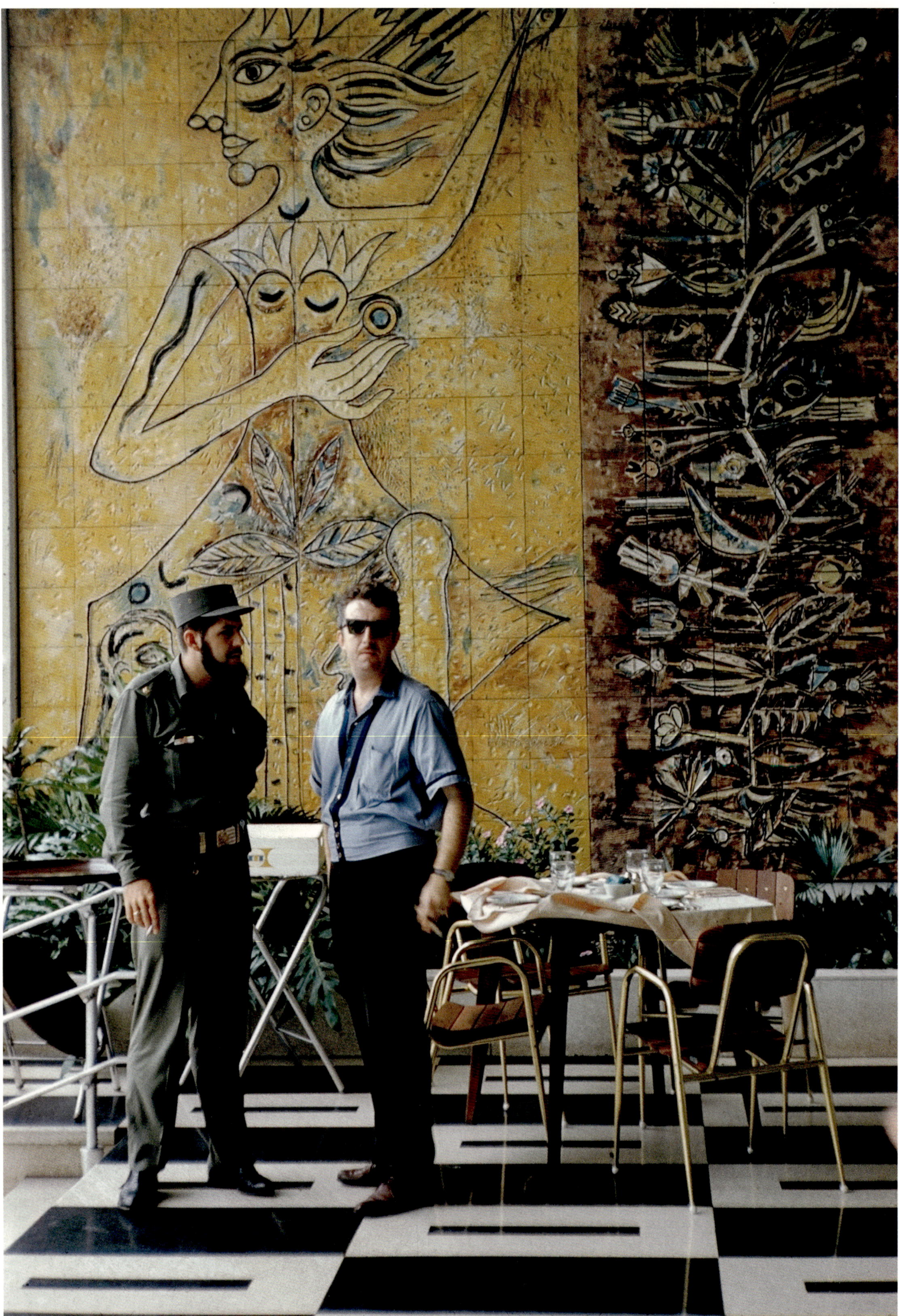

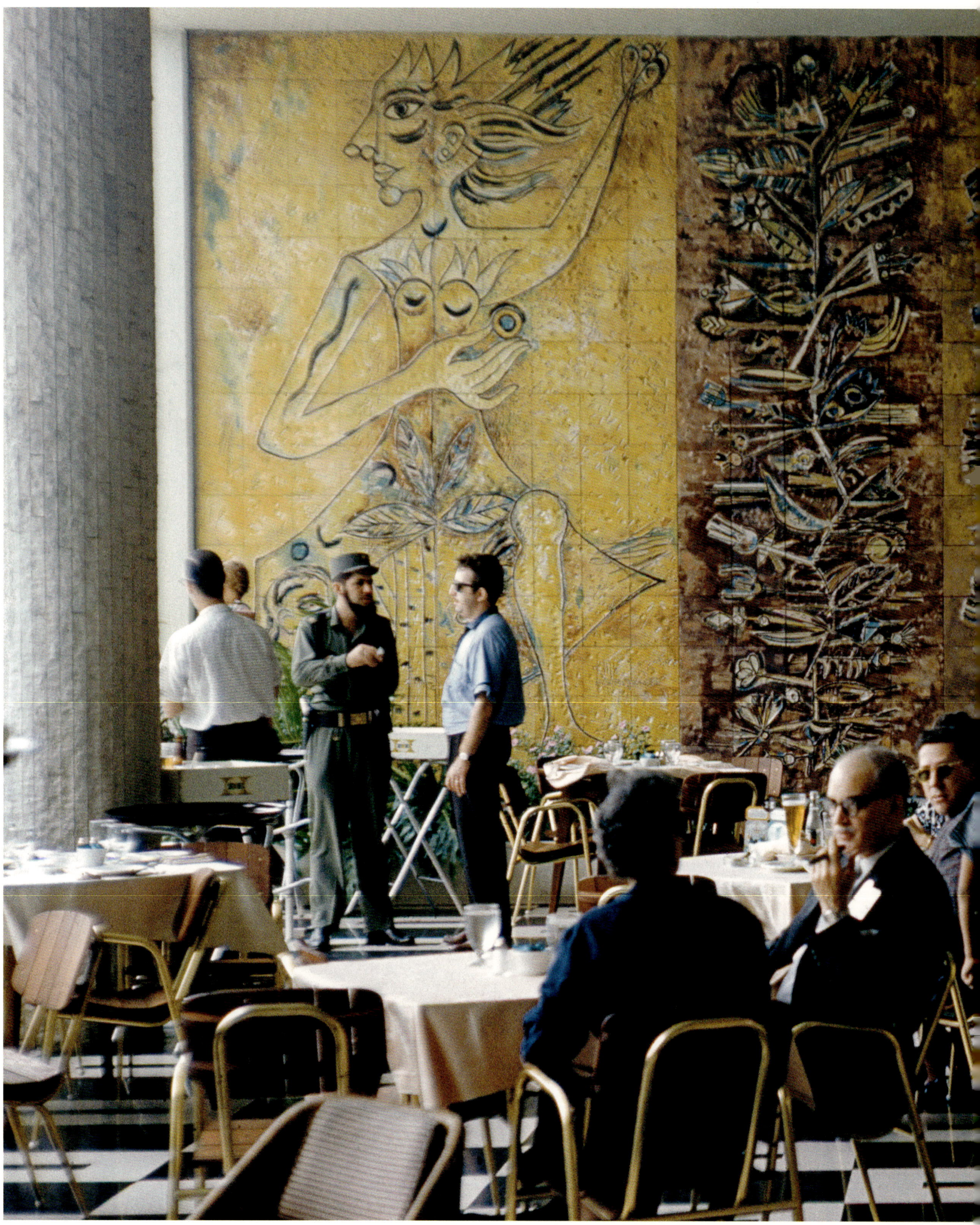

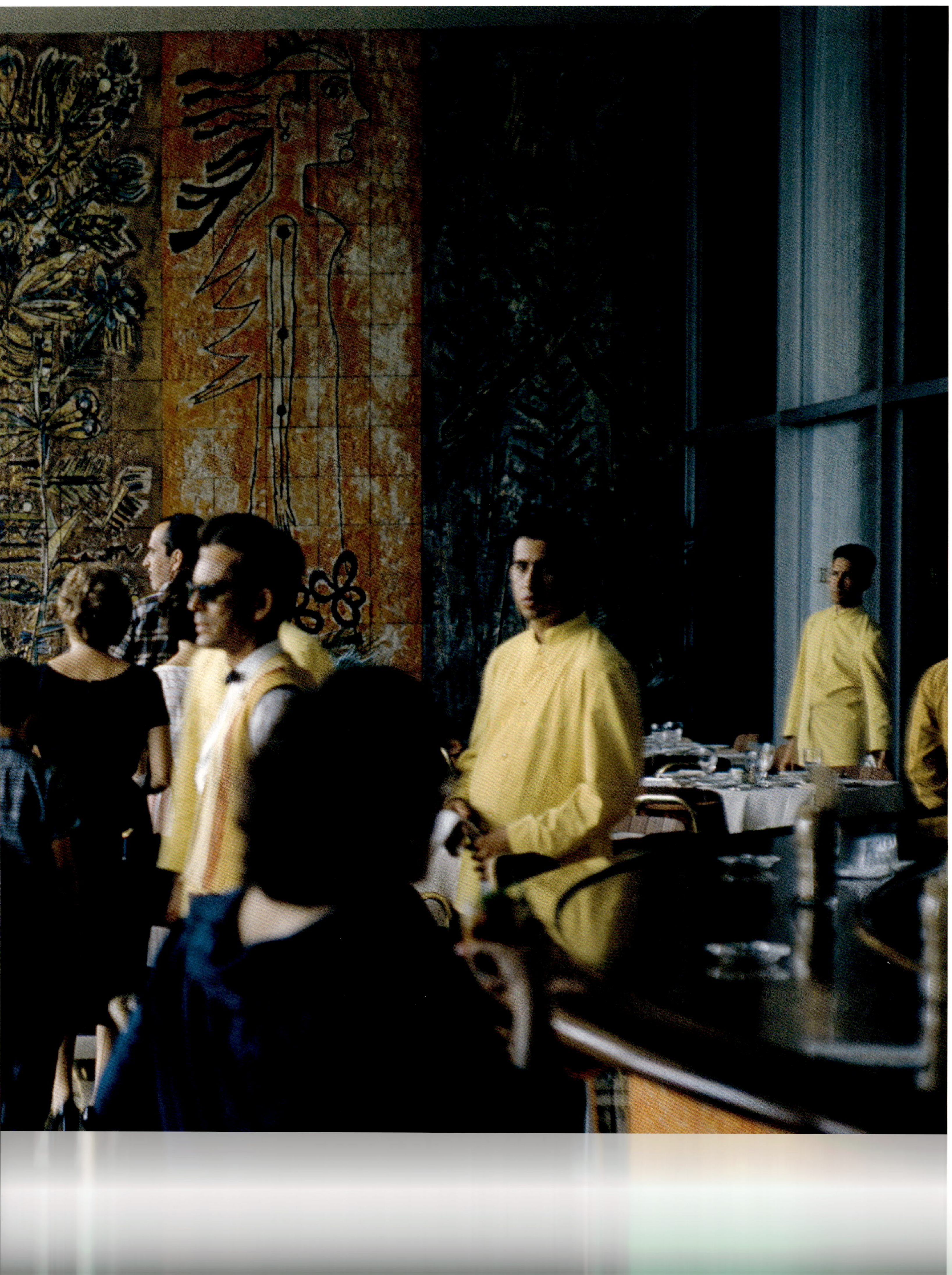

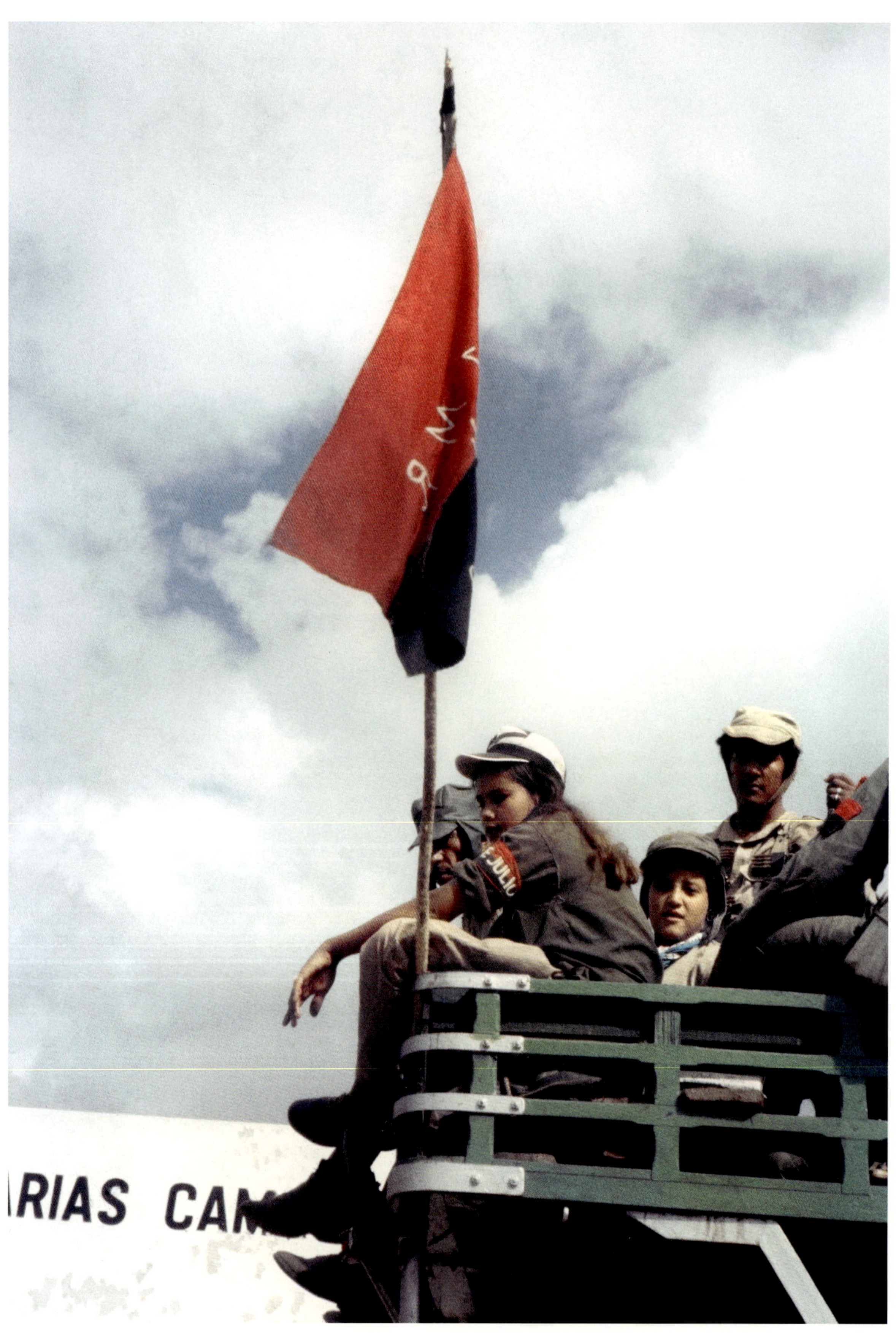

THE DAY HAVANA FELL

The last day of 1958 started promisingly enough. I was living in Manhattan, sharing an apartment with a friend who would turn out, to my surprise, to be legendary magazine editor Clay Felker. This arrangement afforded an excellent inside track on assignments from *Esquire* magazine and, since Clay was so much better connected, it did wonders for my social life, too. This New Year's Eve, Clay's network had gotten us, and two appropriately gorgeous young women, an invitation to a West Side party at Nick Pileggi's. Nick was a reporter at *The New York Times* then, and when we arrived much of the talk was of the Cuban dictator, Fulgencio Batista. The word was that, at that moment, he had backed his trucks up to the treasury in Havana and was on his way into exile. Now I was, and am, a photographer with Magnum Photos. Contrary to the romantic misconceptions about the job, I was not particularly brave. I really hated it when people I did not know began shooting at me. And I was not impetuous. I like travelling to the ends of the world taking pictures, but I like doing it on assignments when someone else has already agreed to cover my expenses and pay me a fee. This night everyone was on holiday and there was no time to get commitments. Under other circumstances, I would have had another drink and stayed at the party.

But this time, pride was involved. Fidel Castro had been an outlaw and rebel in the Sierra Maestra for a couple of years. If you made the right connections and did not mind sleeping on the ground, he was reachable by the press . . .

Without a second thought, I was off. I borrowed whatever money I could from Clay, cabbed home, changed clothes—a tuxedo, even from Morty Sills, my politically radical tailor, is not appropriate for a revolution—packed my cameras and called Cornell Capa, who was then president of Magnum. Cornell knocked on every door in his building and raised whatever cash he could for me. I arrived at LaGuardia Airport in time to make the last Yellow Bird to Miami, with my gear, an Air Travel Card, $400 in cash, and no idea what I was doing.

In those days there was a first come, first serve charter shuttle between Miami and Havana. But at 3 a.m. on New Year's morning, the Miami airport was deserted. There was no one at the other charter counter but there was a phone with a line to the pilot. After a lot of expletives from him about the hour, I explained that there was a revolution going on in Cuba and that I had to get there as soon as possible. He assured me that no matter what hotshot TV journalist came or how much money he offered, I would have the first seat to Havana at daybreak. And for all of twenty dollars I did.

By the time I arrived, it was past dawn in Havana. Batista had fled. Fidel was still hundreds of miles away, although nobody knew exactly where. Che Guevara was on his way to Havana and nobody seemed to be in charge. You just can't hail a taxi and ask the cabbie to take you to the revolution. Without any sleep, I checked into the Sevilla Biltmore in downtown Havana, which figured to be near the action, and I looked forward to a shower, a nap, and a quiet period cleaning the cameras and girding my loins. Not bloody likely. The moment I got to the room there was gunfire in the streets. It's not my favorite sound, but from the hotel window I spotted a couple of photographers running towards the firing. Cursing their industry, I grabbed my stuff and made for the street. Leaderless crowds were gathering, armed with whatever they had at hand: pistols, shot-guns, machetes—whatever. They raided the casino in the plaza hotel and some other office buildings where they suspected Batista sympathizers.

There did not seem to be much opposition, but there was a lot of firing. You could not tell who was shooting at whom. People appeared in the streets wearing "26 de Julio" (the name of Fidel's movement) armbands and helmets with "26" painted on them. On the first day, it was not clear who was a legitimate rebel and who was a summer patriot. I spent most of my time trying to figure out what was happening and mooching as much information as I could from the other journalists who were old Cuban hands.

The remnants of the government Batista left behind had named a provisional president, but it was obvious that this quickly patched-together arrangement would not work. From Santiago, where the rebels had taken control, Castro called a general strike to show the old guard who was really in charge. This may have been great for the Revolution, but it was bad news for the journalists. For the next five days, all the stores and restaurants were closed. So were the bars

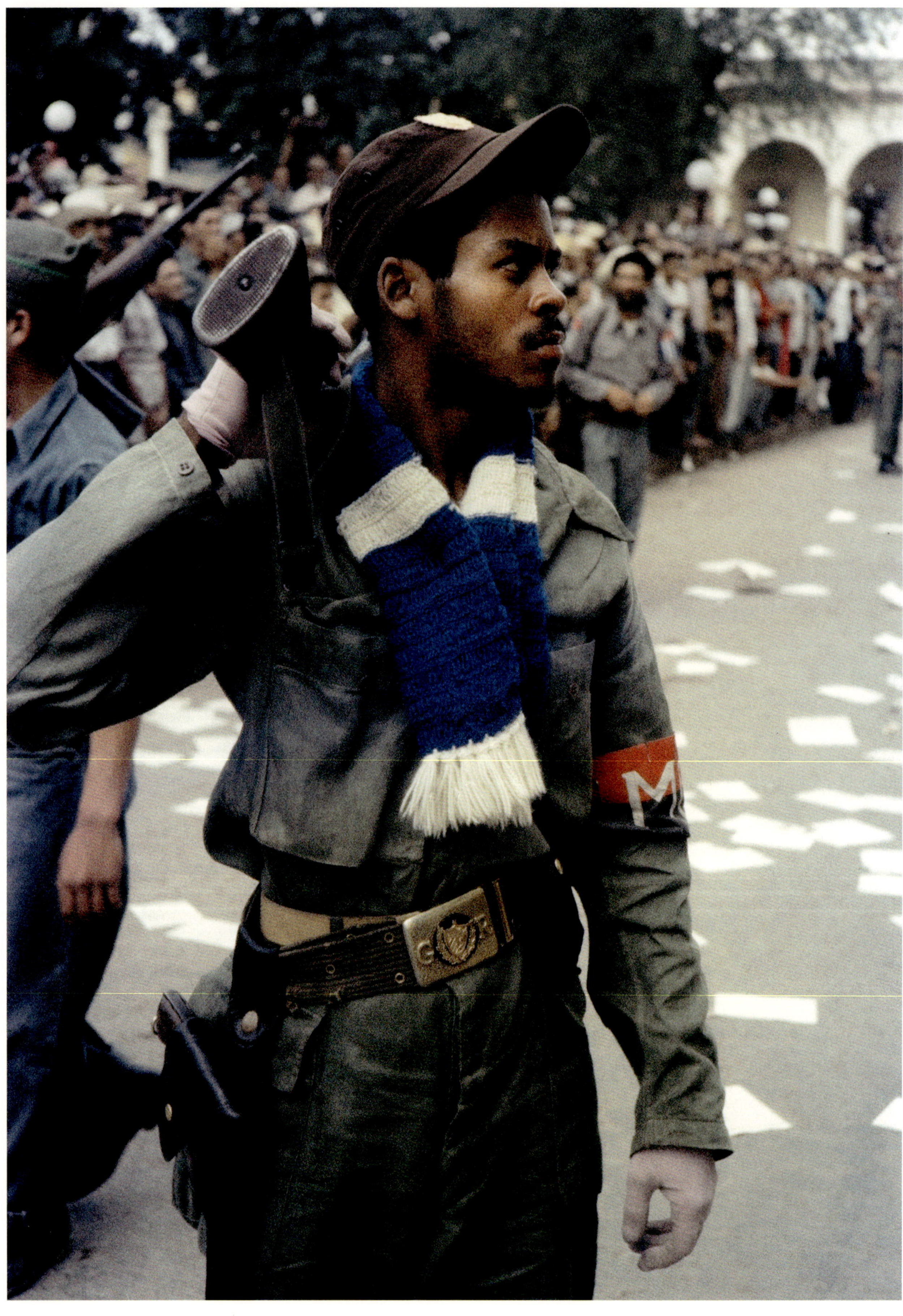

and groceries and liquor stores. Fortunately in Havana, no matter what, you can always find a cigar and a bottle of rum. That is primarily what kept us going.

By the second day, hungry, sleepless, and still confused, I found the police station where the rebels had rounded up Batista's secret police, at least the ones they could find. I photographed all of those newly terrified captives, classic cases of shoes on the other foot. By this time Che had arrived in Havana but was unavailable to us. Rebel general Camilo Cienfuegos was on his way, and the real barbudos, or bearded ones, had begun to come in from the hills. Castro sympathizers emerged from hiding and ecstatic reunions between mothers and sons and old friends were seen everywhere. The abrazo (embrace) was the gesture of the day. Crowds gathered and celebrated.

Everyone was calling for Fidel, but nobody knew where Fidel was. There was no press office; this was not a photo-op, it was a real revolution. The reality of where I was and what I was doing sunk in. I was exhilarated. I was in one of the great adventures in my life.

In the meantime, the *Life* magazine team—writers Jay Mallin and Jerry Hannifin and photographer Grey Villet—had organized their own transport and teamed with a Venezuelan photographer. At this distance, no one can remember his name, but everyone called him Caracas. I think he must have been a good photographer, but I know he was a hell of a quartermaster. He could always find something to eat . . . He kept us in enough chicken sandwiches to survive and enough rum and cigars to prevail. And it was Caracas who finally spotted Fidel on the road between Camagüey and Santa Clara.

After an all-night speech in Sancti Spíritus, the Castro group had dwindled momentarily to four cars, carrying Fidel, his aide Celia Sánchez, and an escort of about eleven bearded ones. We had made contact with Fidel but it was hard to keep track of him. He had started in the Sierra Maestra without any official vehicles but as he progressed from Santiago, Camagüey, Santa Clara, and Cienfuegos toward Havana, the column grew. Somehow the rebel entourage acquired tanks, trucks, buses, jeeps, cars, taxis, limousines, motorcycles and bikes.

Castro kept changing vehicles and we kept playing tag with him all the way, trying to spot him in the column on the road. As the caravan traversed the countryside, it would roar through towns where people lined the streets, cheering.

At Santa Clara, about 180 miles from Havana, the momentum really grew. The column arrived in a disorganized frenzy. Nobody knew which car Castro was in but they were delirious. Santa Clara had been the site of the one big battle of the Revolution, and when Che Guevara took the city it was a signal to the army that it was finished, and Batista fled. Although the city was already in rebel hands, Castro's arrival was greeted like the liberation of Paris.

In Cienfuegos he started speaking at 11 p.m. and went on until two in the morning. He involved his listeners, asking them for advice on how to run the country. He climbed down from the platform into the crowd and discussed farming methods with them and exchanged jokes about the deposed Batista. It was an incredible demonstration of two-way faith. Considering the situation, his entourage was worried about an attempt on his life, but Castro was fearless. Fidel spouted no Marxist jargon in those days. He made contact with the people all along the route from the mountains to Havana. Sometimes he would stop to buy gas for the column. He would sip a beer or a coke and ask the attendants for directions along the road. He talked with nuns, with middle-class matrons, with children. None of the conversations were political. The euphoria was incredible and permeated the whole country.

How sad to think of what has become of that moment. Che may have been right, but I wonder what would have happened if we had made an all-out effort with Fidel. Certainly anyone on this mystical magic tour to Havana would have known better than to believe the exiles' theories about Castro's unpopularity that two years later became the foundation for the US-financed invasion now known as the Bay of Pigs.

After leaving Cienfuegos, the route became so unruly that we lost Fidel until we caught up with him on the entry to Havana. By now the crowds were so tumultuous and the ranks of the marchers so swollen that it was impossible to differentiate the procession from the audience. Arriving in Havana, the crush along the seaside Malecón was so great that I lost my shoes while struggling to get my pictures.

We neither slept nor ate regularly nor bathed on the nine-day trip to Havana. But those were great days. I did learn then that a good cigar can be life sustaining. But I also remember the wild hopes and the ominous portents that filled those few brief days. I only wished in all these years since then that Fidel had done the Cuban people better and that we had been smarter.

I think I would trade all of these, my favorite pictures, and all of the great cigars I have had from Cuba, if we could do it all over again. Only better this time.

Burt Glinn, 2001

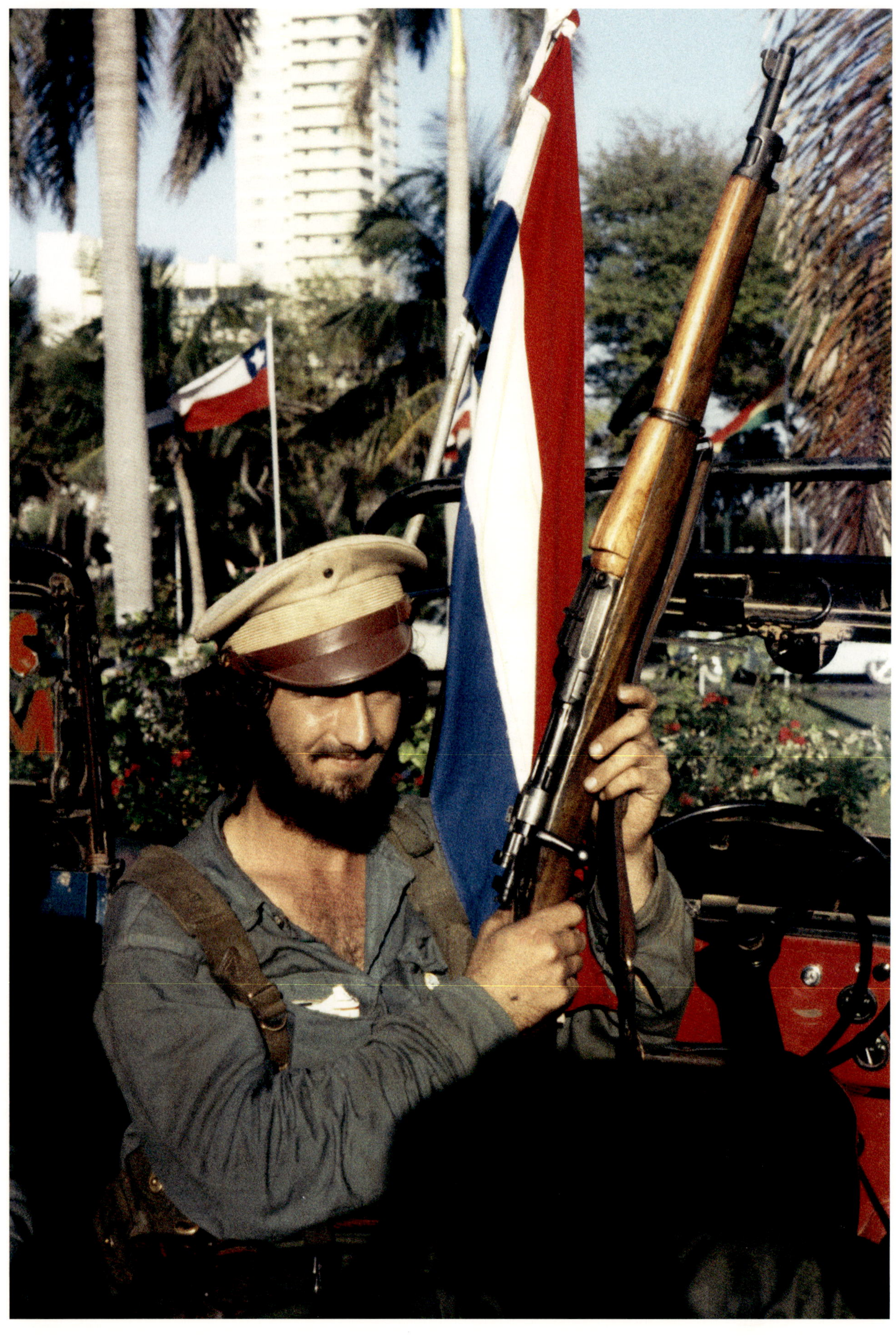

REBEL VICTORY IN CUBA

Just over three years ago on December 2, 1956, an exiled law student with eighty-one companions-in-crusade made a clandestine landing on the south beaches of Oriente Province in Cuba. Within a matter of hours, the eighty-one had been reduced to twelve, by the combined air, sea and land forces of Fulgencio Batista's strong-arm government.

The twelve, led by Fidel Castro the law student, fled to the shelter of the wild Sierra Maestra mountains to teach themselves guerilla warfare, to collect men and arms for their cause—the overthrow of Batista whom off and on since 1933 had dominated Cuba, an island of 6.5 million peoples and a yearly income of more than two billion dollars from sugar, cattle, tobacco, minerals and tourists.

It took Castro three long hard years, but on January 8, 1959, a twenty-one-gun salute heralded his triumphant entry into Havana at the head of an armored column, part of the 8,500 men and women partisans who had joined his 26th of July Movement. Of these, about three thousand were trained guerilla fighters, trained by the experience of fighting with pistols, home-made grenades and their wits against the tanks, jet planes and mortars of the government forces. But the Movement had the strongest armament that exists—the will to free their country from a man who ruled by terror and suppression. Every time that Batista's brutal police tortured or shot, each time they arrested students or jailed citizens without trial, Castro won a victory in recruits and arms. And three weeks ago, even Batista's loyal forty-six thousand-man army was surrendering its garrisons in the heart of the island to the Castro forces as they pushed forward on their campaign across the 750-mile-long island. So, by the time Castro took the main city in the provinces, Santiago, he had tanks and armored cars, as well as several captured planes. On his victorious march into Havana, he was preceded by his hard-won armed might. Overhead, the planes dipped their wings in salute. Around him were his partisans, ragged, still wearing the rough beards which, like their chief, they had sworn not to shave off until Havana was theirs. Delirious crowds wept with emotion, embraced the soldiers, waved the rebel colors, red and black.

Actually, Castro's victory was already nine days old when he arrived in Havana. Dictator Batista, his family and his henchmen had fled in droves on New Year's Eve. Happily for them, their life-in-exile would not be financially difficult. Their reign in the small but wealthy island had brought them riches. Some received it from deals with the gambling casinos in the luxurious hotels, others from Batista-bestowed import privileges, others from dipping their hands into the leaky government treasury. Even lesser army officers managed to rake in a profit by demanding "protection" money from American-owned and managed factories and plants.

The rebellion against this graft and its patron Batista cost Cuba over $100 million, and the lives of eight thousand of its people. At the time of the victory, business in most parts of the island was at a complete standstill.

The Nicaro mines, source of eleven percent of the world's nickel, were closed down. So was the Bacardi Rum's main plant, for the first time since 1862. In many parts of the

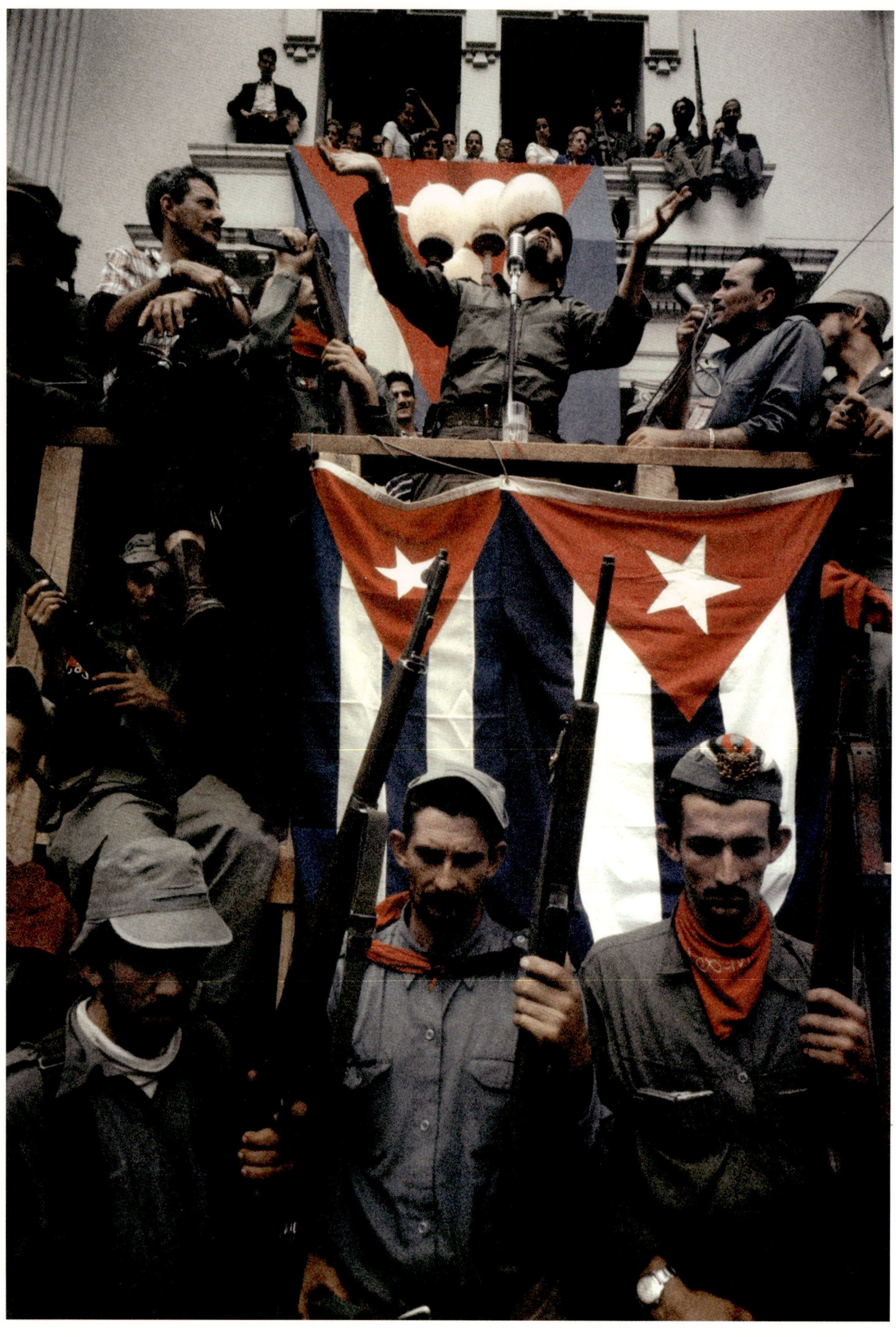

island, townsmen were forced to use horse-drawn wagons because there was no gasoline. And if the island economic life-blood is to be saved, quick work and organization will be needed to harvest the six million ton sugar crop which supplies the USA with a third of its needs. Railway transport is non-existent, owing to the dynamiting of bridges. Central Highway, the main road running the length of the island is pitted with craters, a result of the home-made grenades and bombs of the rebels. Telephone and telegraph lines have been destroyed, the poles carried off by the rebels. In Havana, where a fifth of all Cubans live, there are iron shutters on the shop windows, restaurants and hotels for fear of looters who raided the city after Batista's flight. Once the dictator had lost control of his police and army, the Habaneros went wild. Typical of the fury of the crowd were the broken gambling machines ripped out of American run casinos, and the smashed parking meters recently installed by Batista.

Doctor Manuel Urrutia, President-Designate of Fidel Castro (too young under Cuban law to serve as President) flew in from his exile in New York to form a provisional government, and promptly banned gambling and cockfights; organized the harvesting of the sugar crops; took steps to stop the flight of Batista-government funds out of Cuba; and started war crime trials against the more than thirteen hundred suspected collaborators of the Batista regime in the Havana area. Already some forty followers are reported executed.

And so Cuba entered the ranks of the four other Latin American countries who have chased out their dictators in the past four years.

The triumphant rebel chief, Fidel Castro, took his time in coming to Havana, interpreted as a deep disdain for this center of intrigue and gambling wealth. He declared Santiago in Oriente Province the provisional capital until Urrutia took office in Havana. Then he started his 500-mile-long march of love through the heart of his land, riding in a jeep, guarded by four bearded ragged stalwarts, and cheered deliriously at each town by thousands, many of whom wait through the night to see their hero. There was no schedule. People never knew when Castro would show up. Thousands stood along the road for thirty-six and forty-eight hours just for a glimpse of him. He strode through the people with amazing energy and deep contact with them. He joked, he talked, he planned Cuba's future with them, keeping going for twenty hours at a stretch. His speeches lasted three and four hours, and the people loved it, even at four in the morning.

As yet the Movement has no political credo. It was plotted in yachts carrying rebel arms off the coast, in elegant Havana clubs, in the rugged mountains of eastern Cuba, in the offices of leading Cuban lawyers, and amongst the Havana University students who have been locked out of their classrooms by Batista. The only motive needed was the strong hatred of him and his ilk.

For the American, both government authorities and businessmen who own large parts of the sugar and other industries in Cuba, the big question is: what is the rebel's attitude toward the USA?

Barbara Miller, 1960

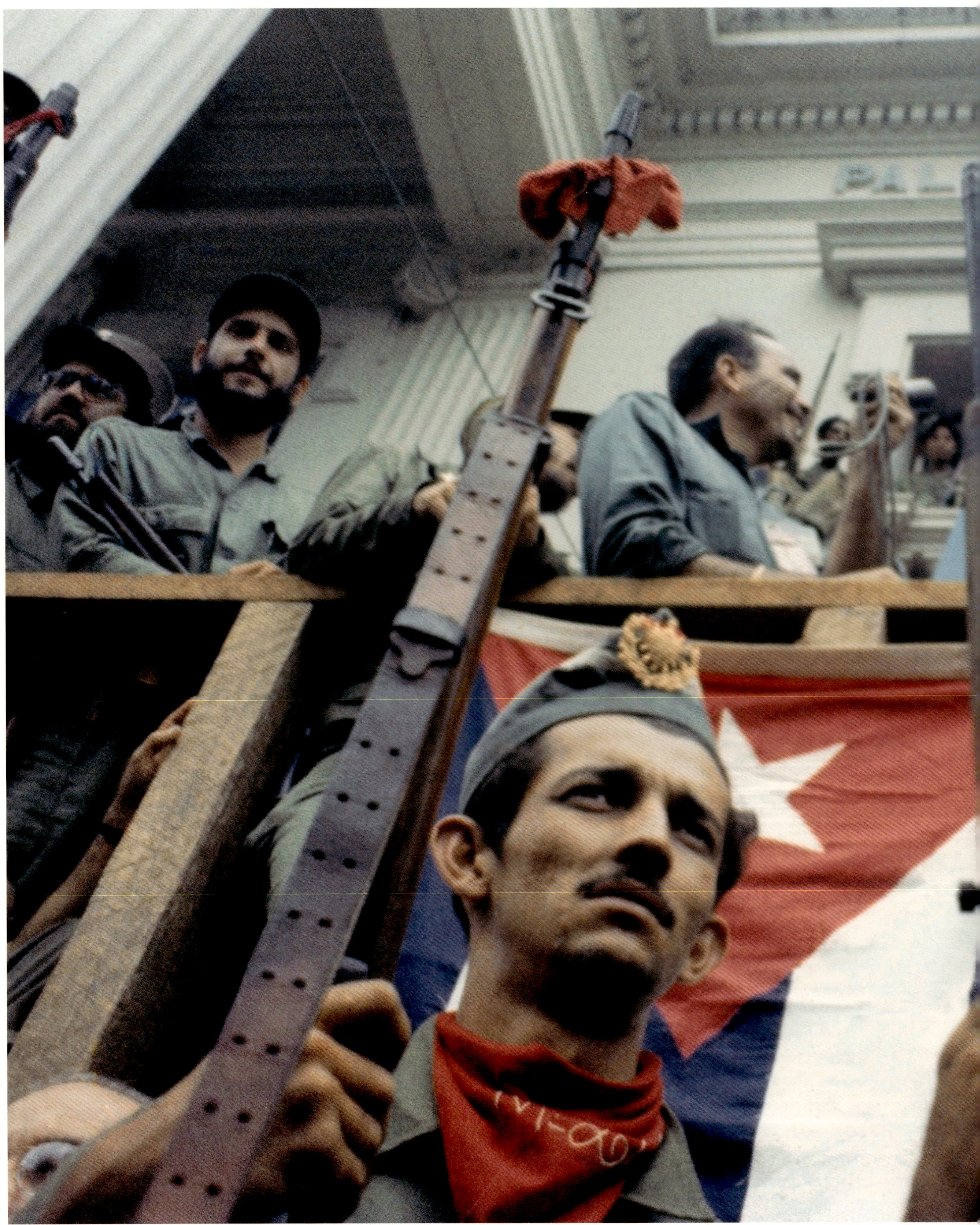

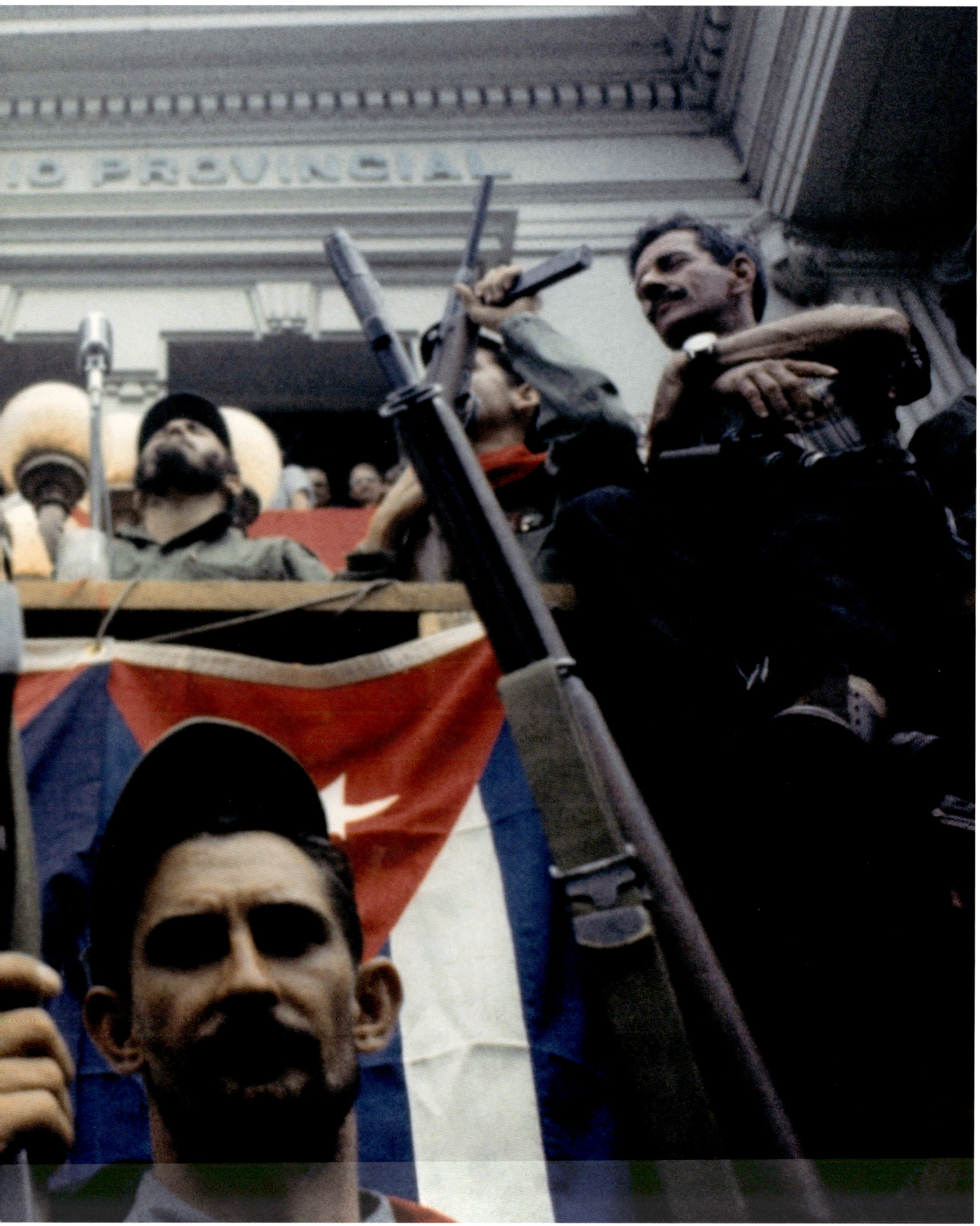
PROVINCIAL

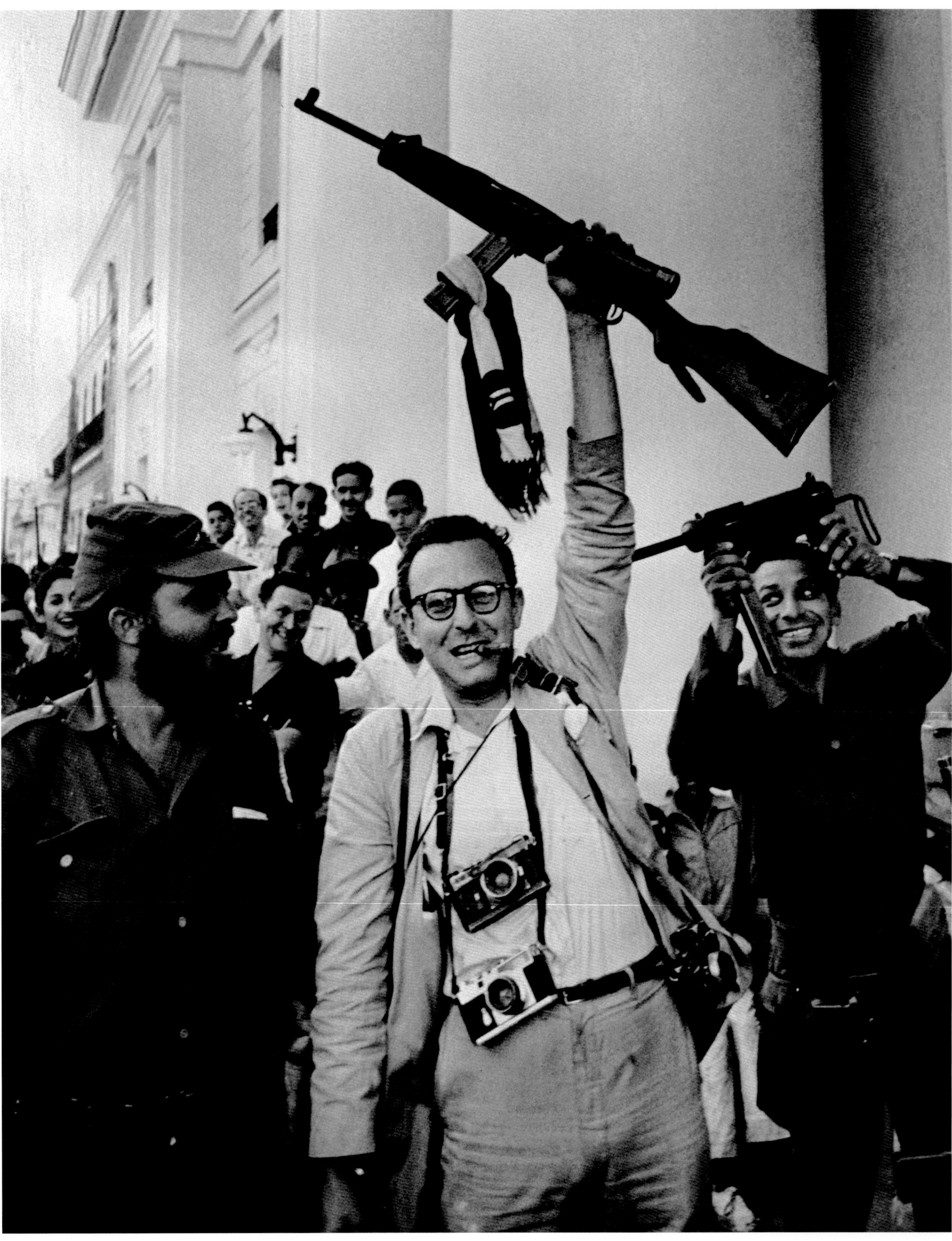

CUBA

January 1–10, 1959

At 11 p.m. on December 31, 1958, I decided to fly to Cuba. At daybreak, I was sharing the streets of Havana with hundreds of delirious Cubans. Within four days, I had found Fidel, and by January 10 this project was completed.

Burt Glinn

Havana Airport, January 1, 1959, 7 a.m.

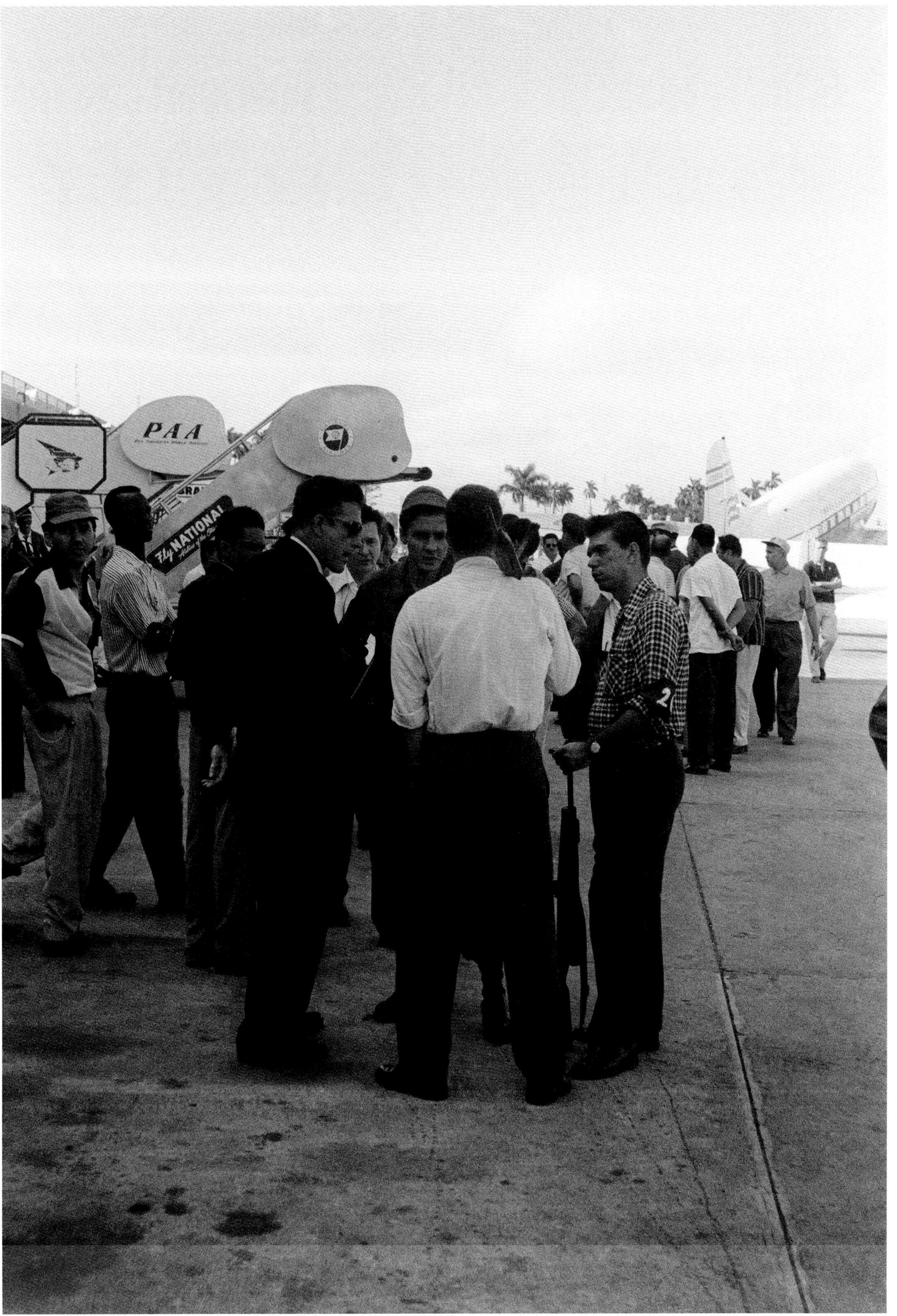
PAA
Fly NATIONAL

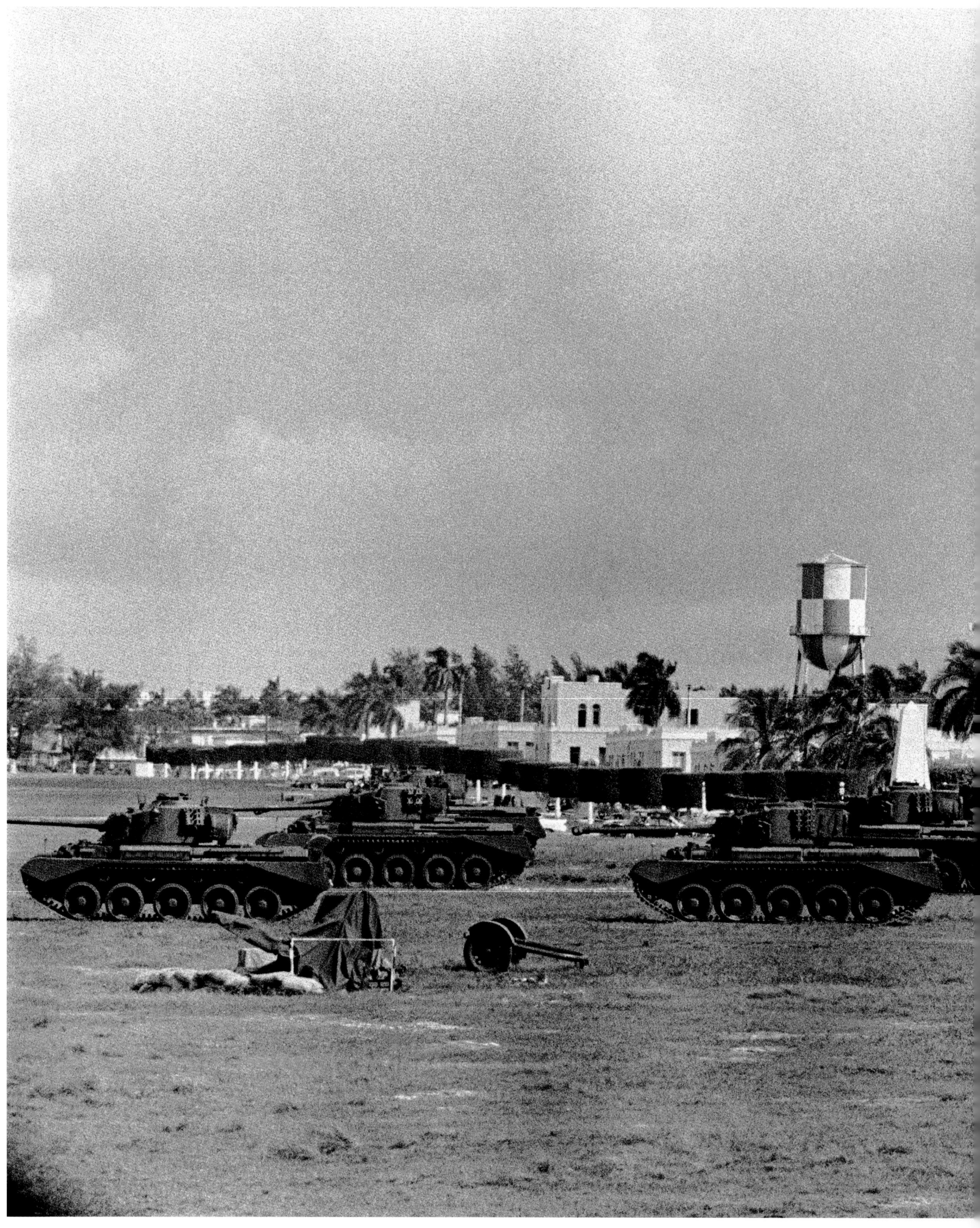

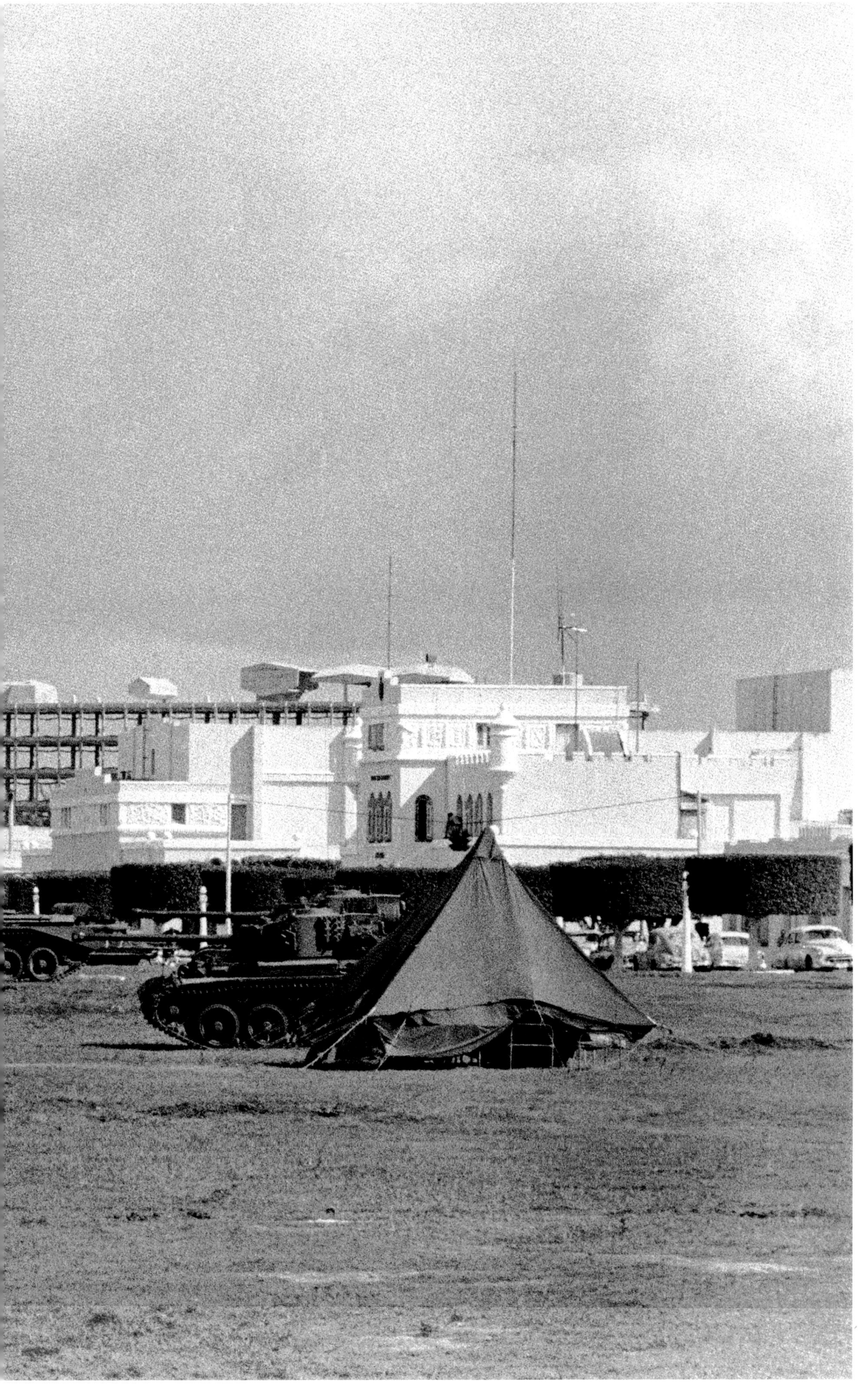

There is a lot of gunfire in the streets although I see only two people hit. I am not sure whether they are hit by friendly fire or opposing fire.

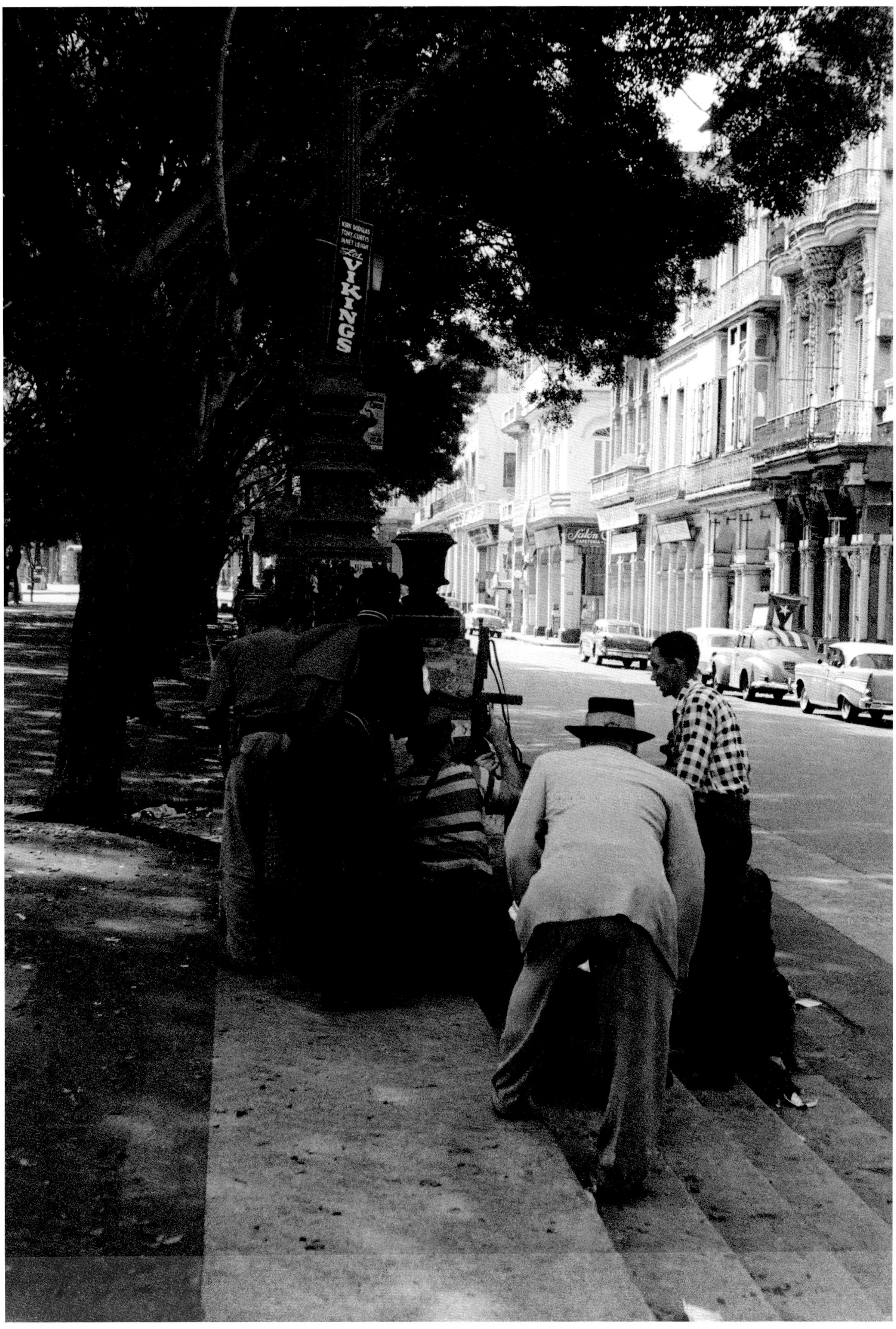
KIRK DOUGLAS
TONY CURTIS
JANET LEIGH
Los
VIKINGS

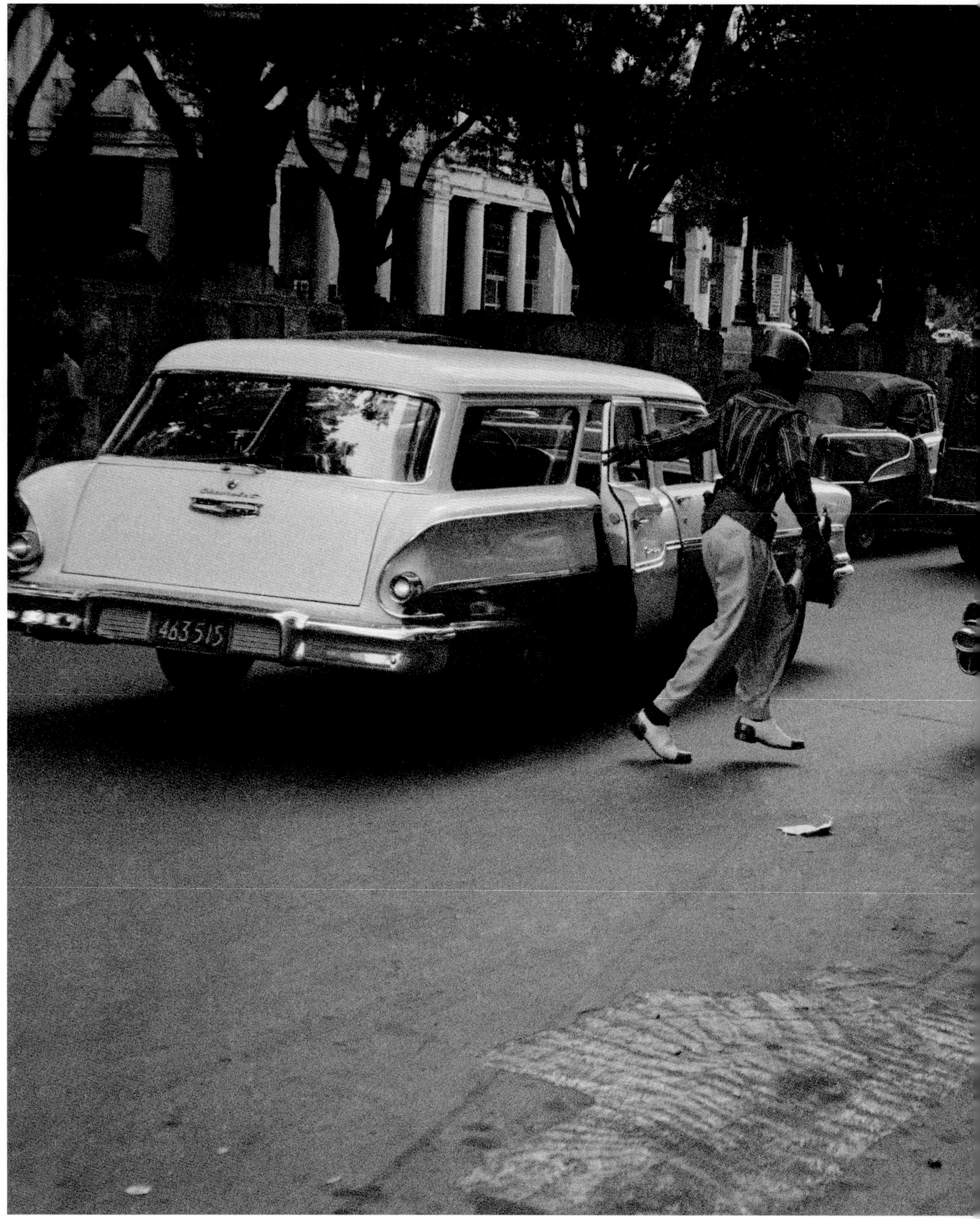
463515

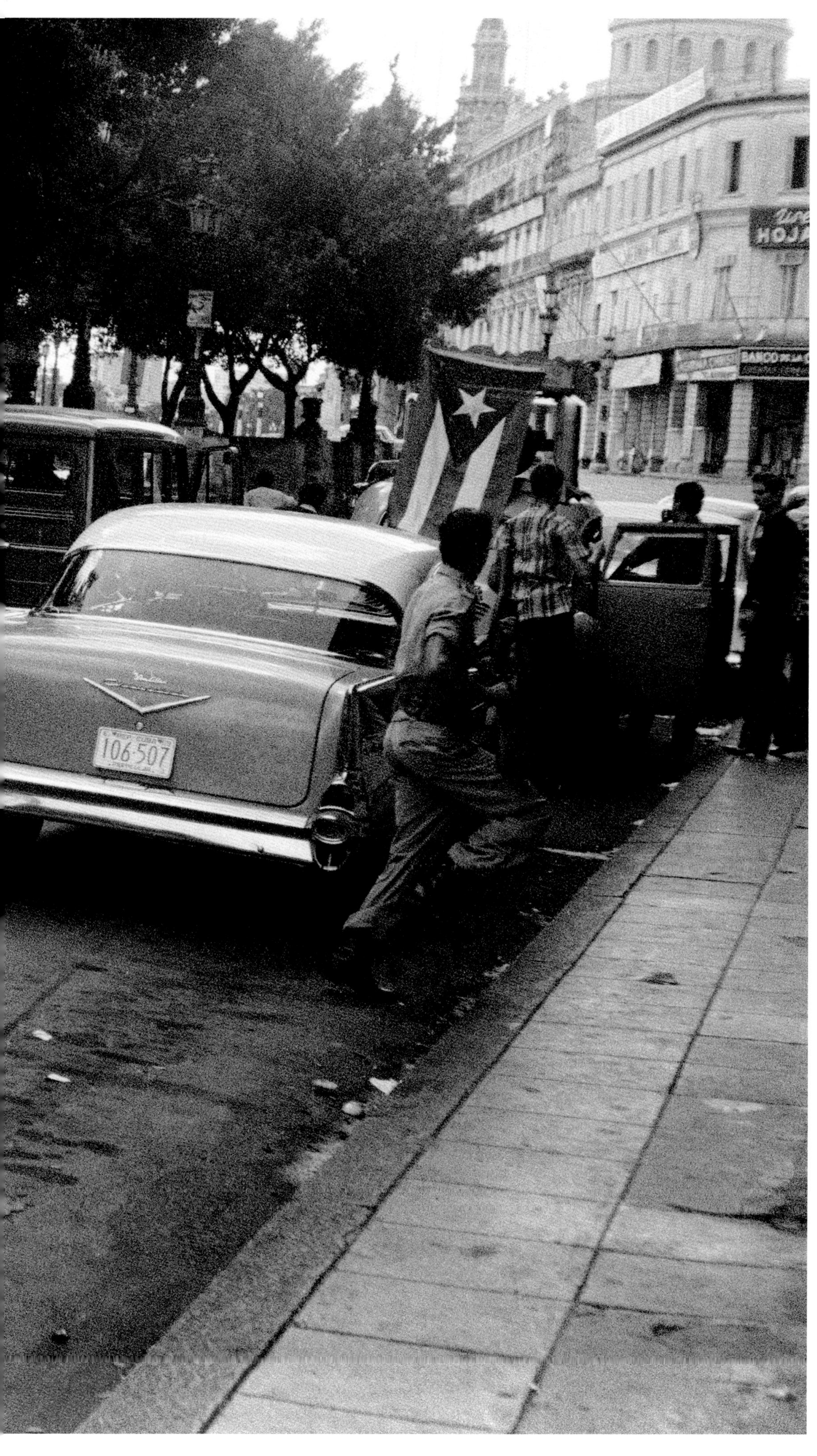
106·507

Castro sympathizers take to the streets with small arms. There is firing between rebels and Batista men. Early reports indicate as many as fifty people killed in such encounters. Tensions run high.

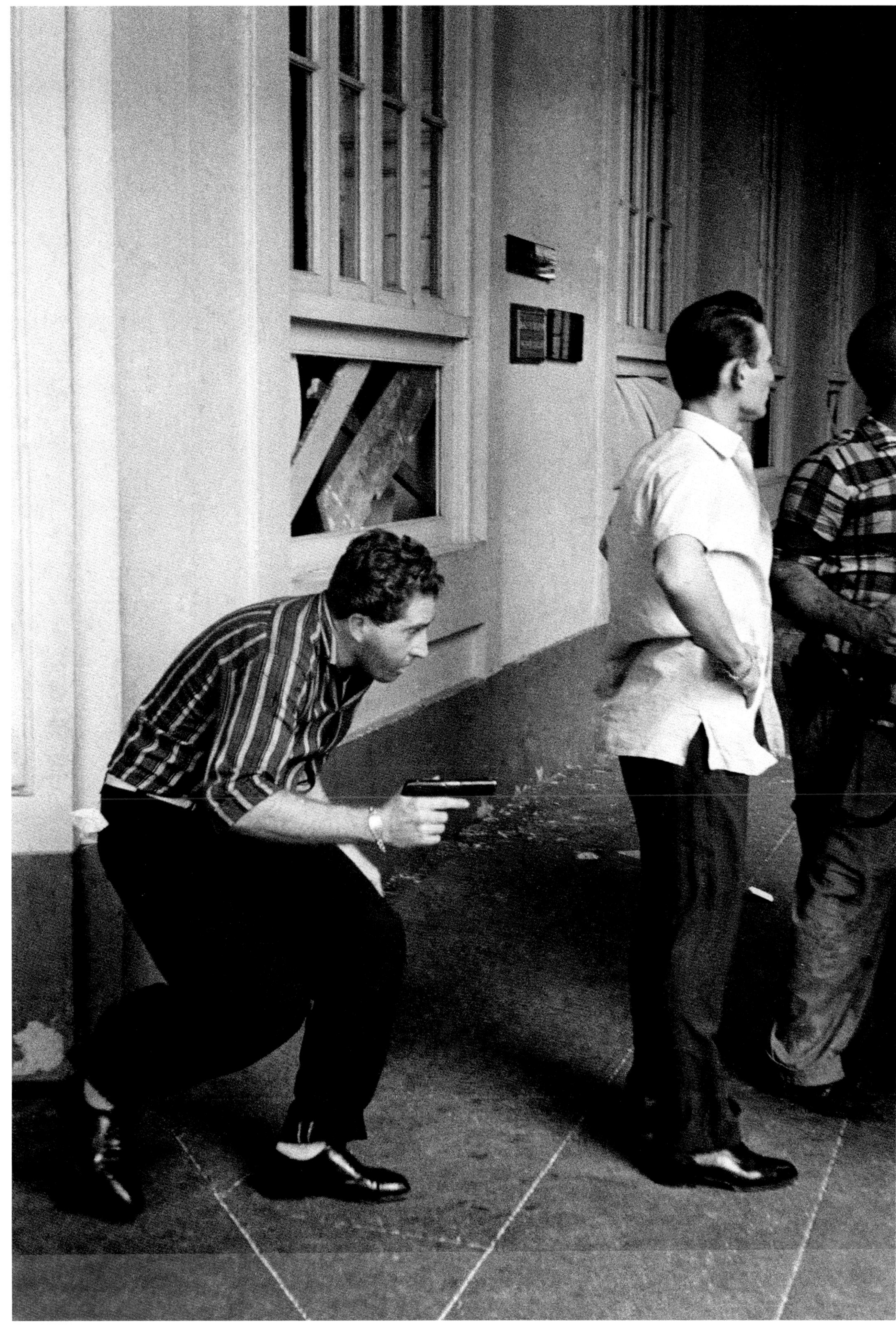

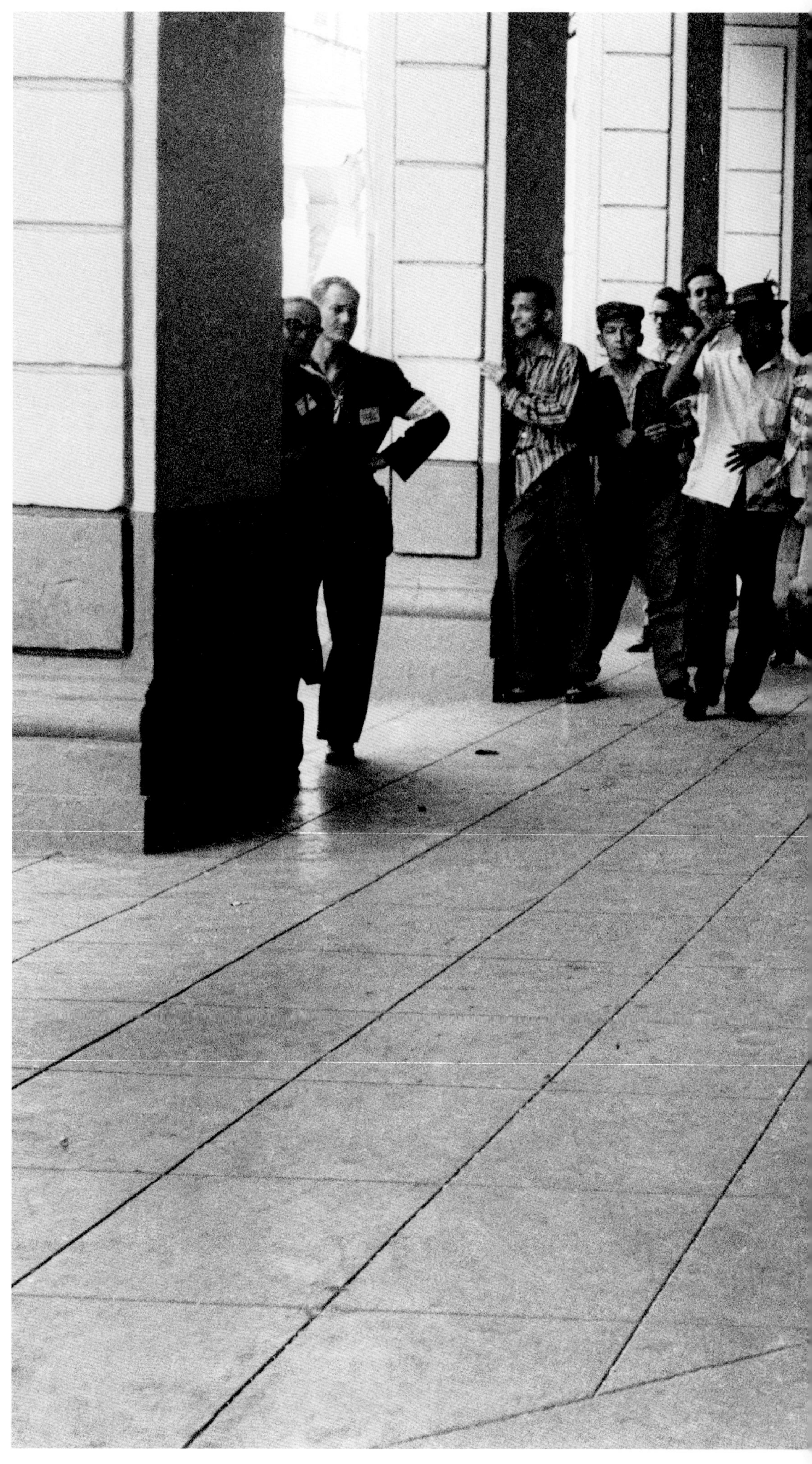

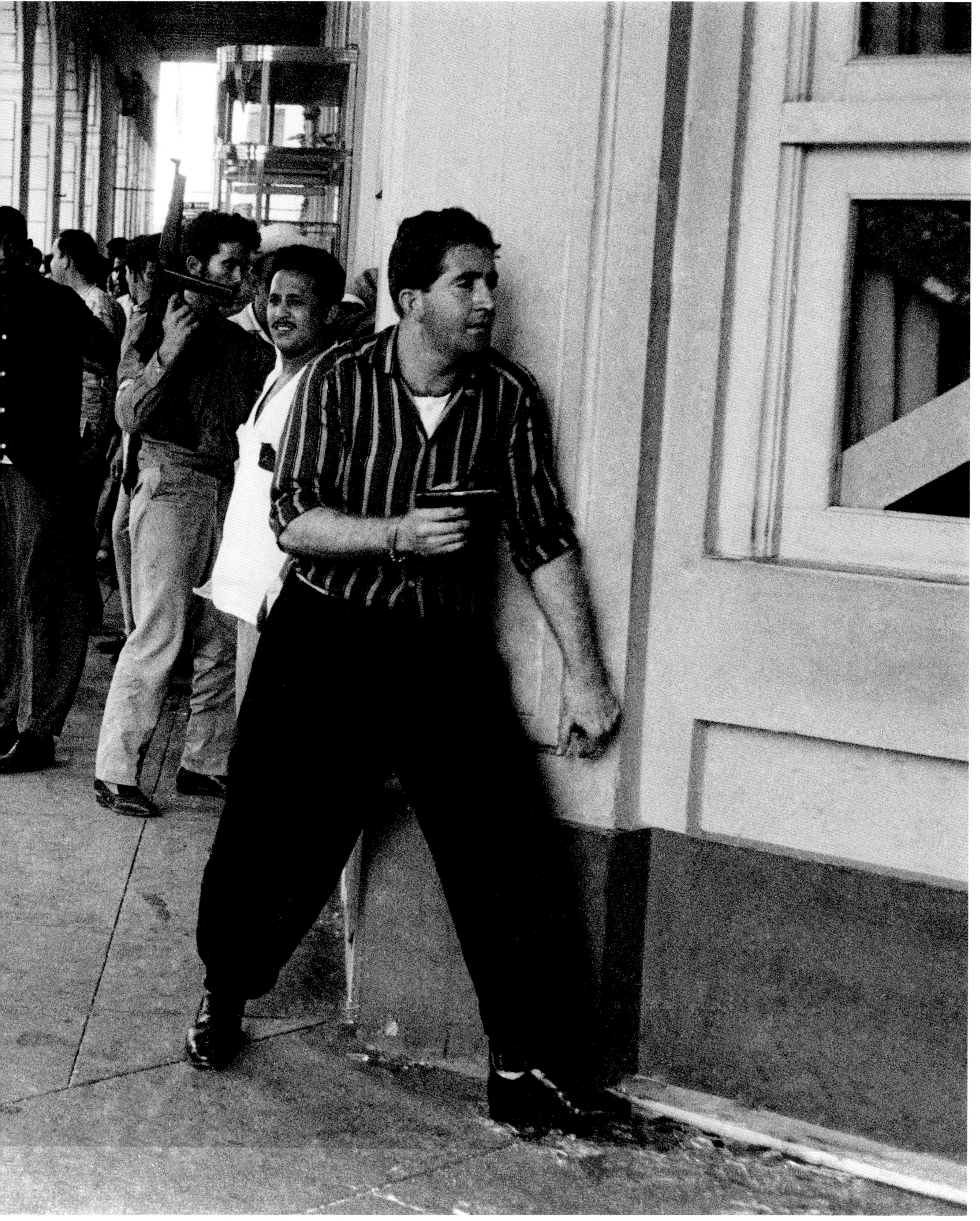

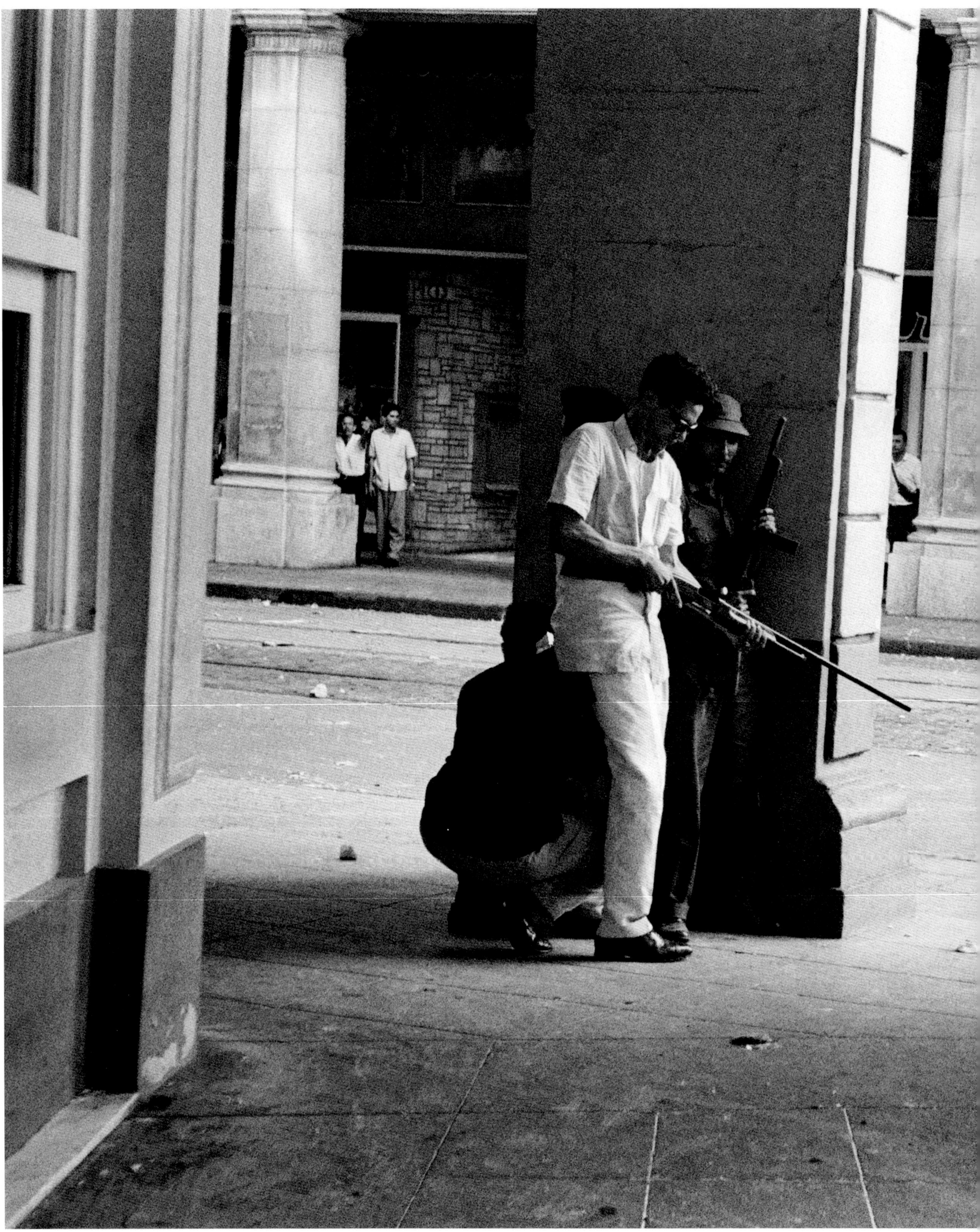

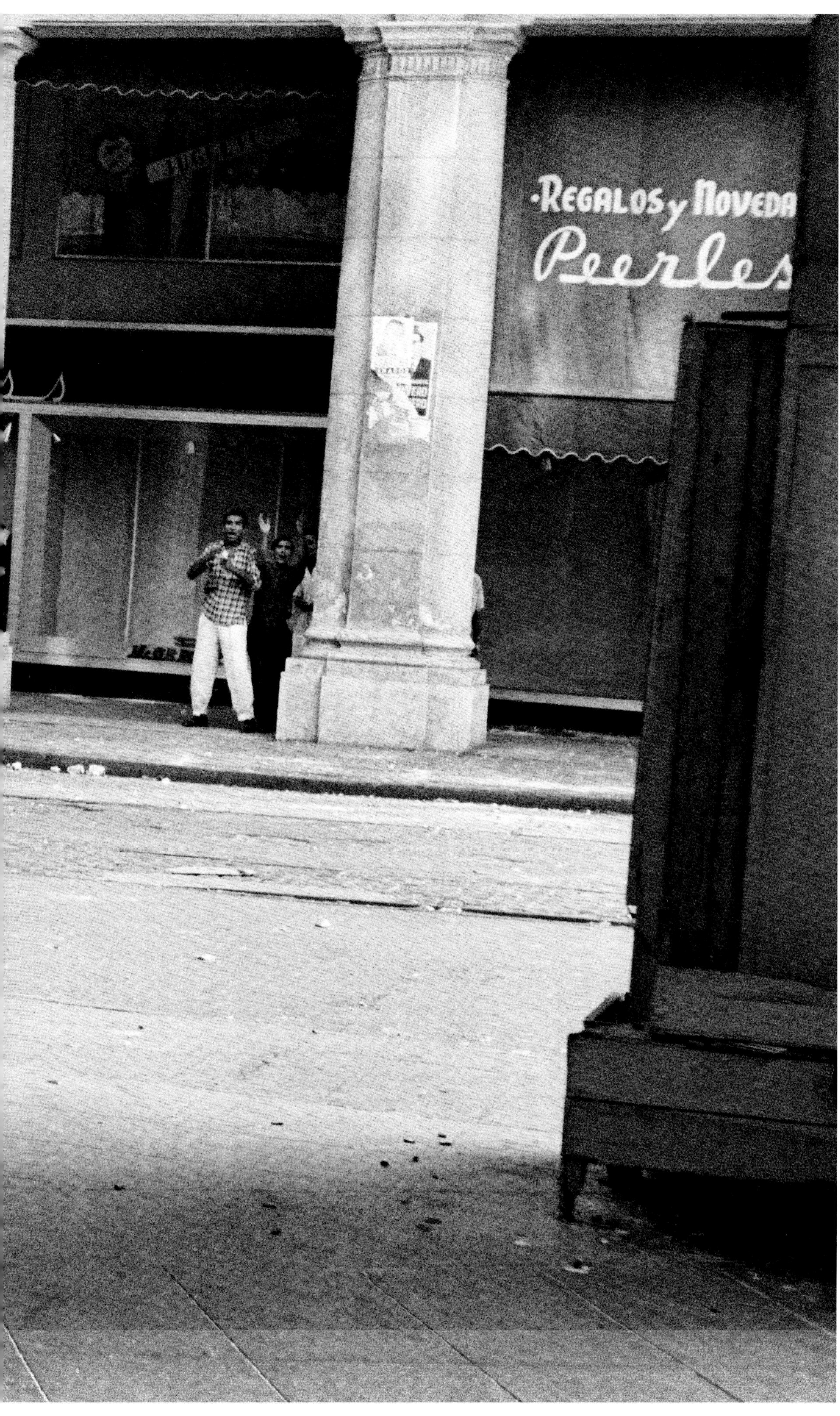
·REGALOS y NOVEDA
Peerles

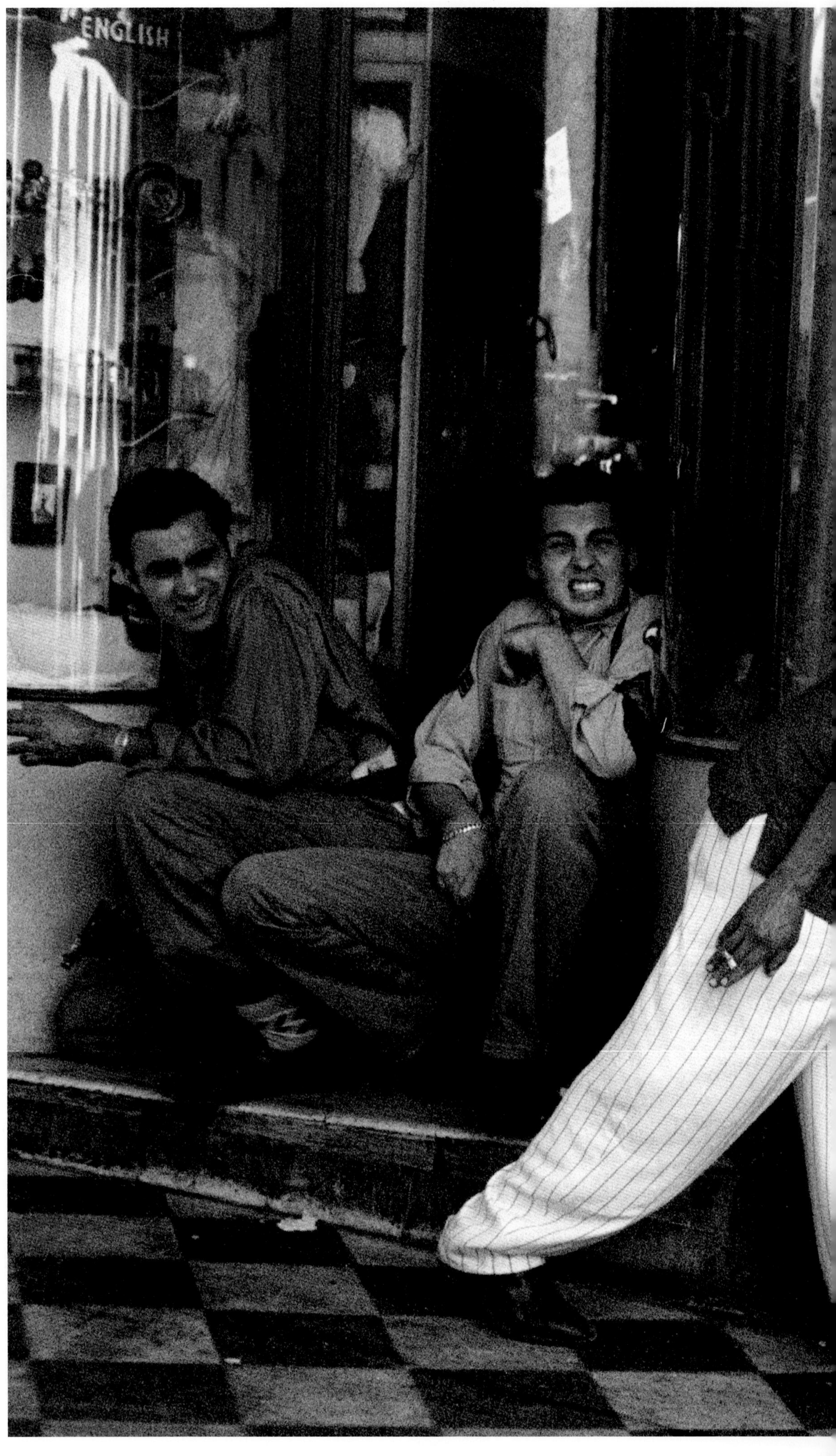
ENGLISH

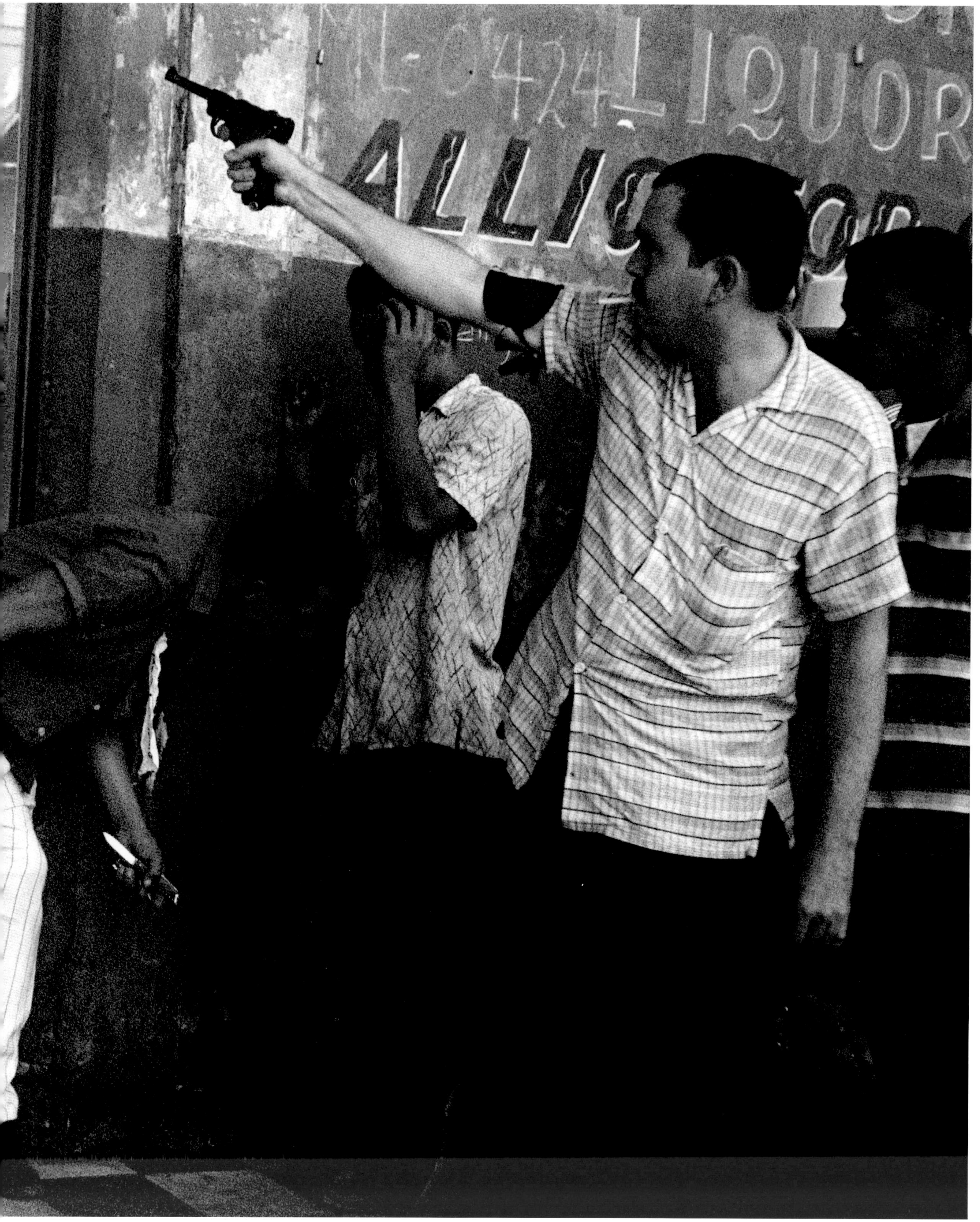
ML-0424 LIQUOR

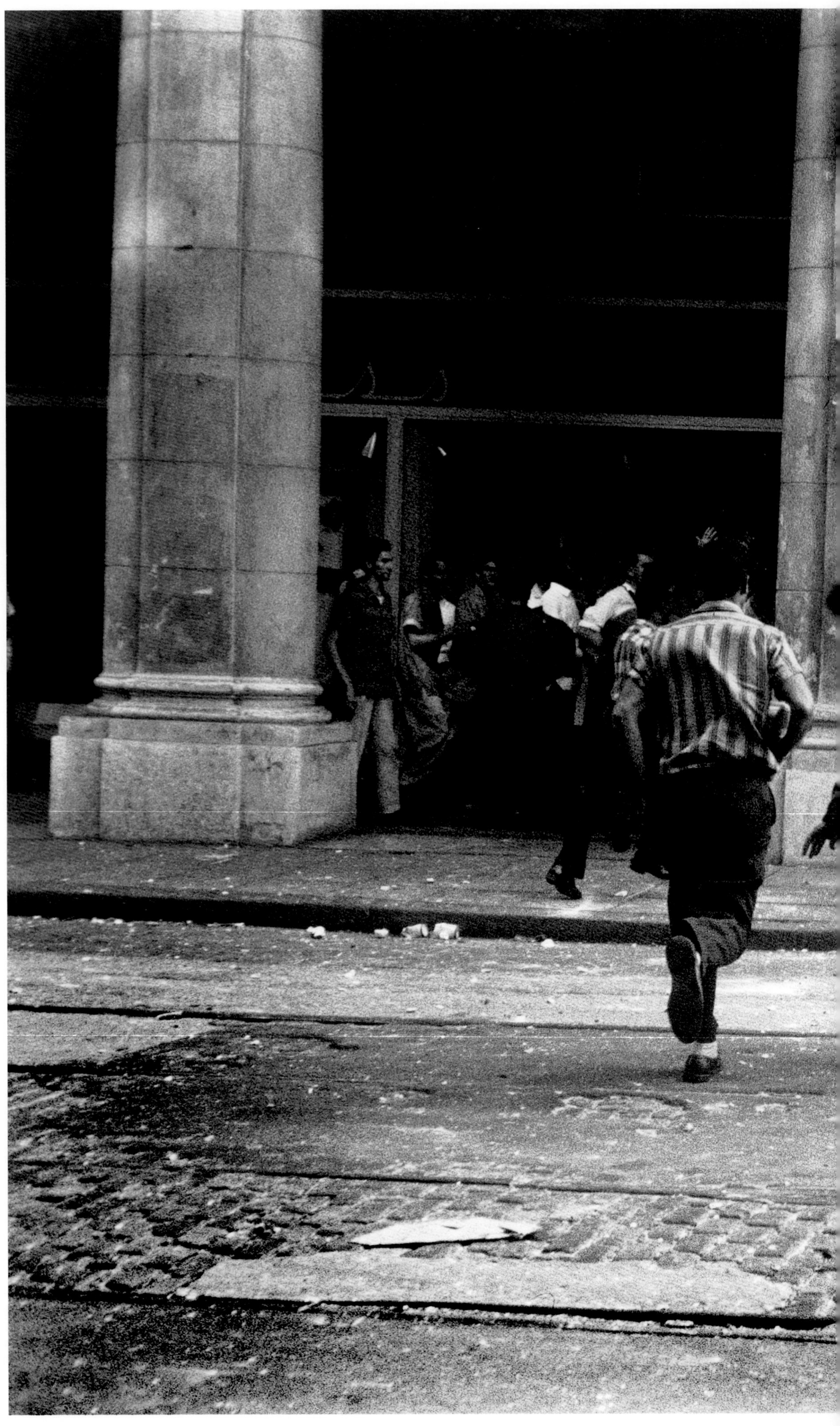

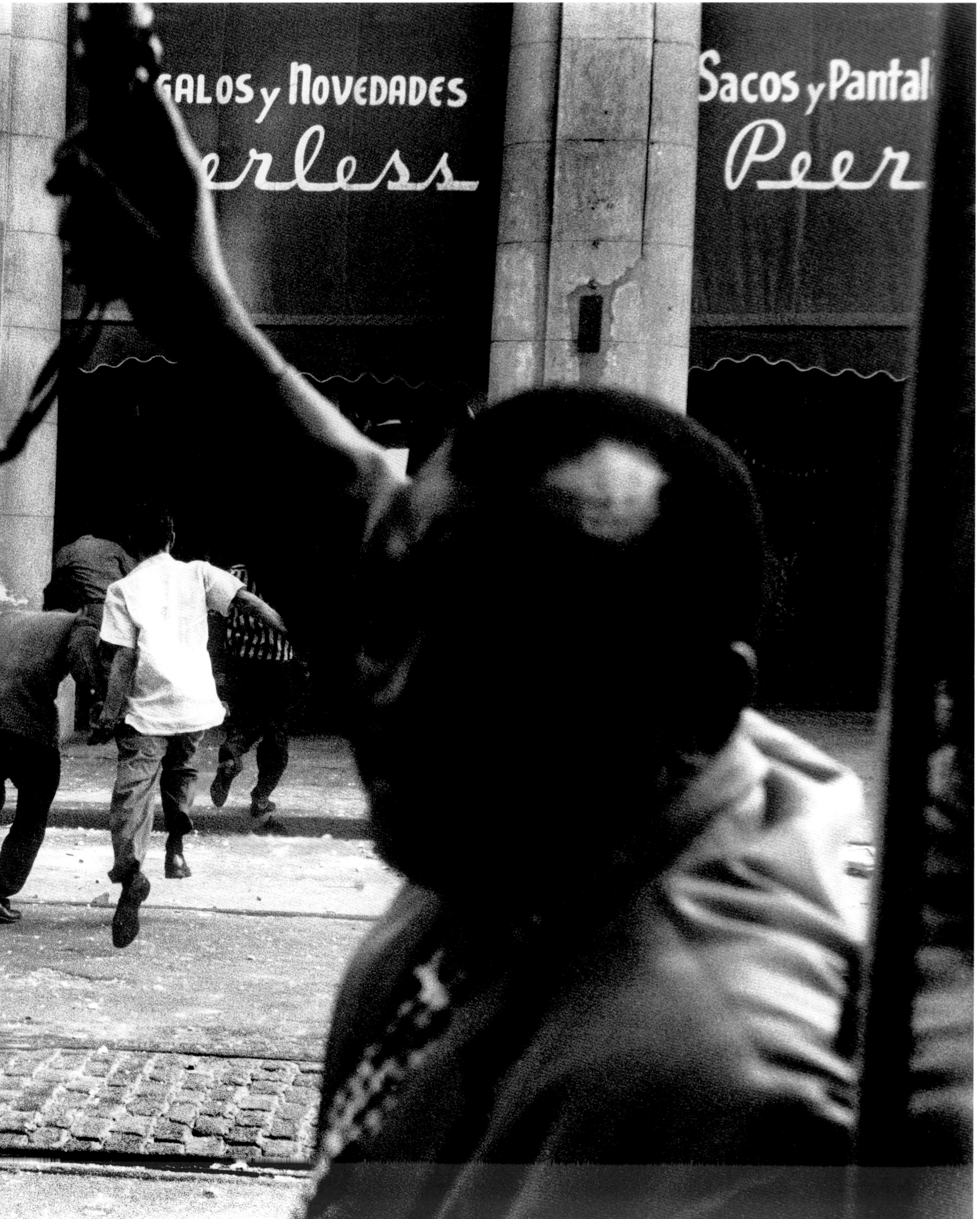
GALOS y NOVEDADES
erless
Sacos y Pantal
Peer

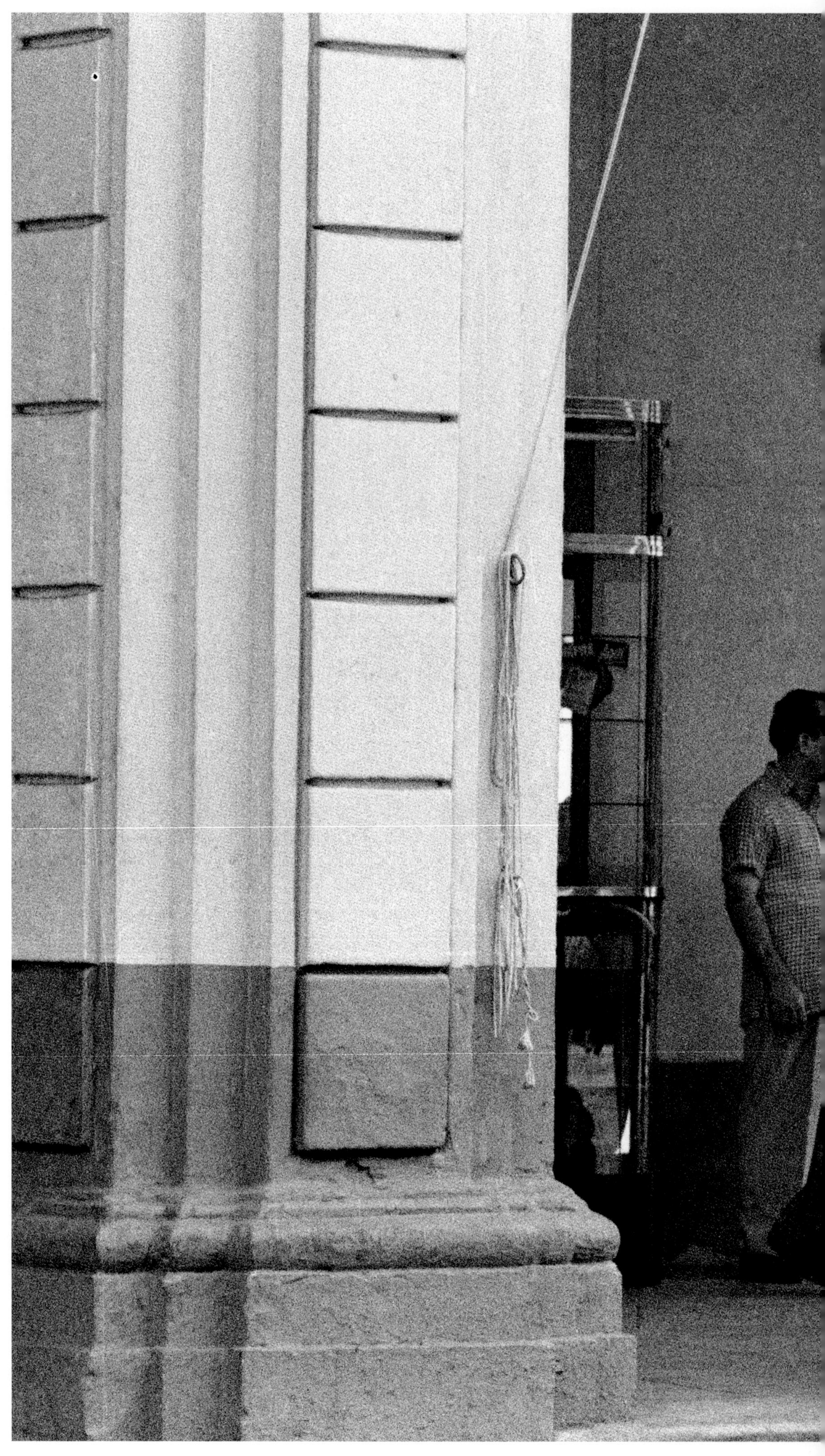

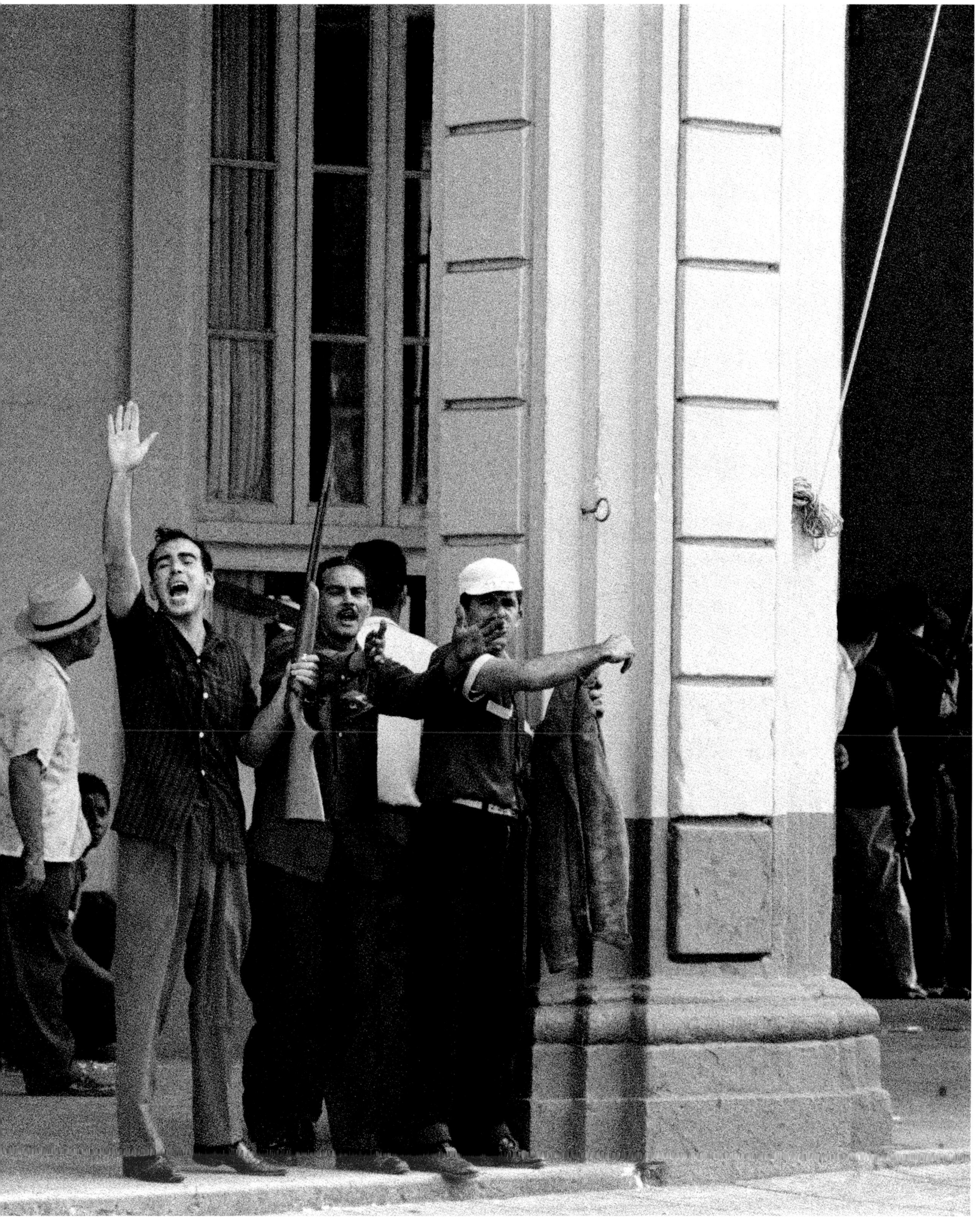

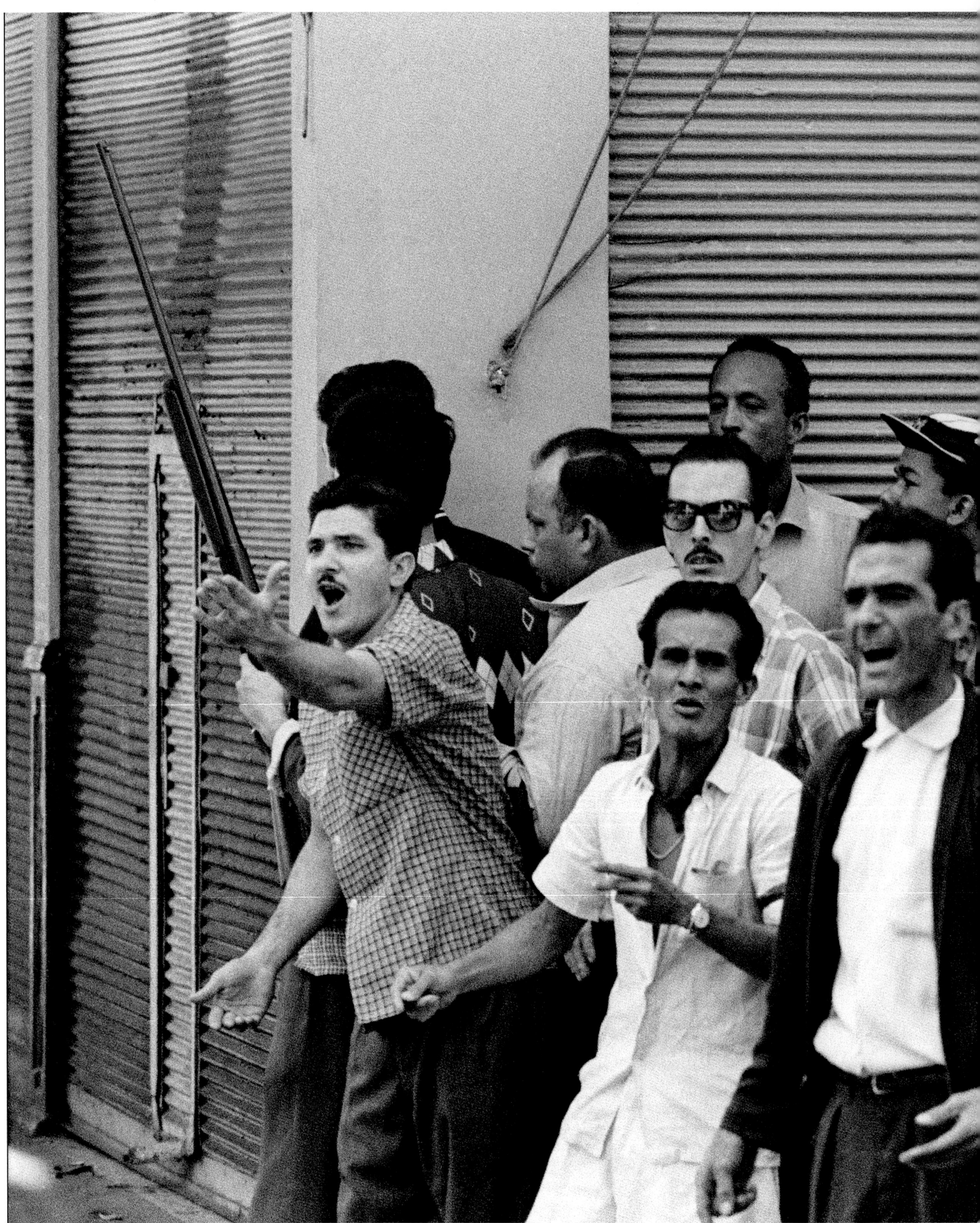

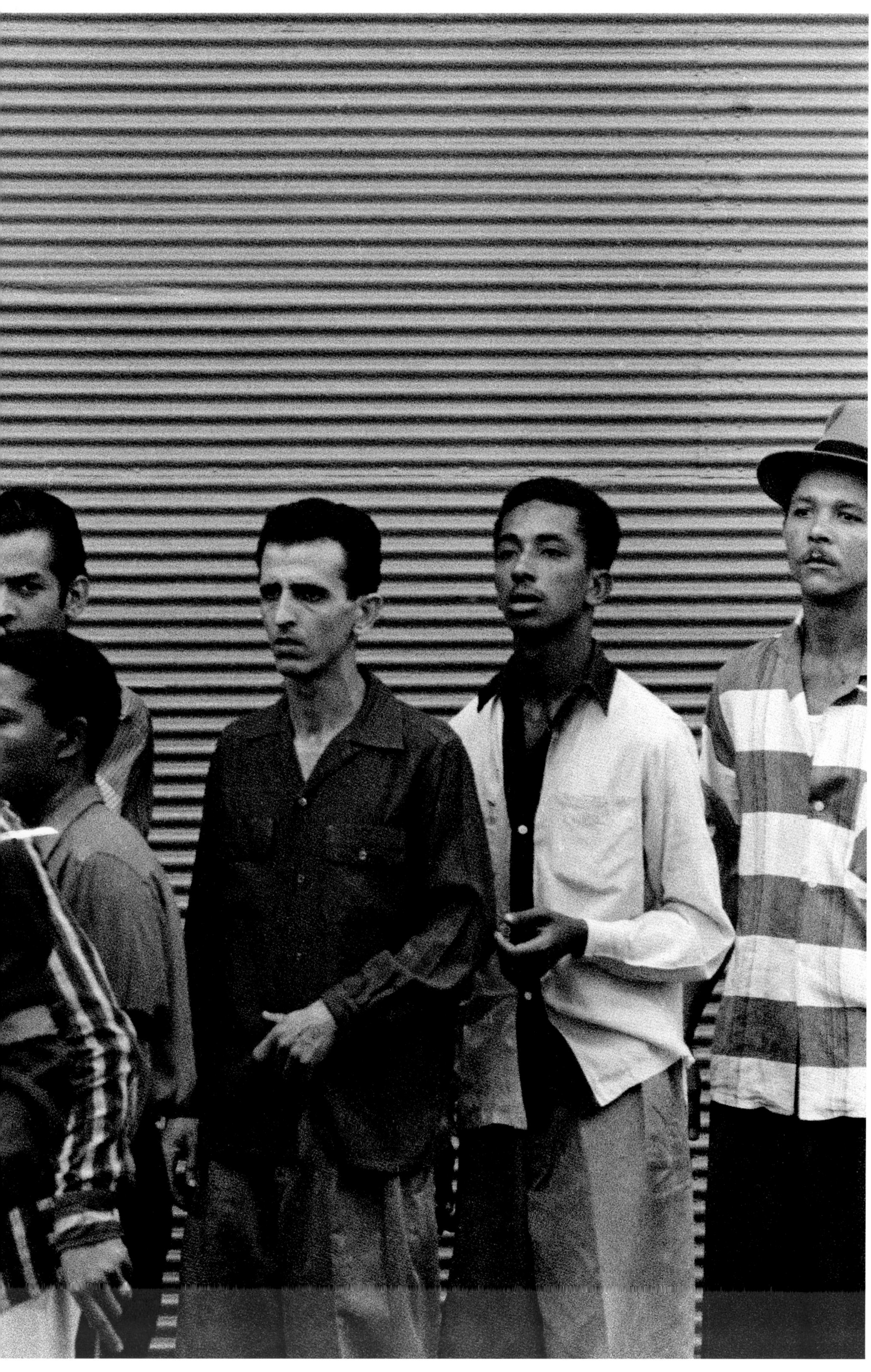

The people have begun to sport "26 julio" armbands and are searching buildings for informers and former policemen.

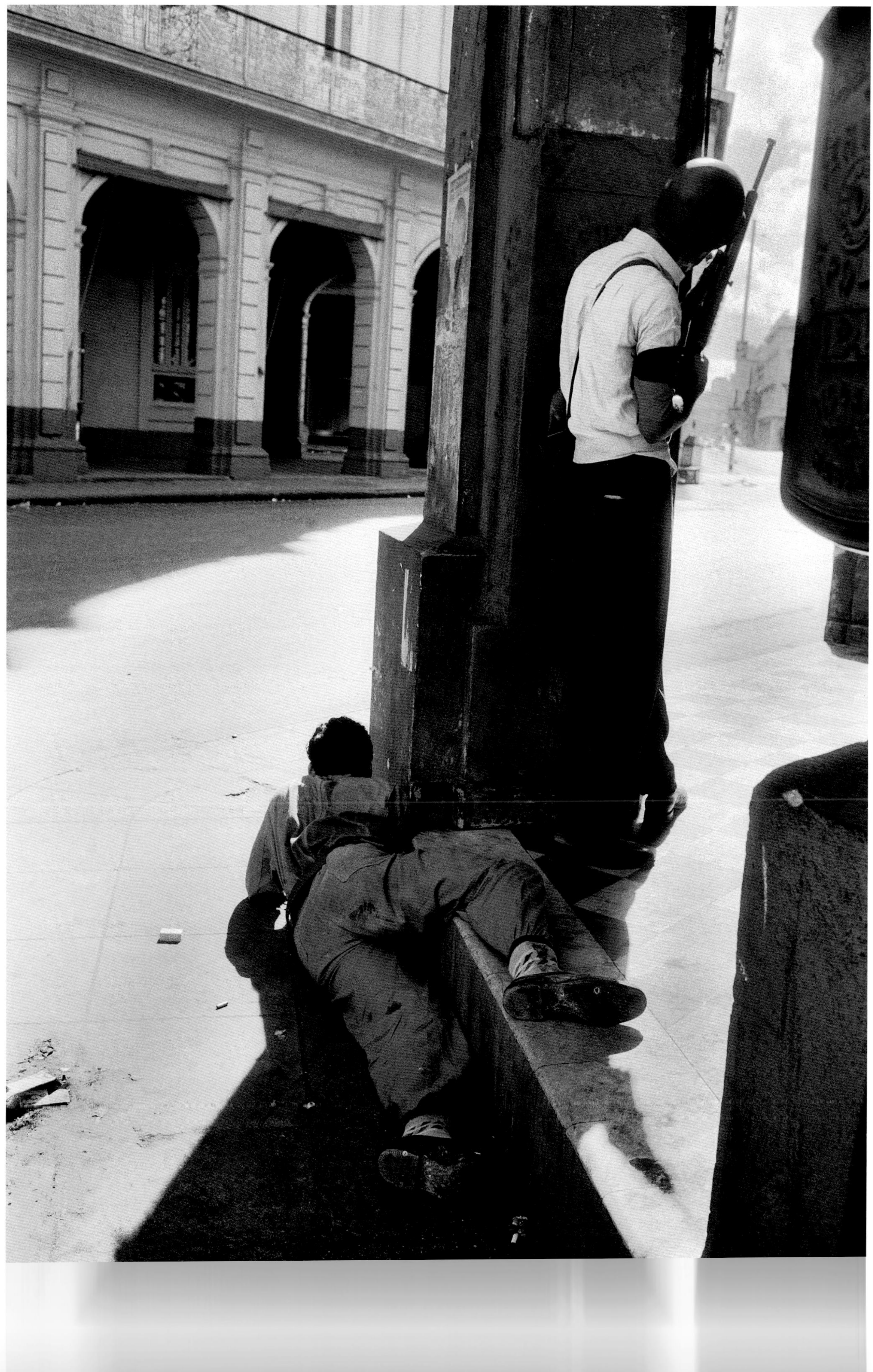

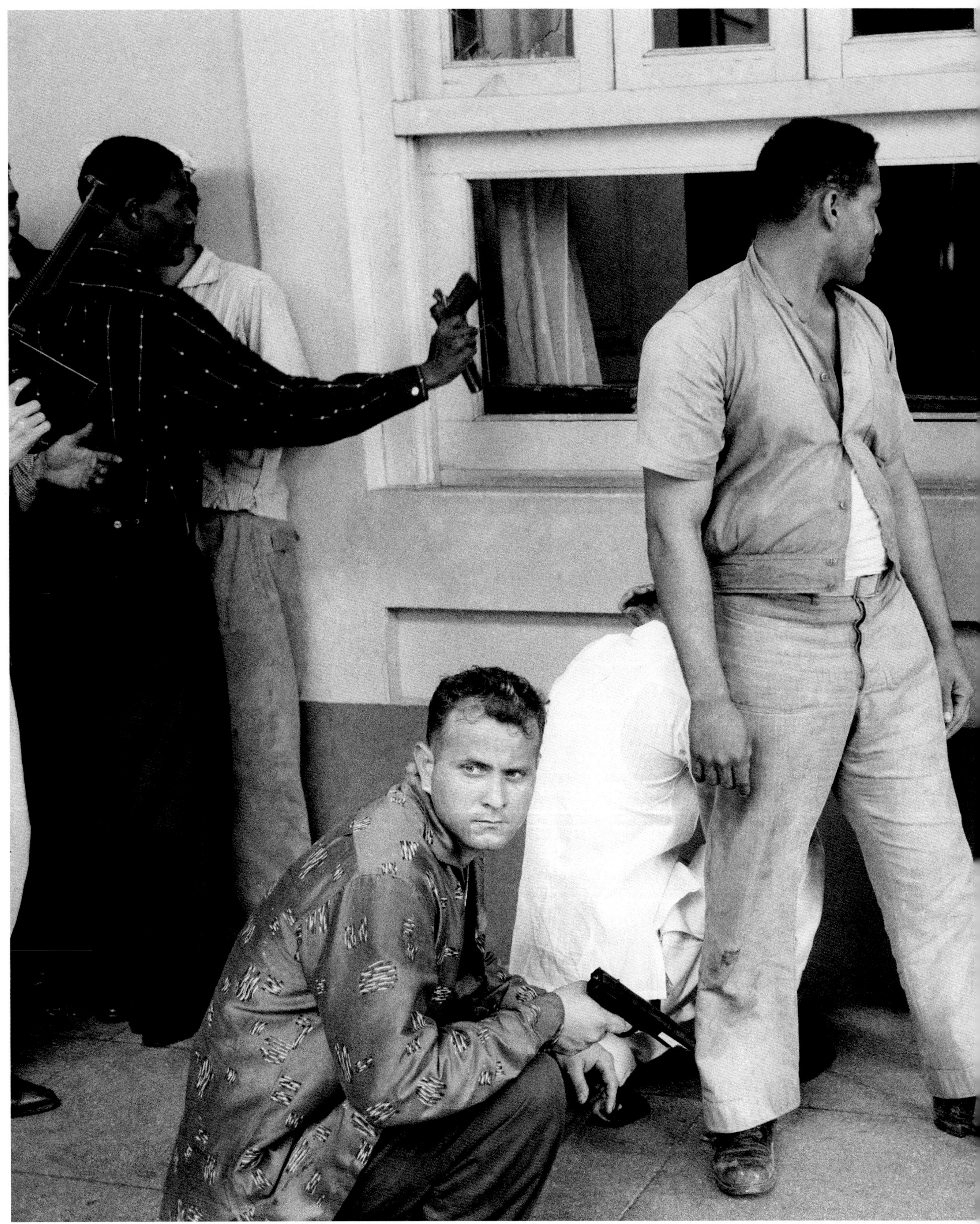

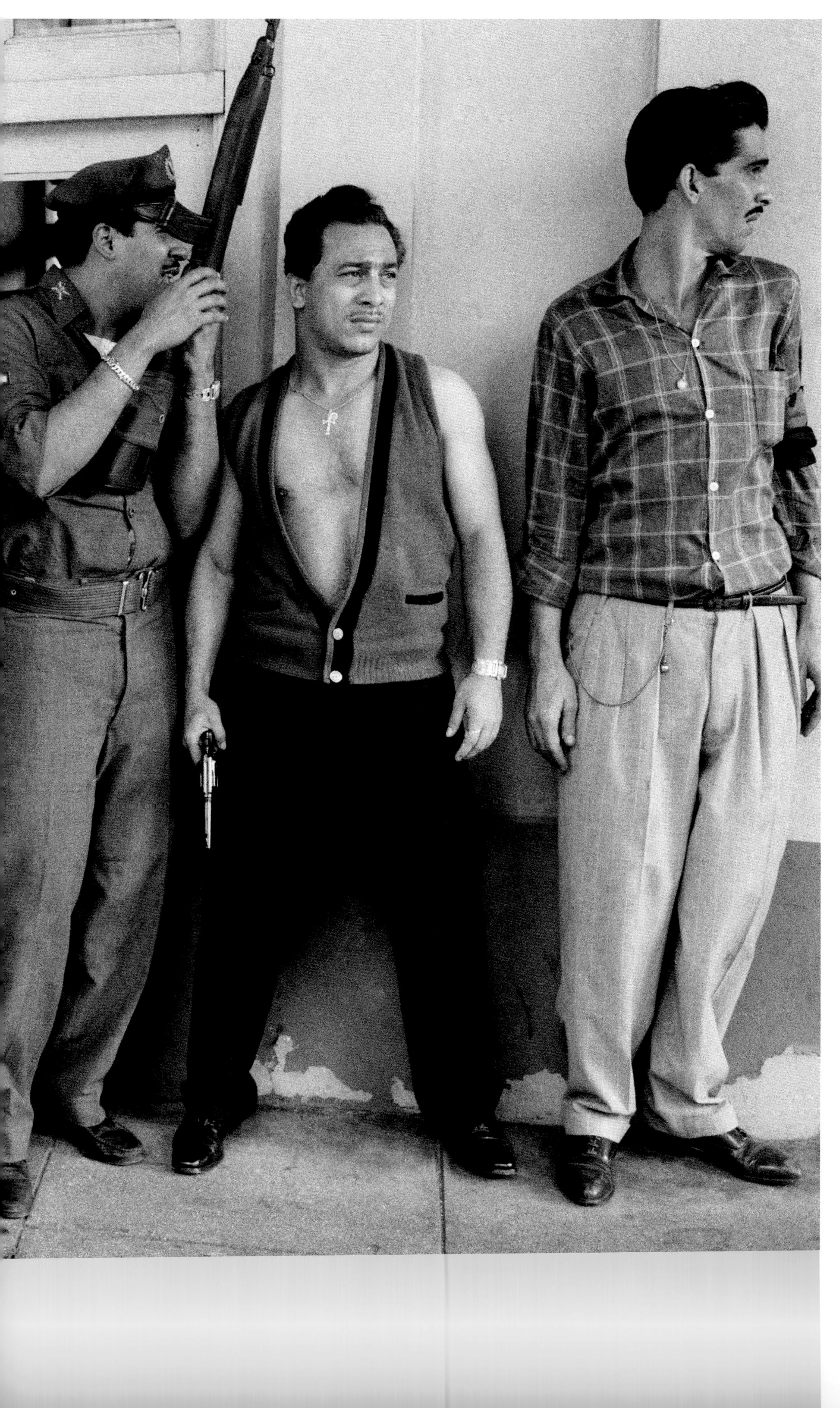

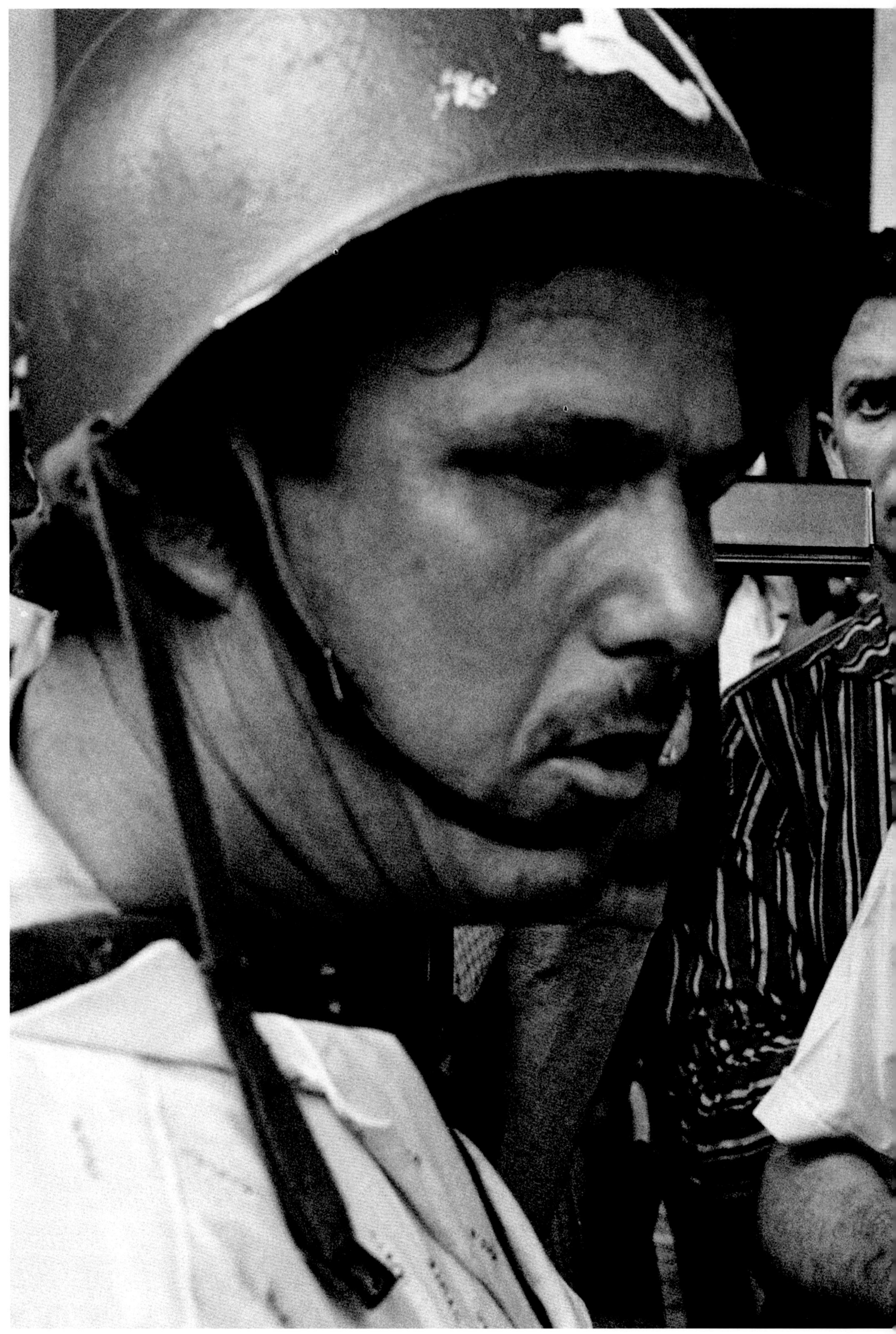

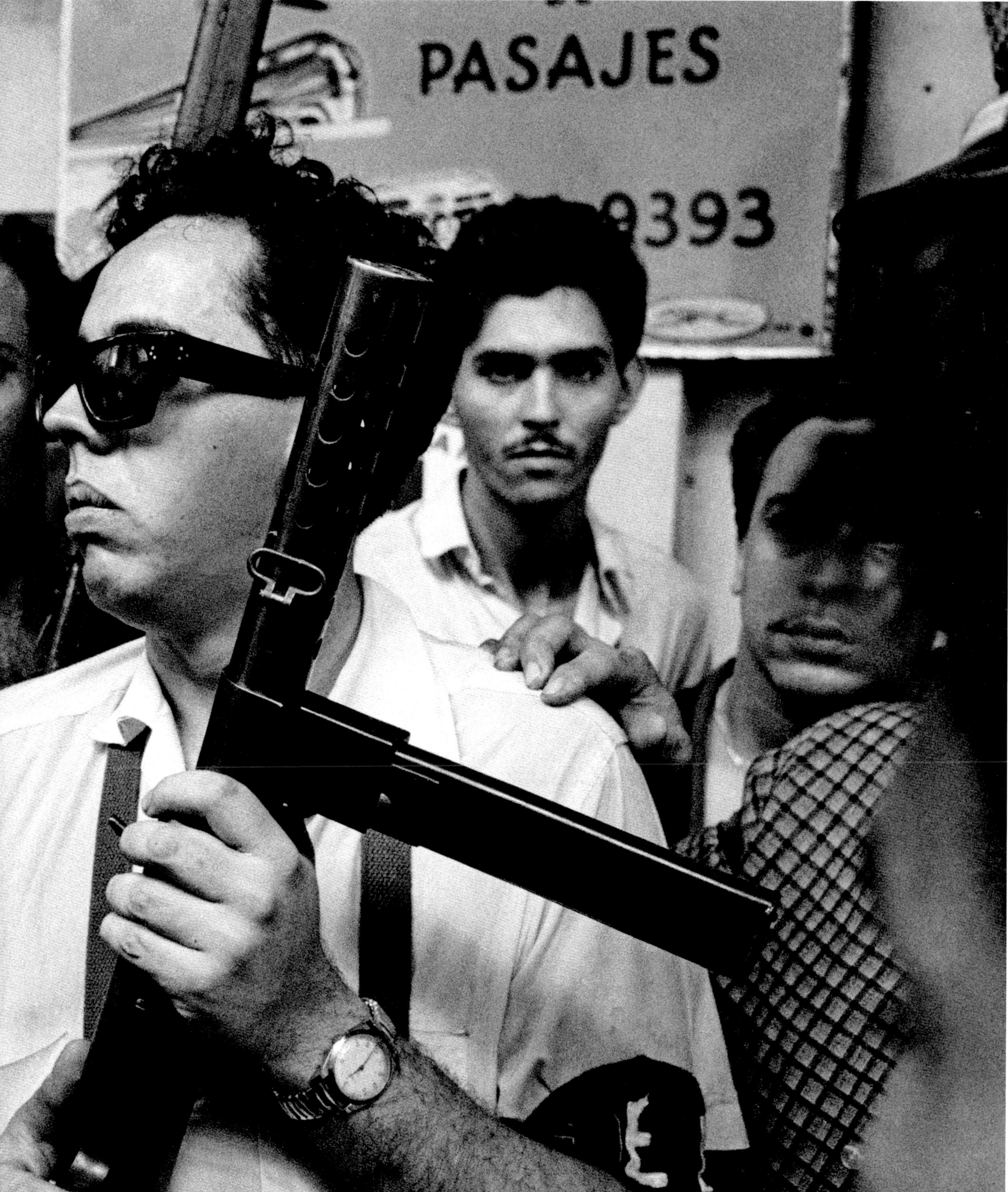
PASAJES
9393

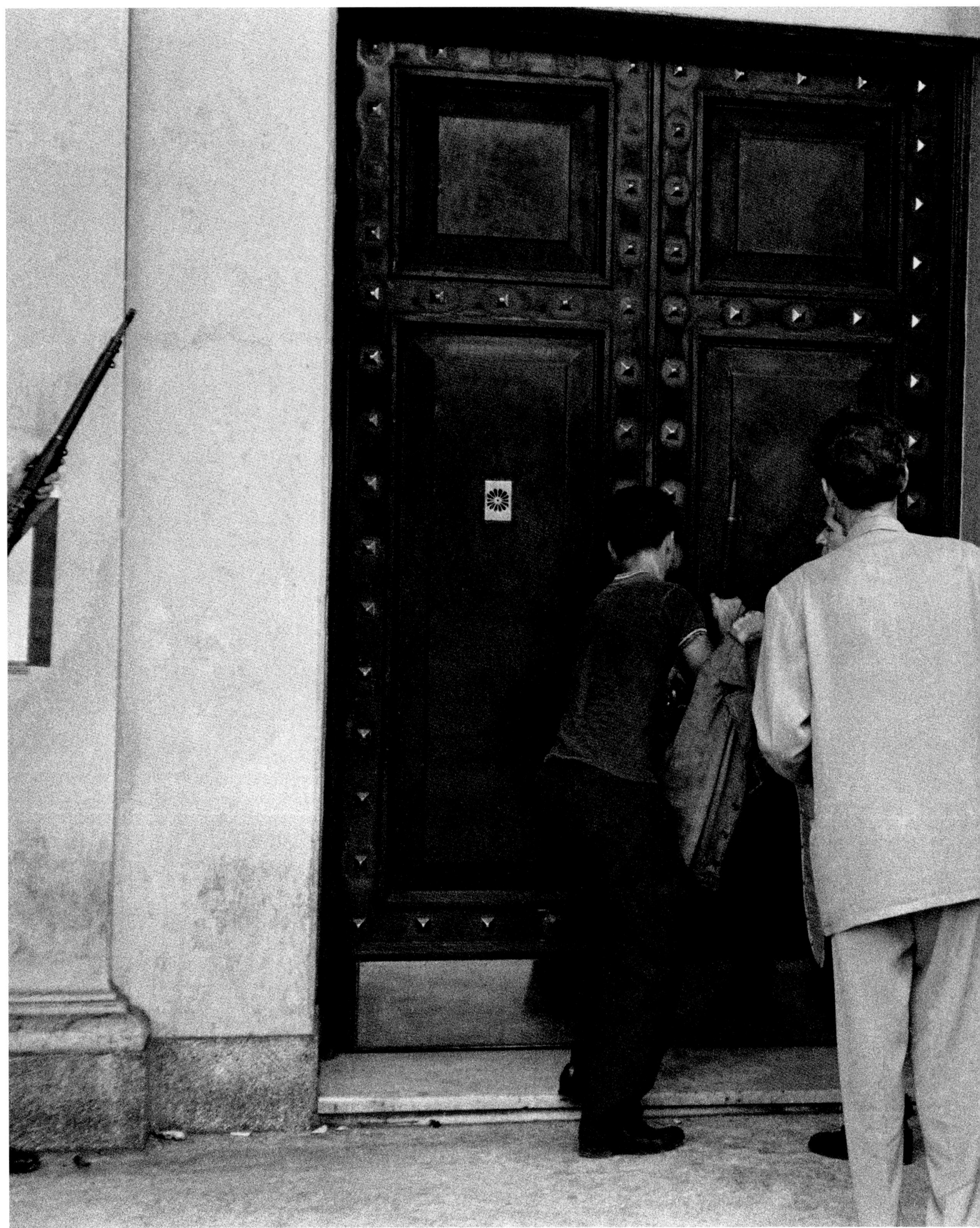

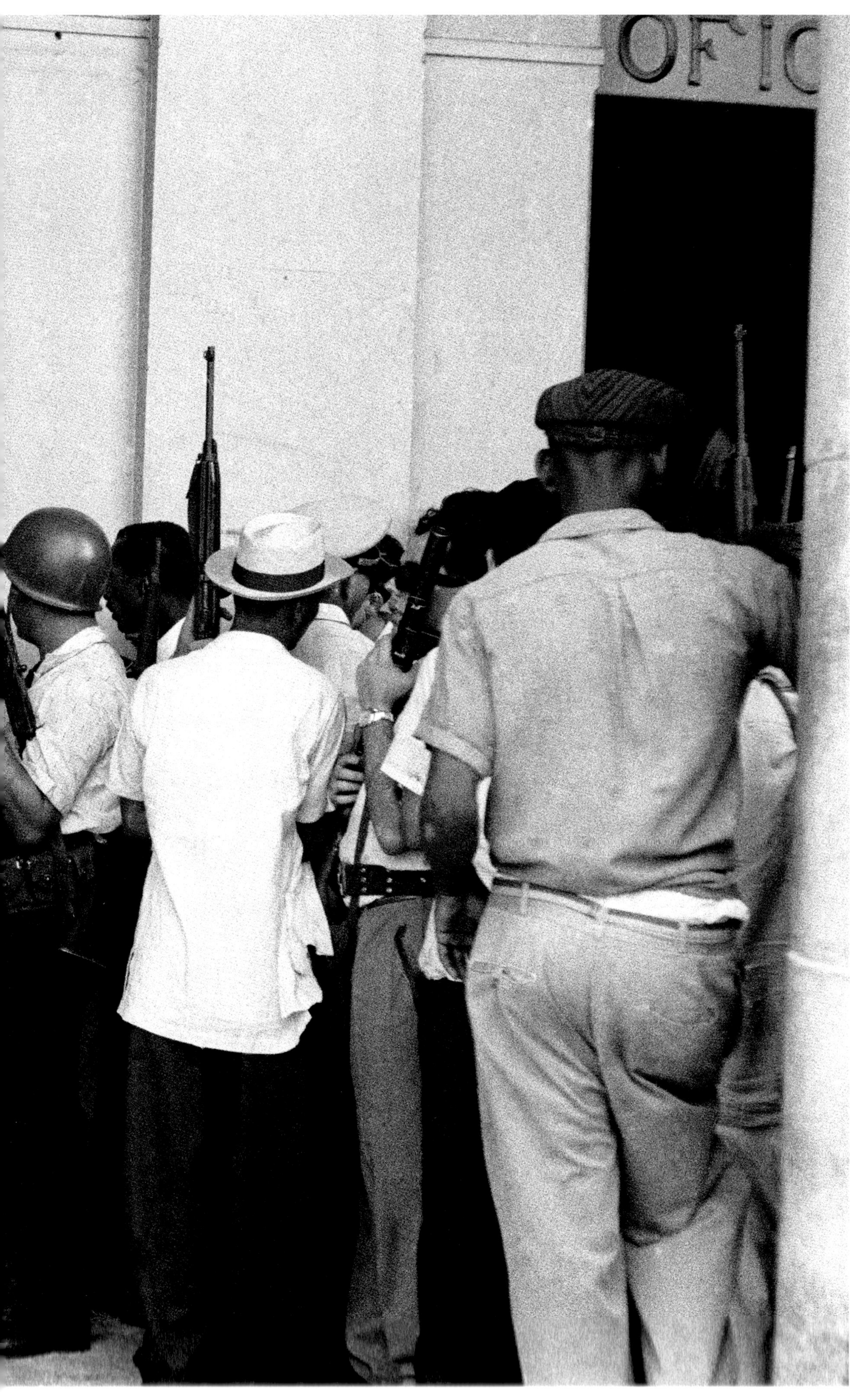
OFIC

There are floor by floor searches in the downtown office buildings, where Batista supporters are believed hiding. Police and communications facilities are also seized. In one building, members of an infamous private army of Batista men, notorious for their atrocities against rebels, held out until all were killed or captured.

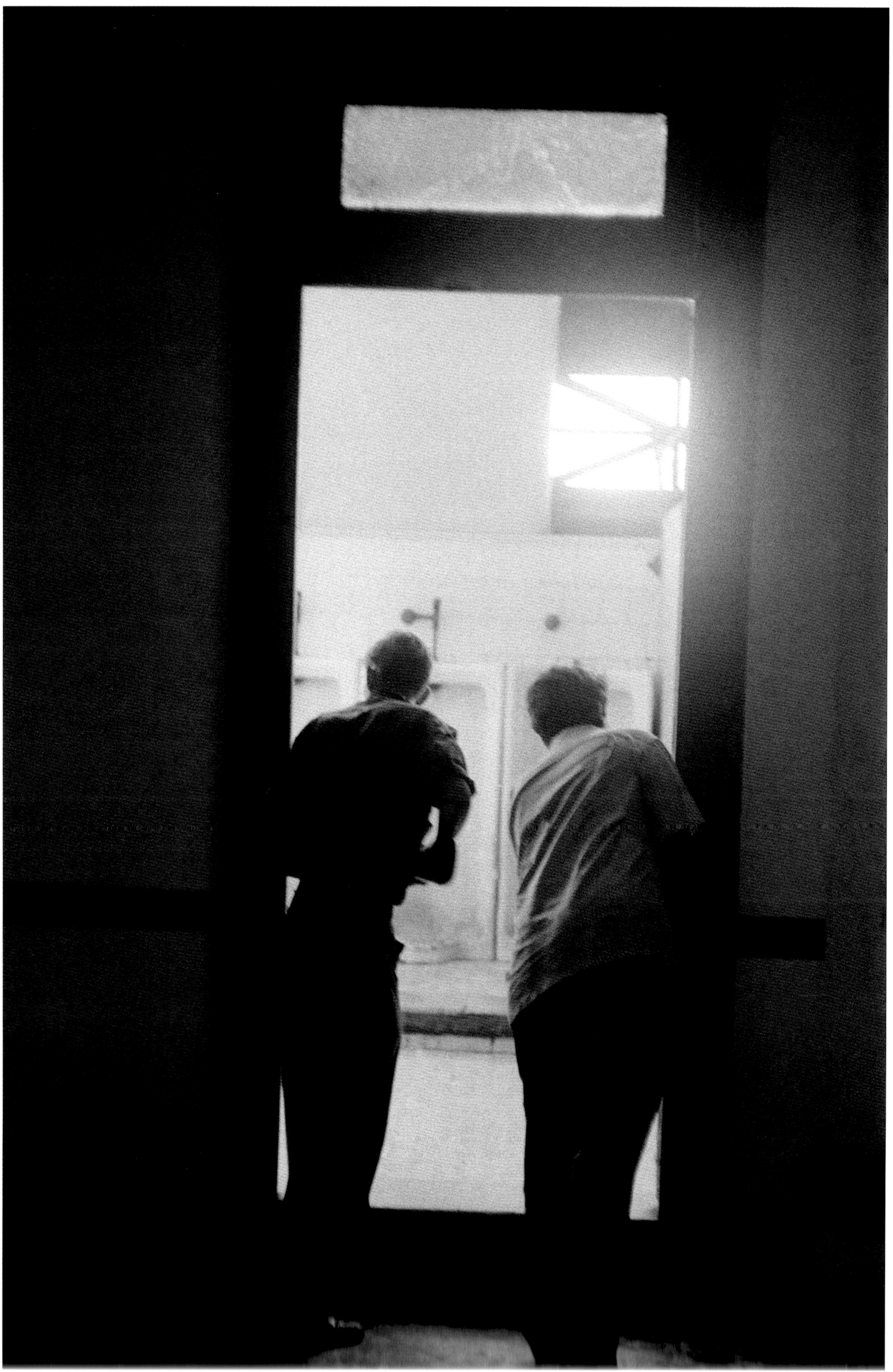

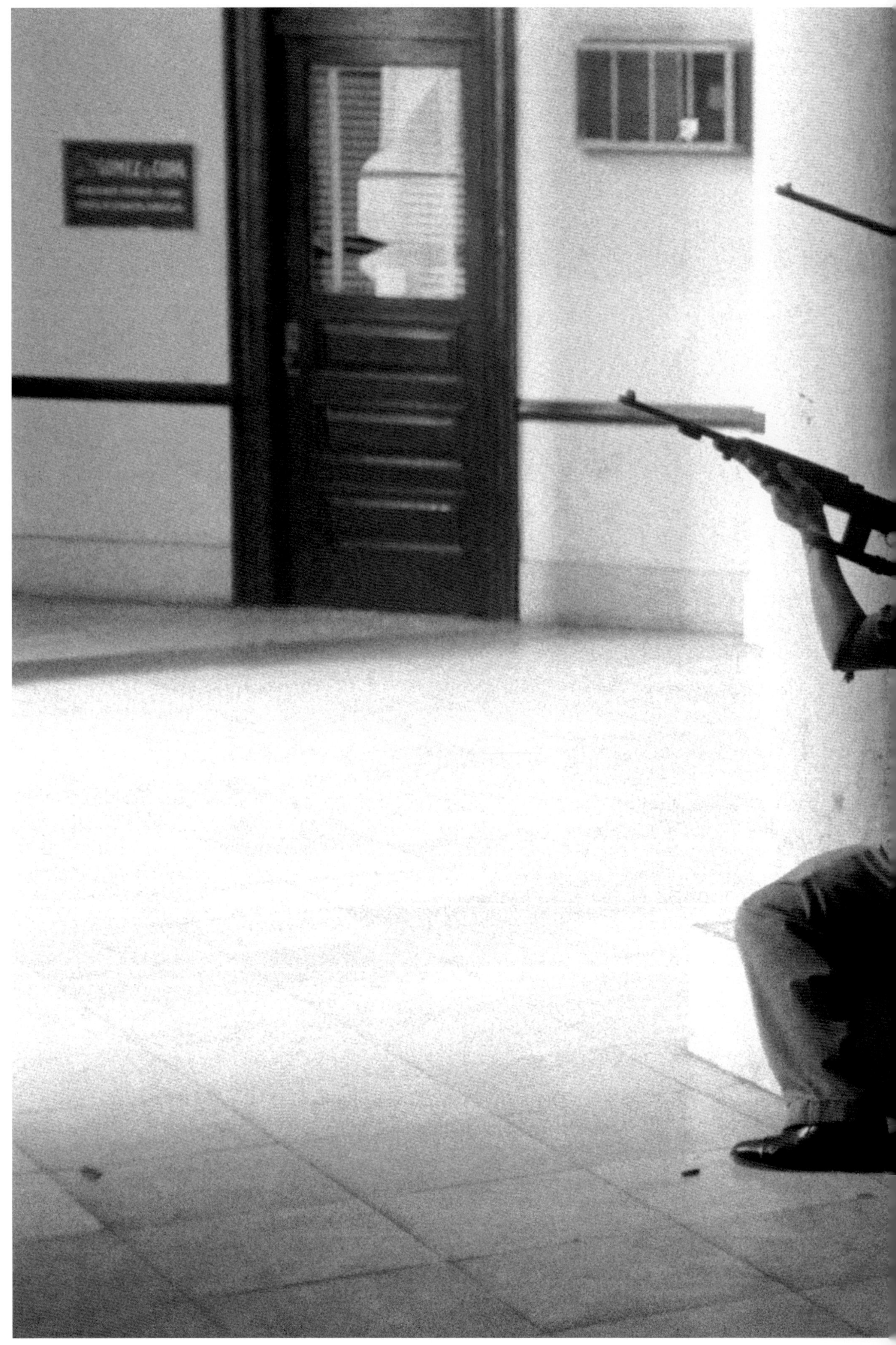

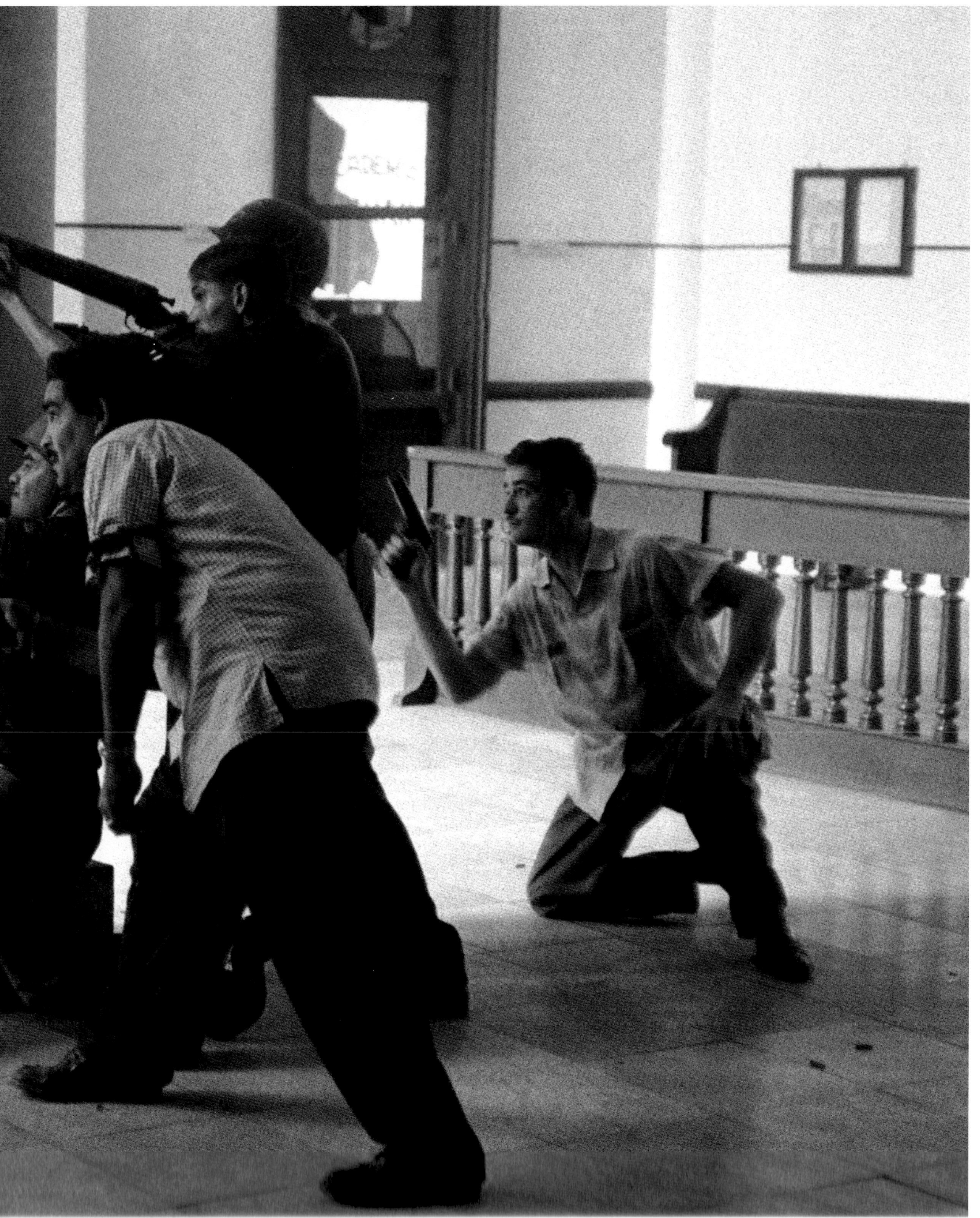

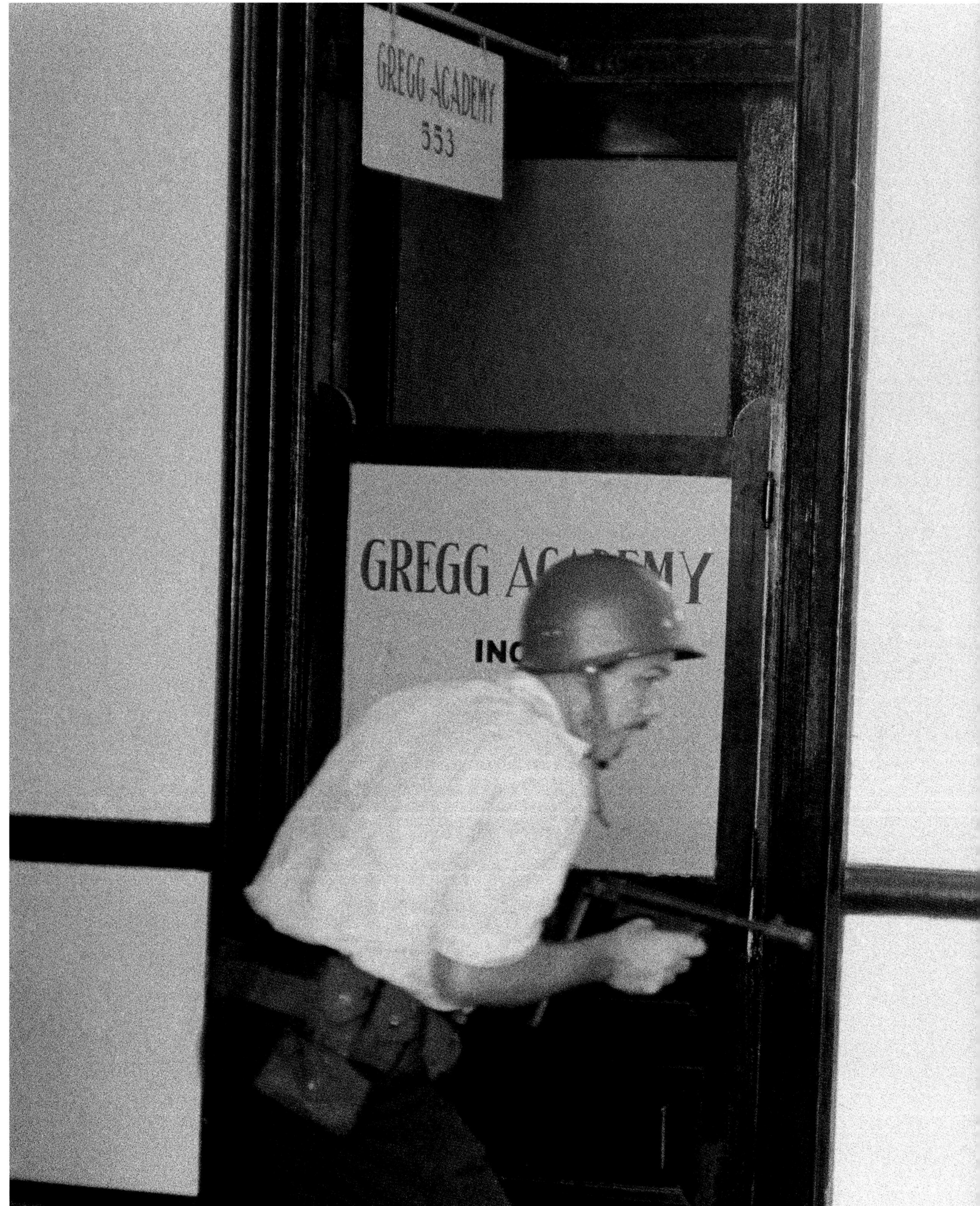
GREGG ACADEMY
553
GREGG

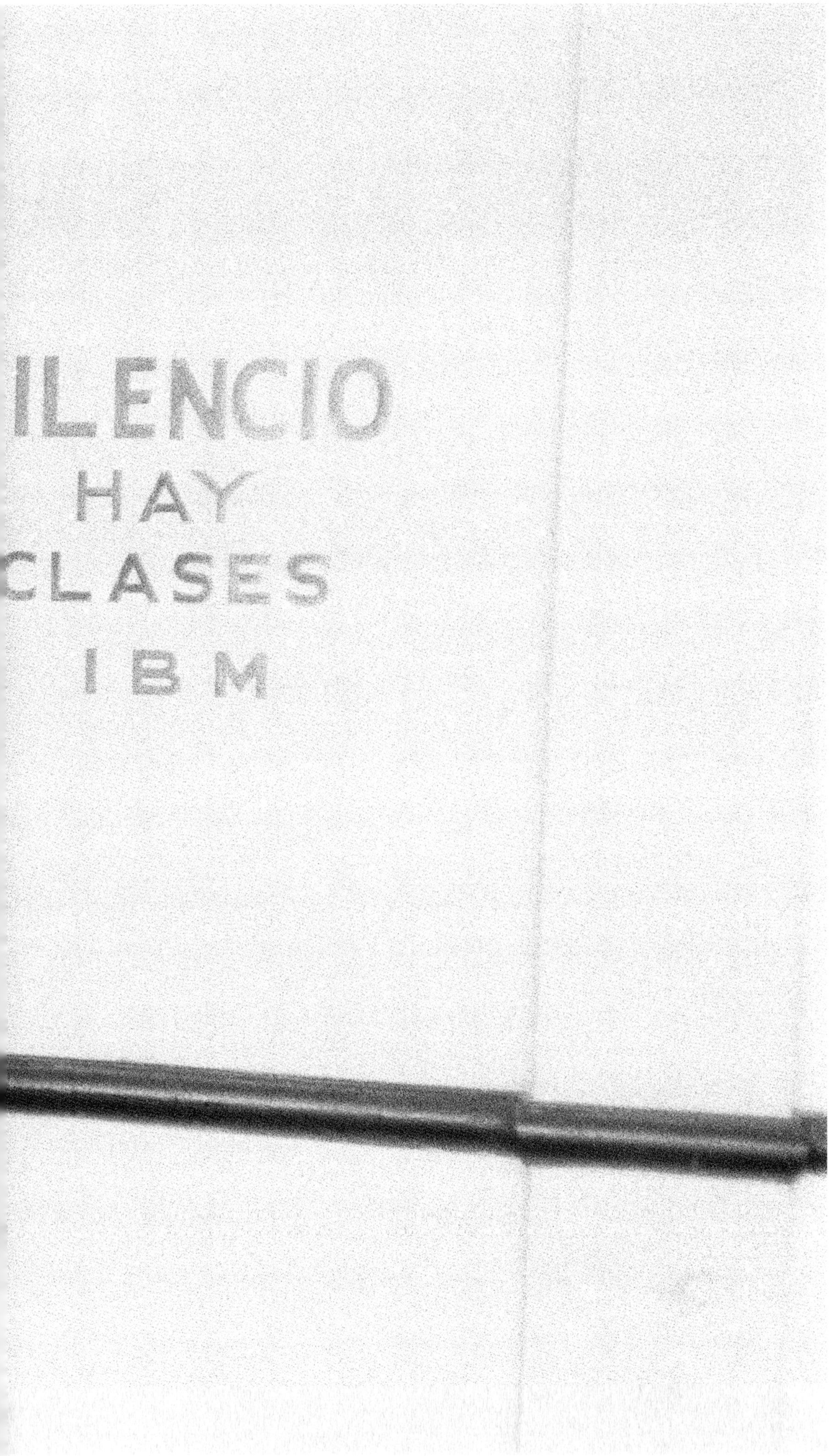

ILENCIO
HAY
CLASES
IBM

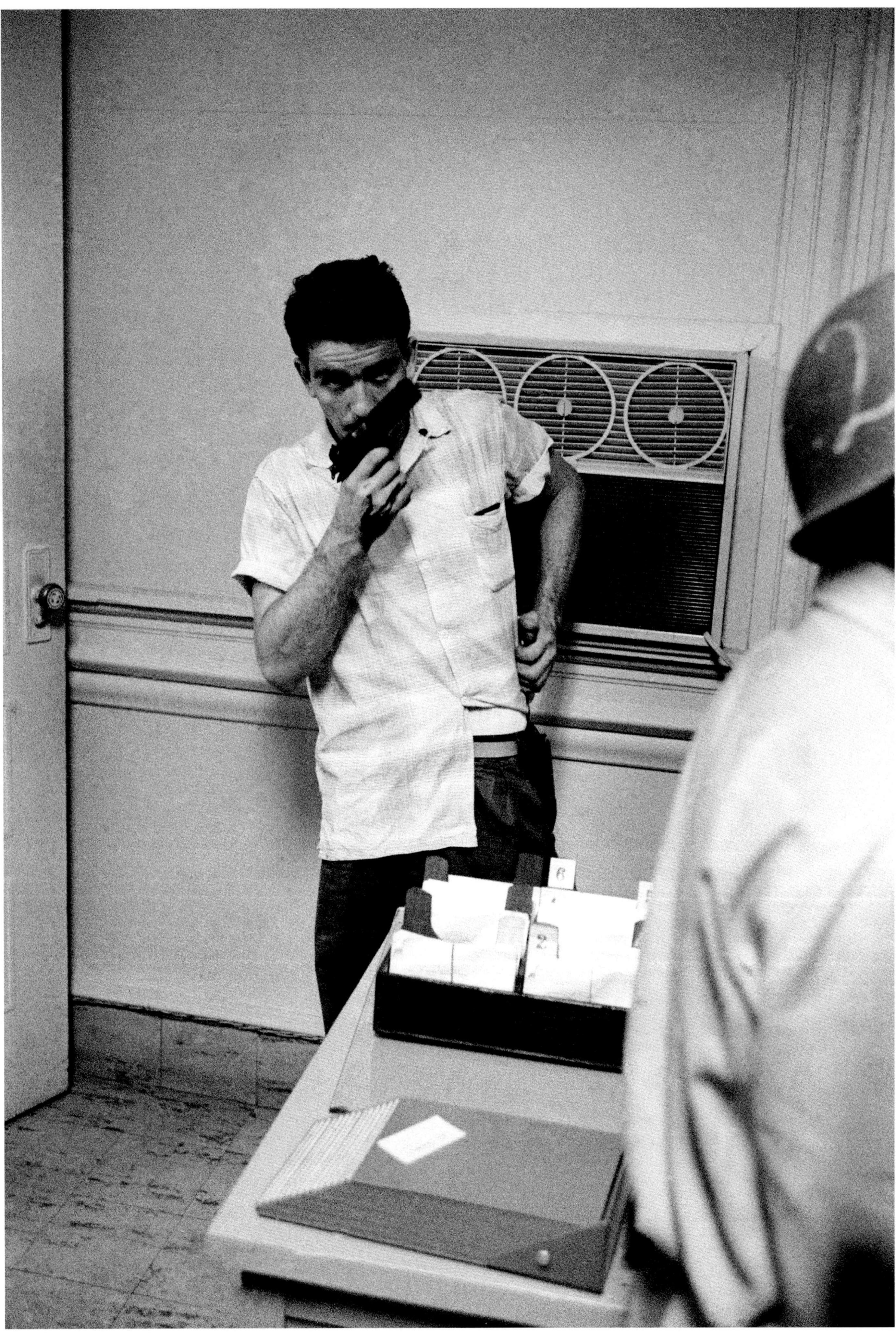

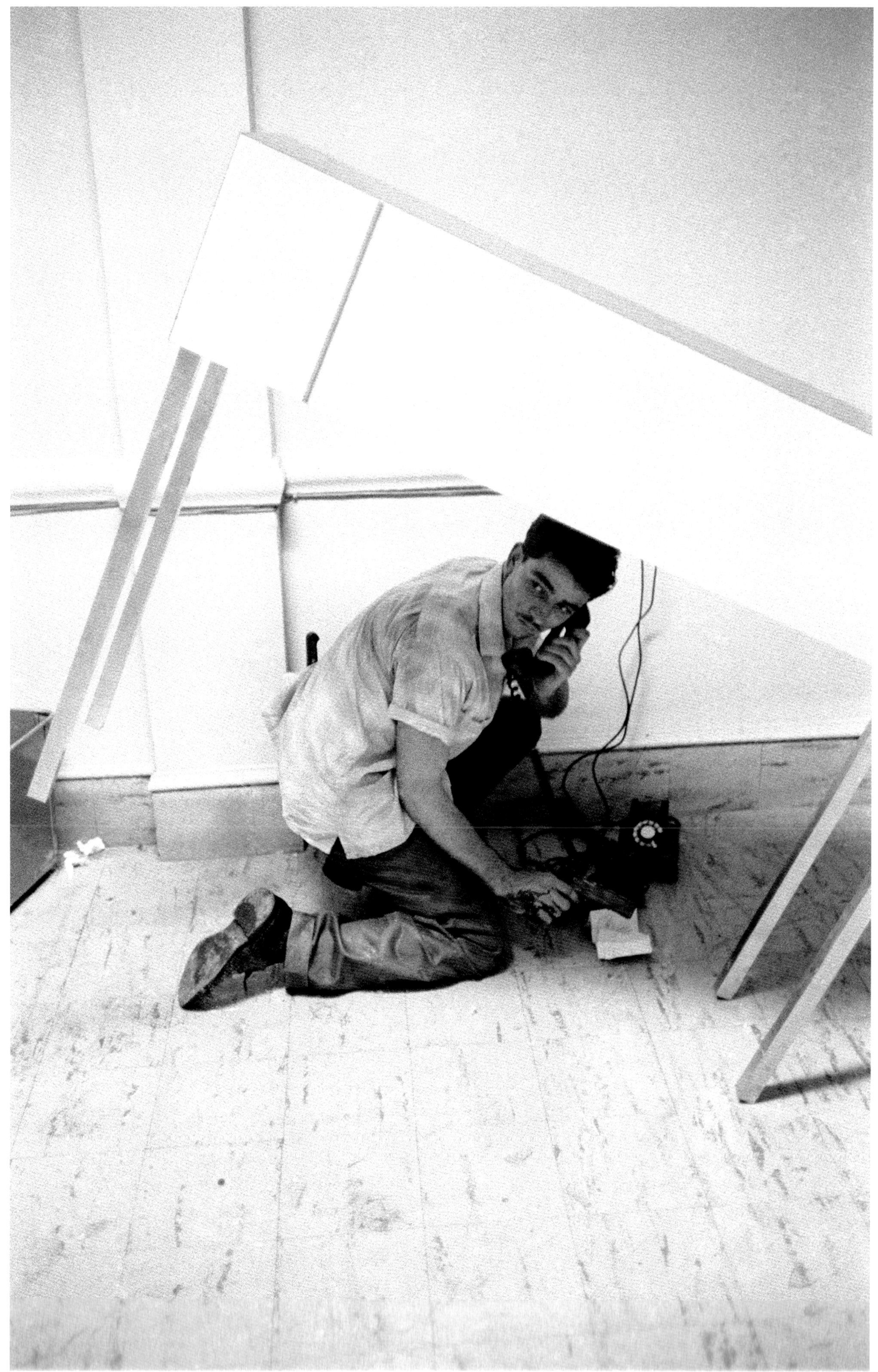

The militia make a search from office to office under the belief that unfriendly fire had been coming from this building. Nobody was found after a great deal of tension and the search. Somebody wearing a helmet, looking a bit more regular than the other odd folk, has come in. They wave to the crowd outside that all seems to be clear.

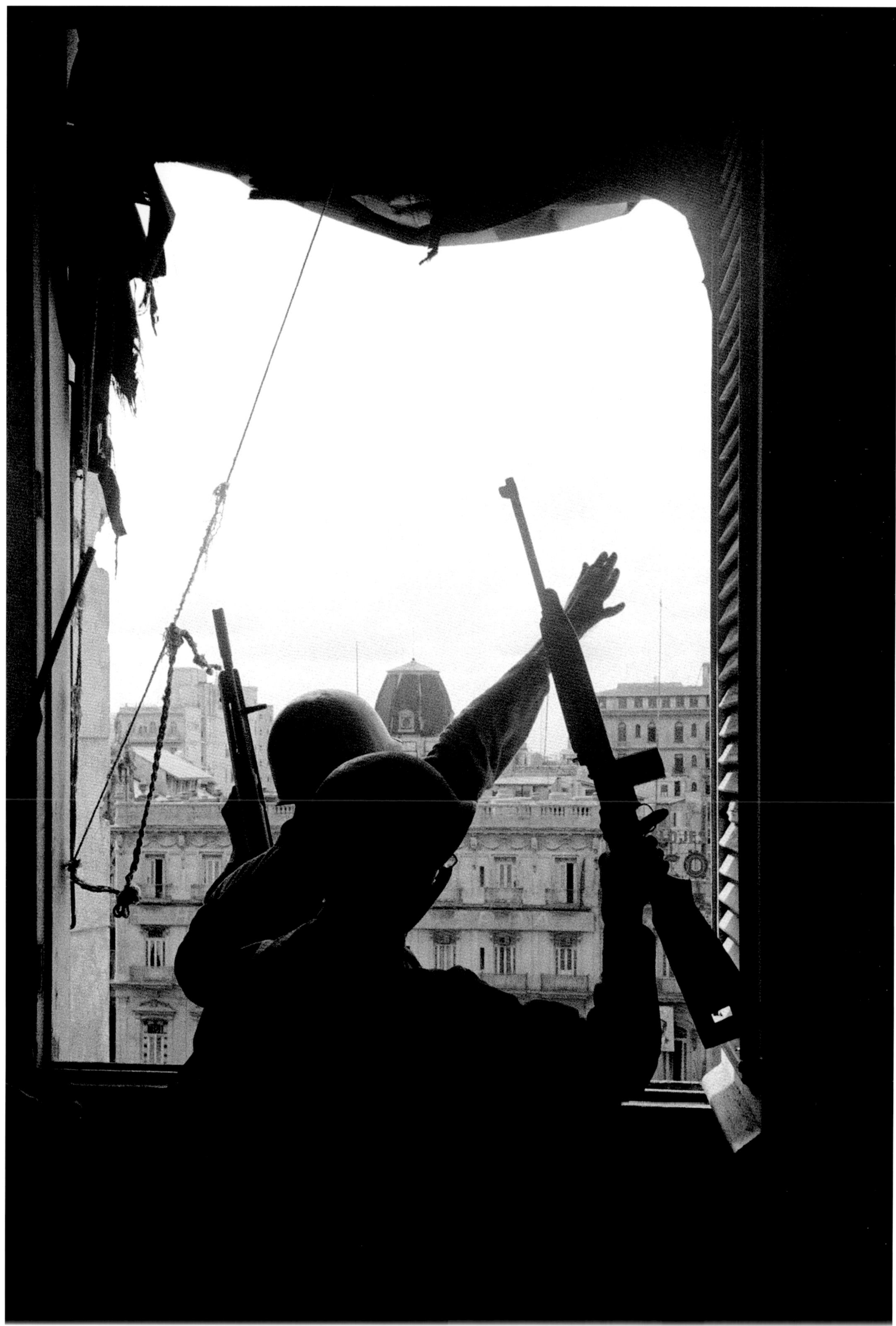

These were the first people I saw who seemed official and had authority. Wearing the "26 julio" armband, they have begun to set up almost a city headquarters. They rounded up former secret police and suspected Batista collaborators, most of whom were absolutely petrified with fear and undoubtedly "got it" during the very early days of the Castro regime.

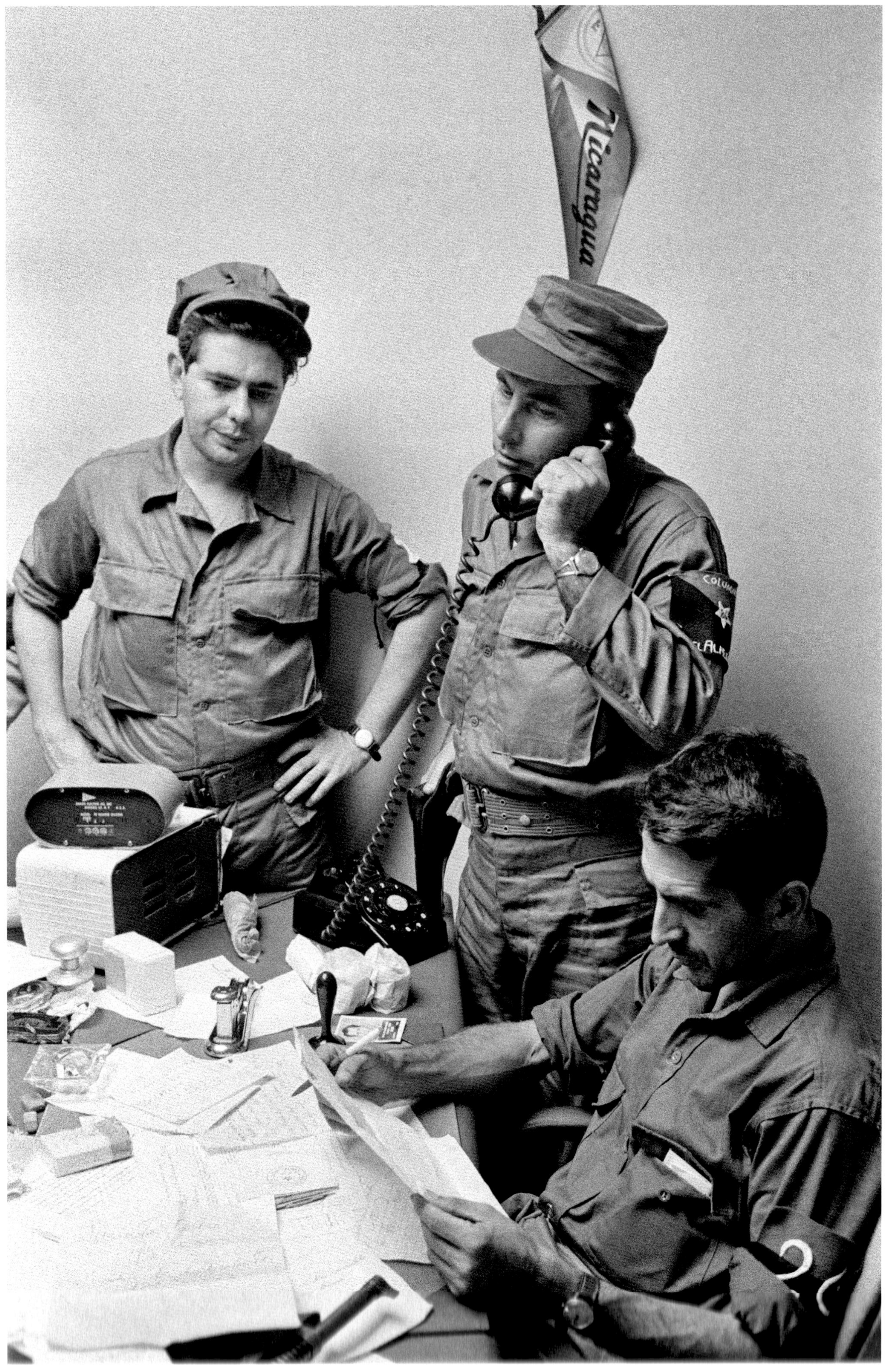
Nicaragua

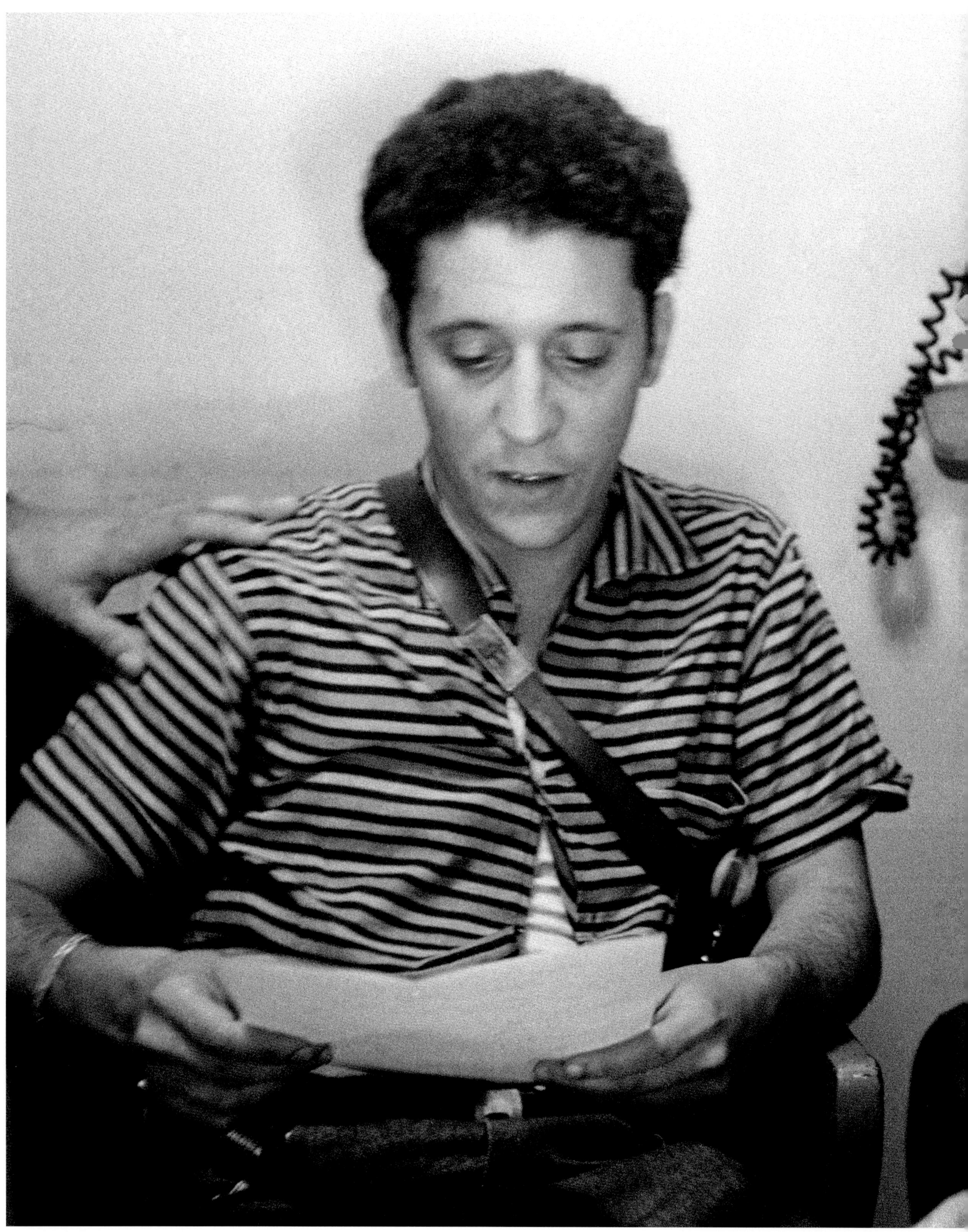

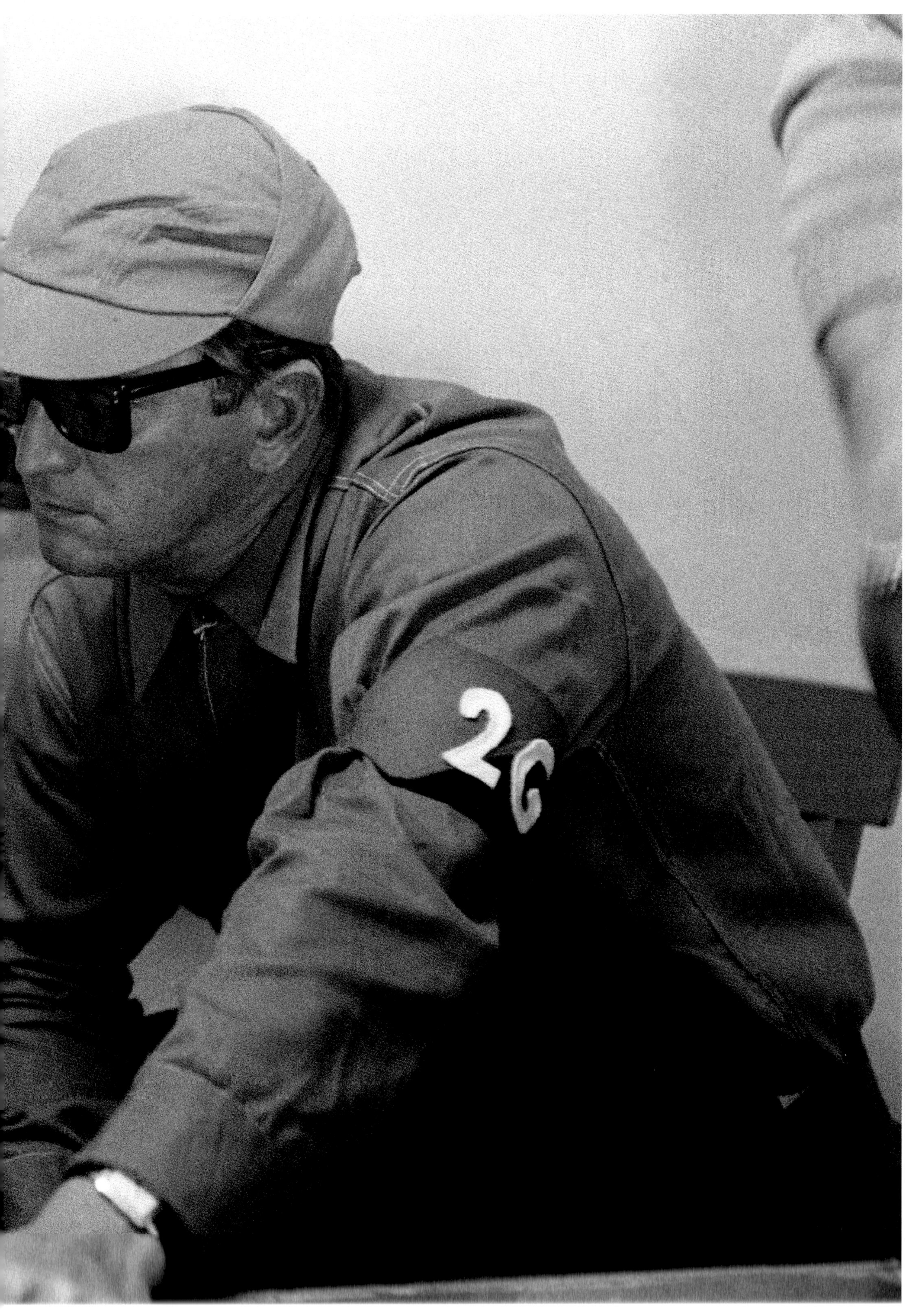

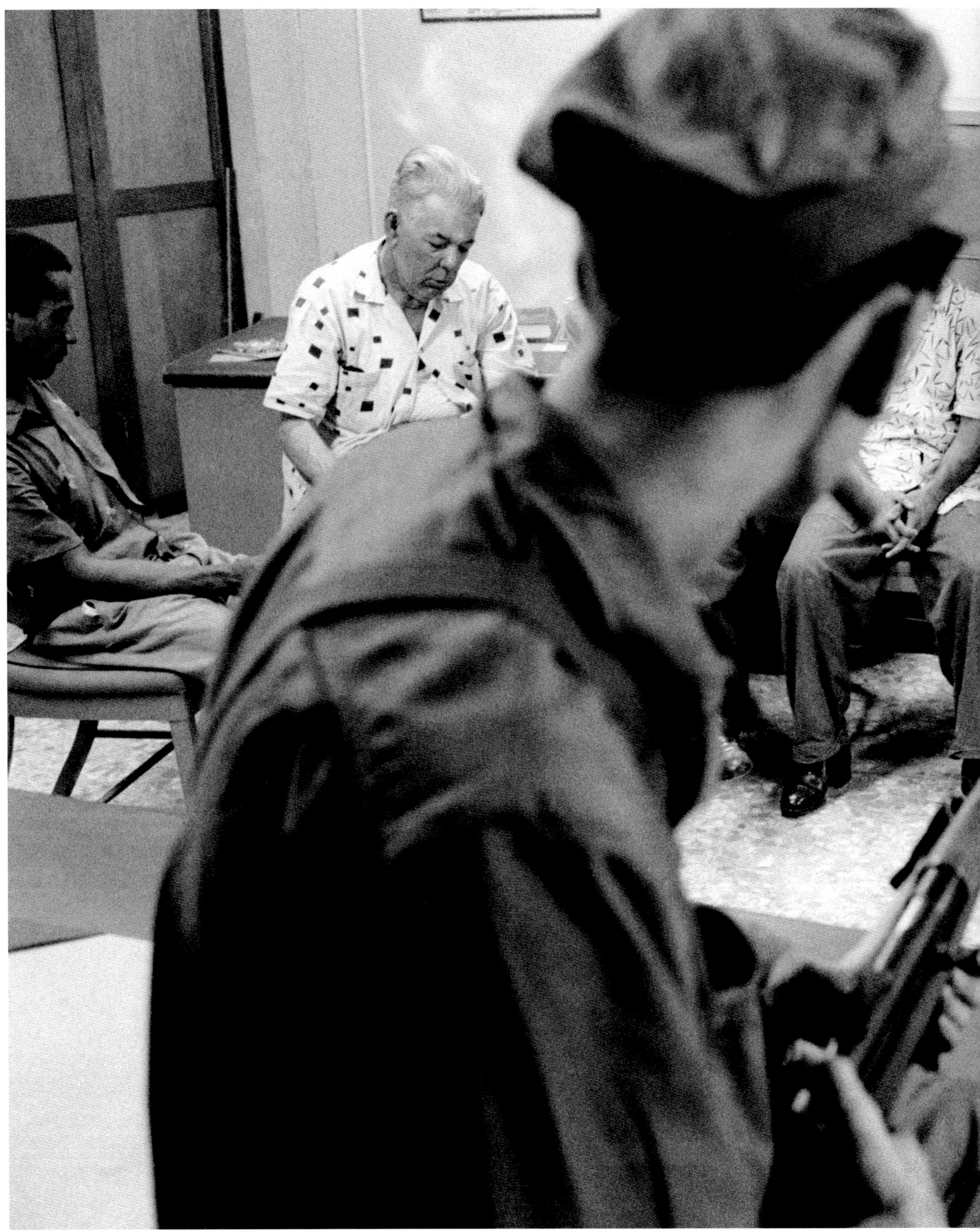

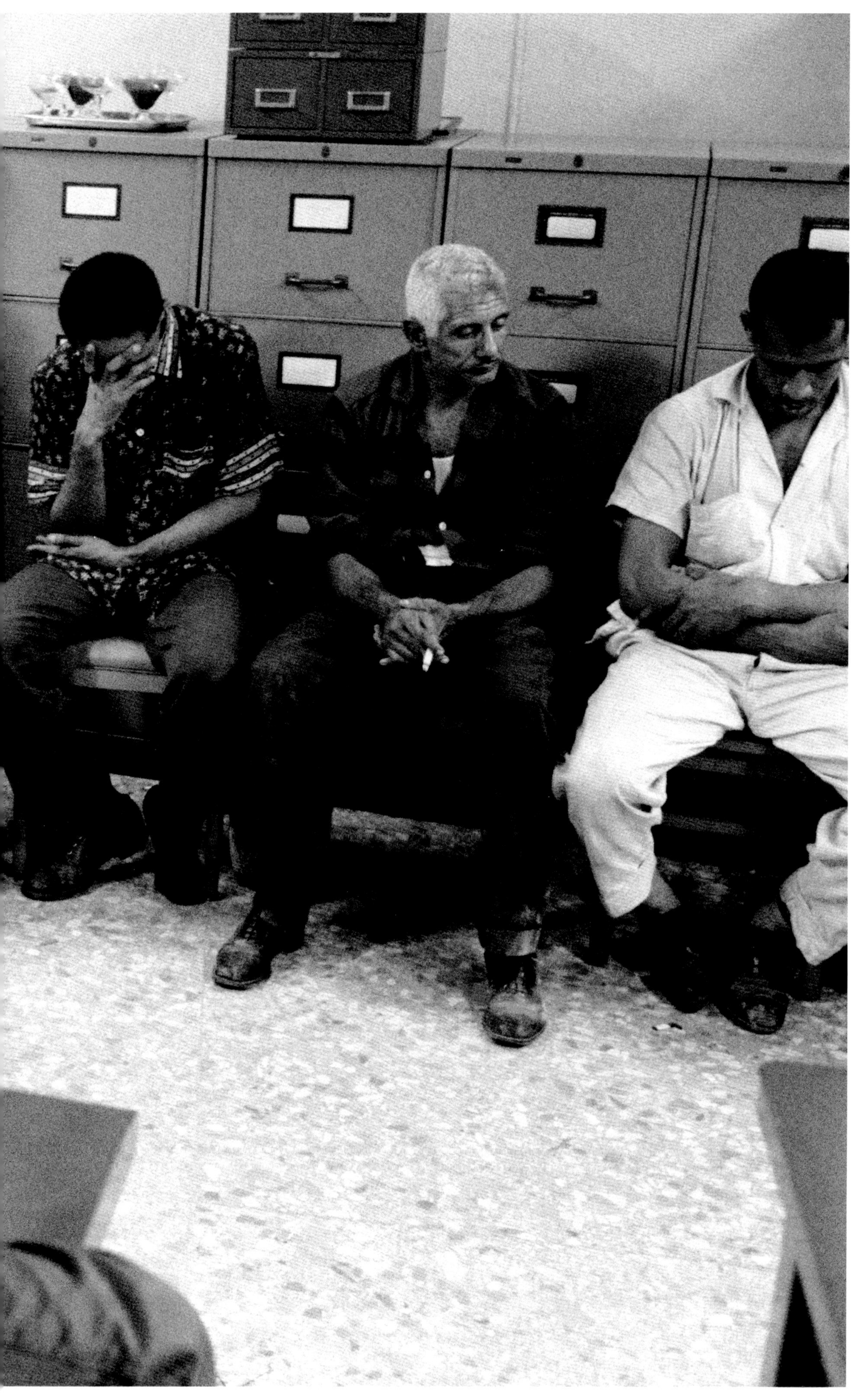

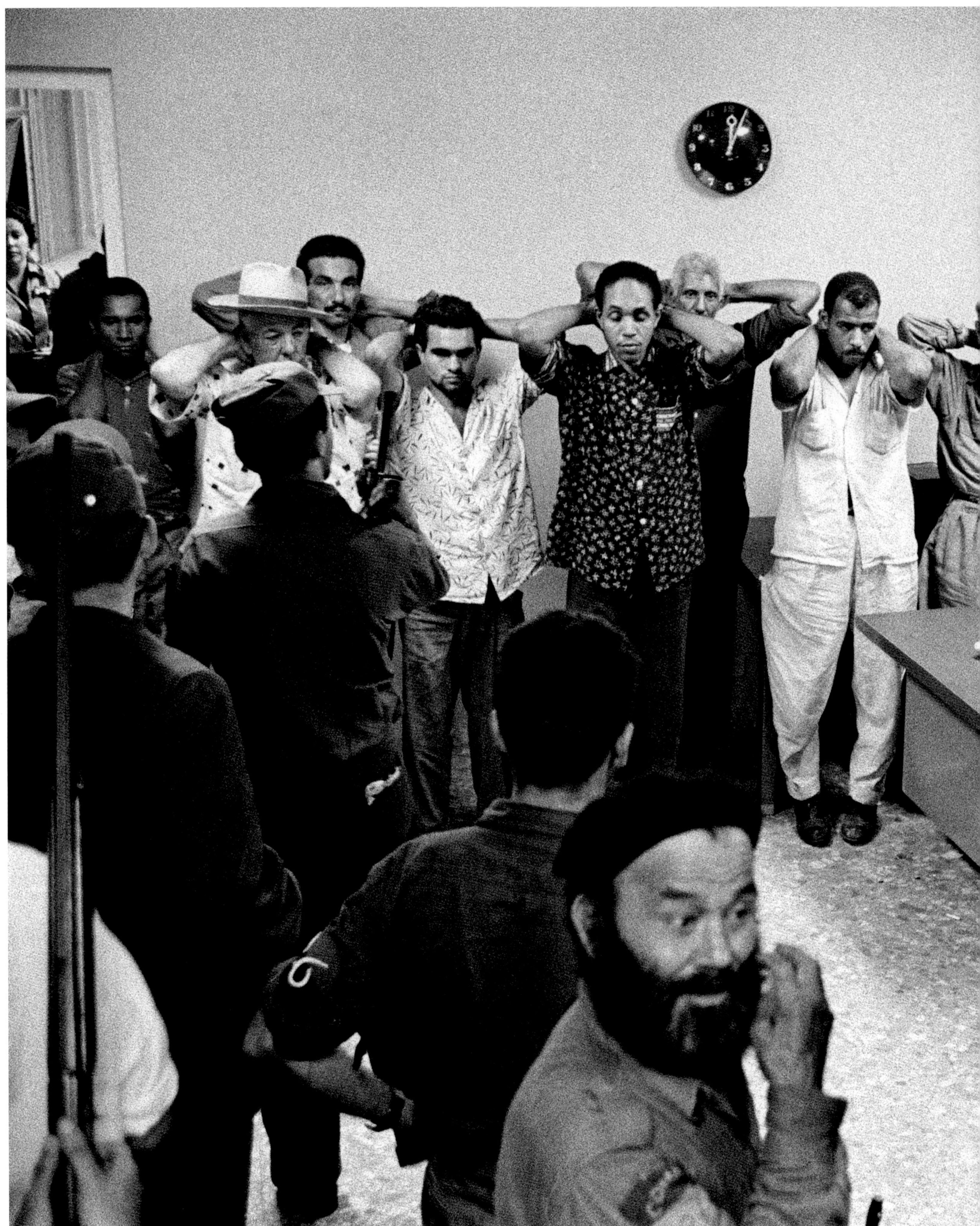

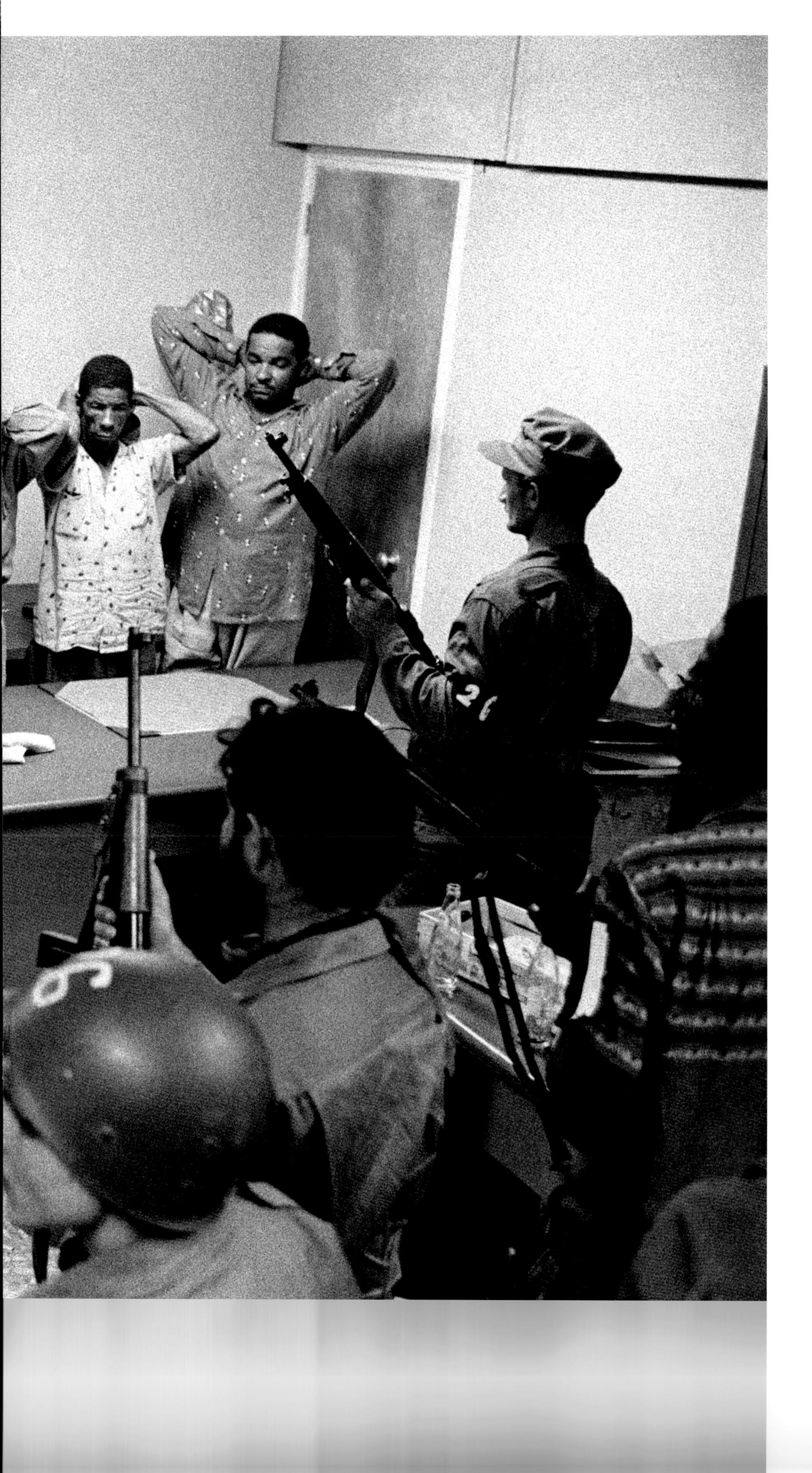

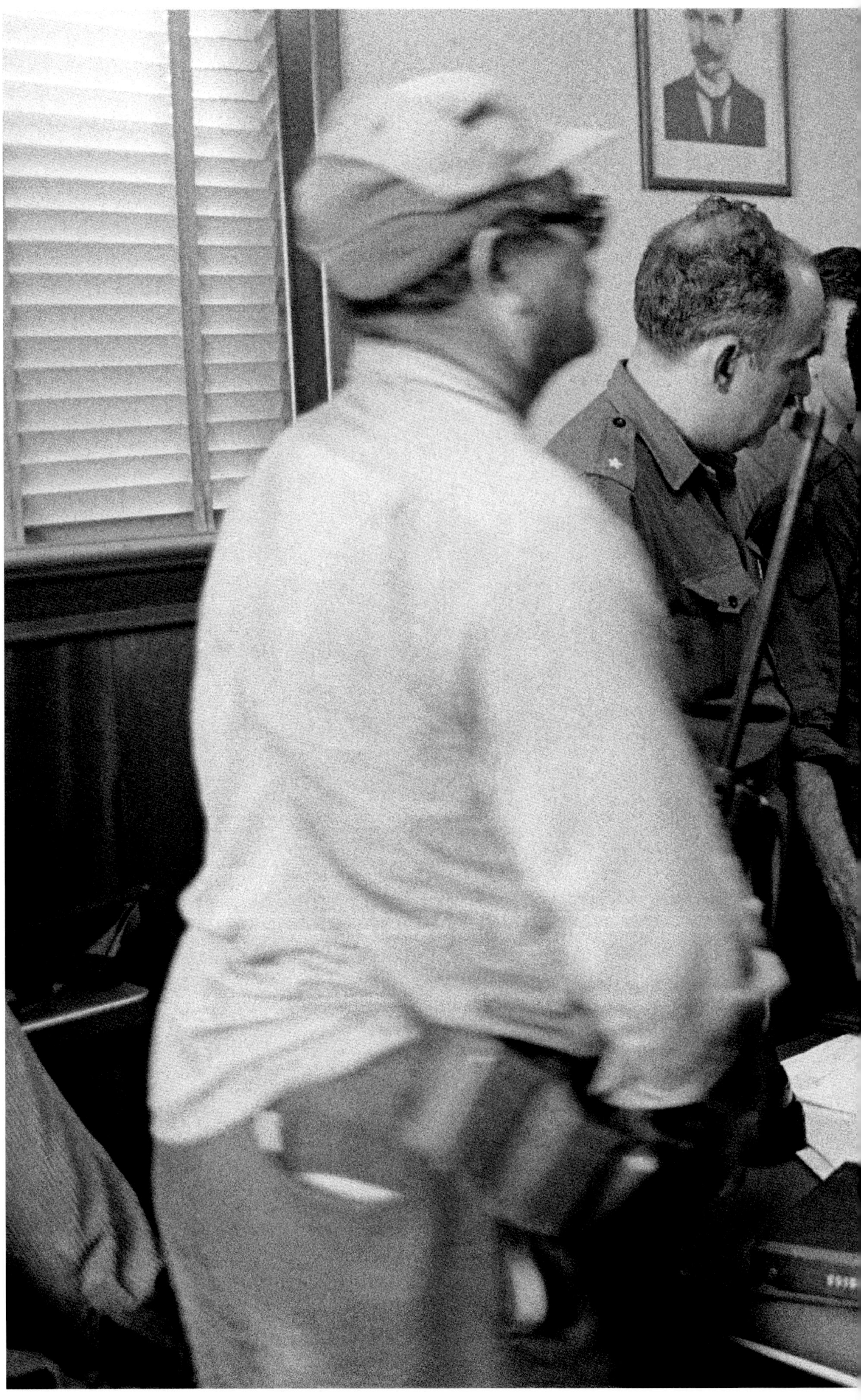

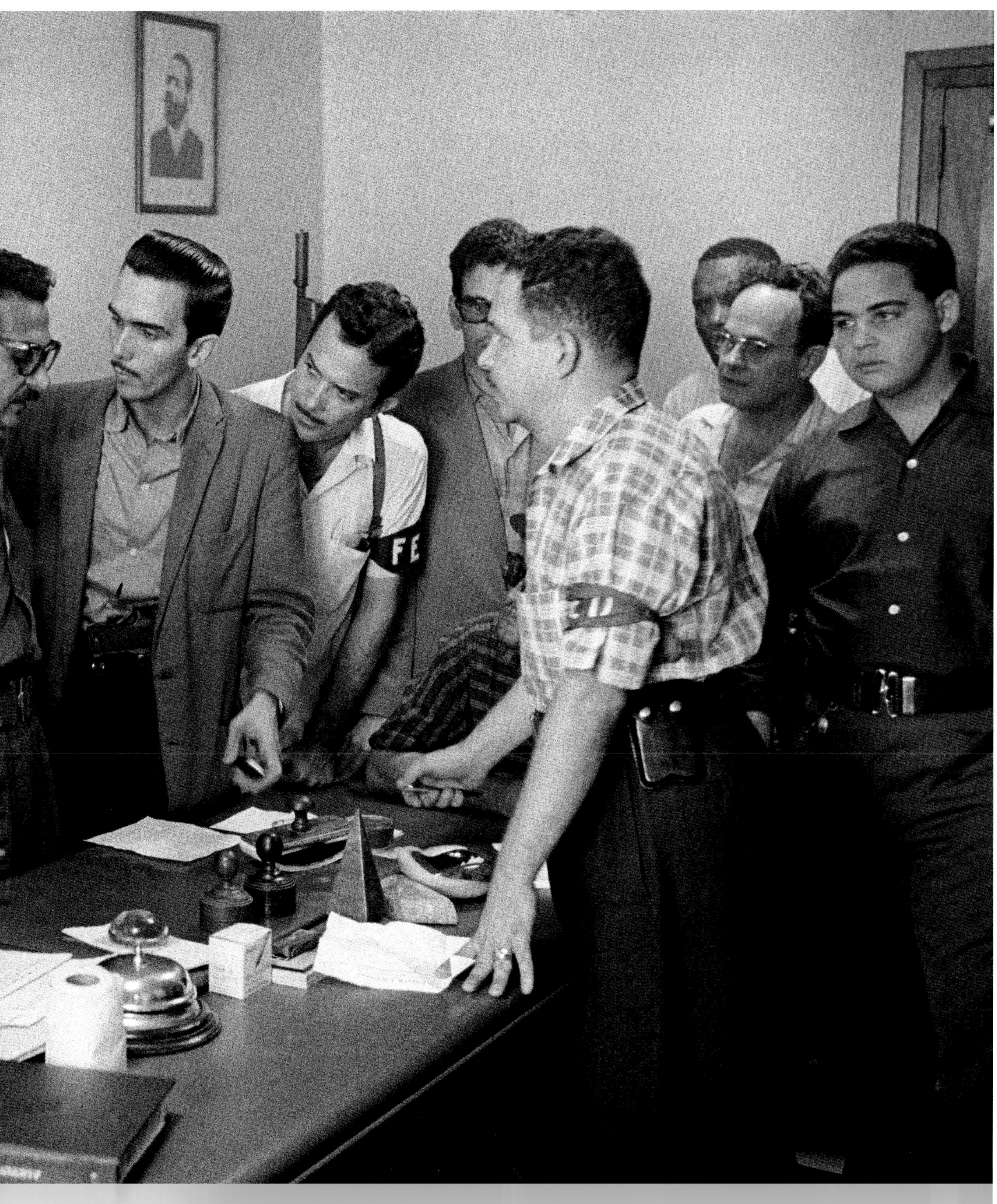

The first few days of January, the people in the streets of Havana were warlike and had armed themselves in a very irregular manner. This was not a gentlemanly revolution.

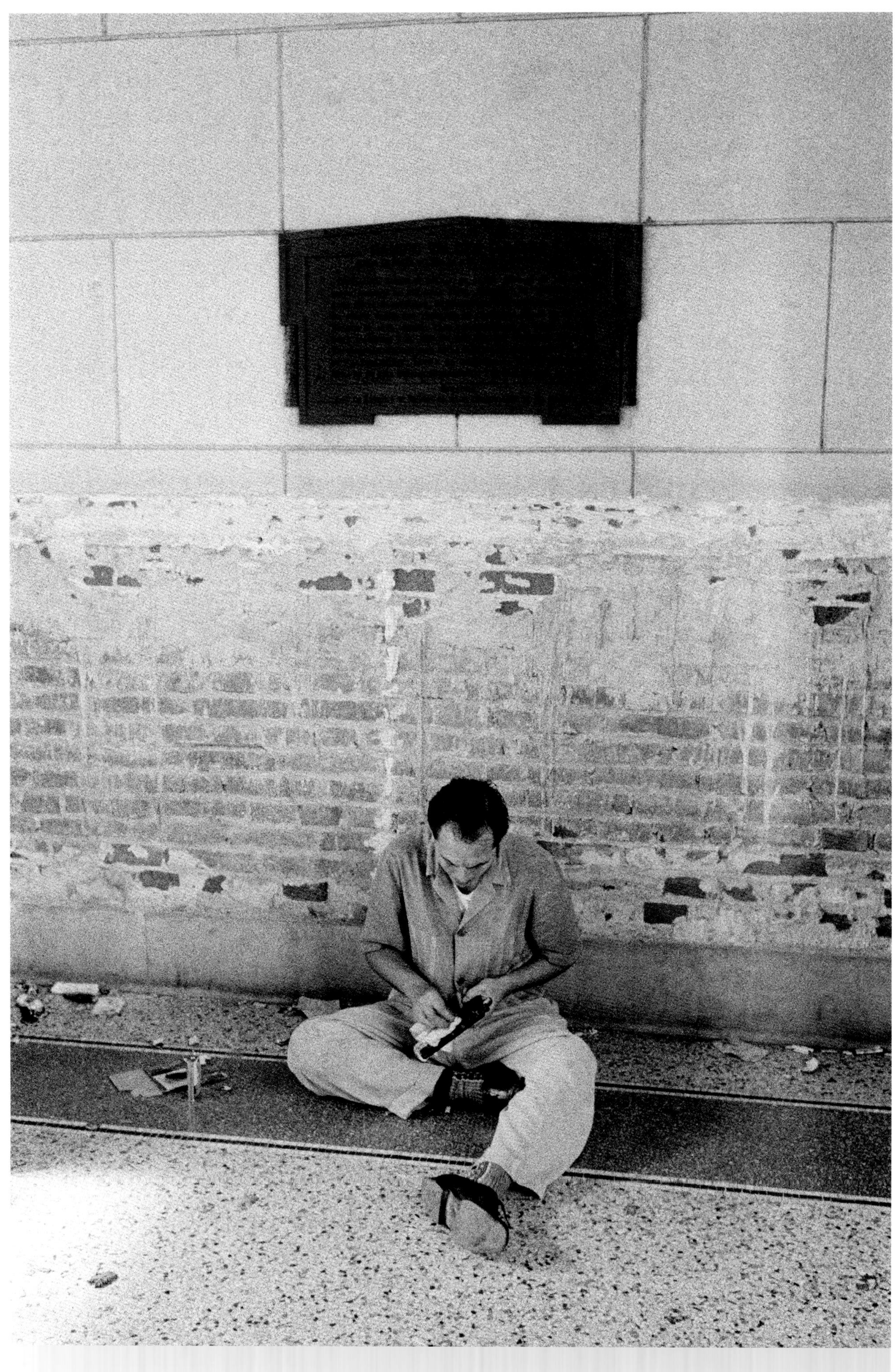

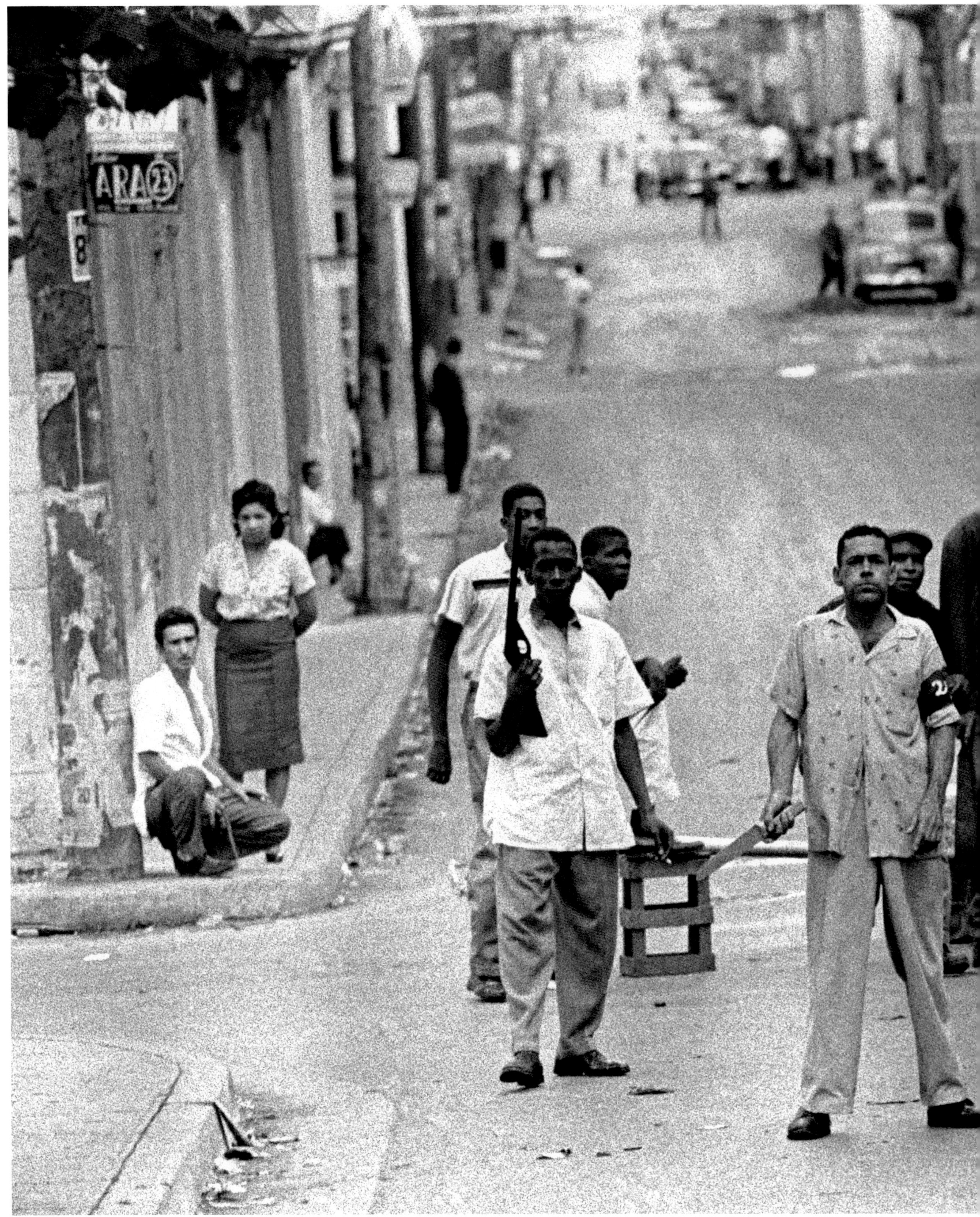
ARA
23

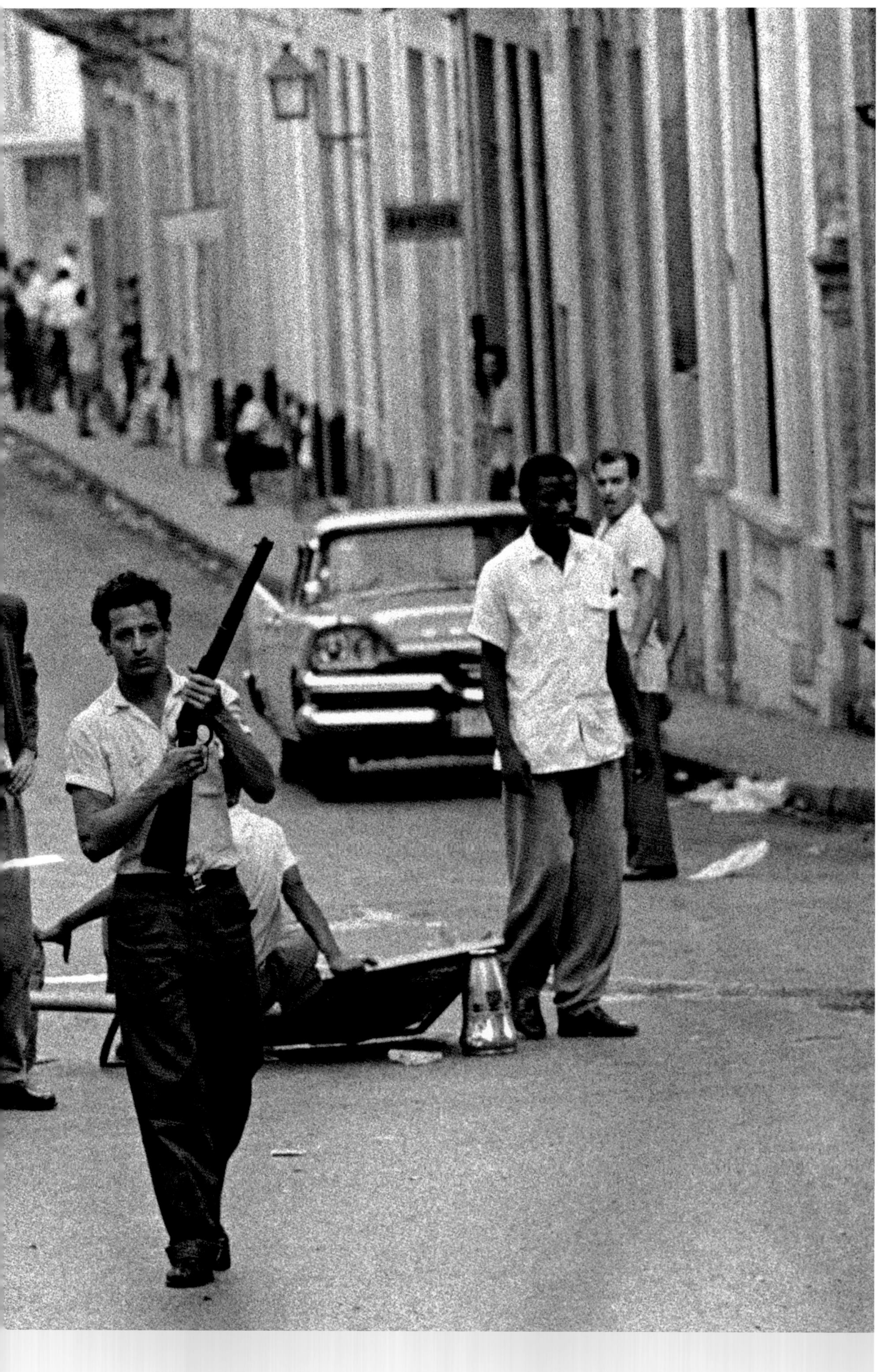

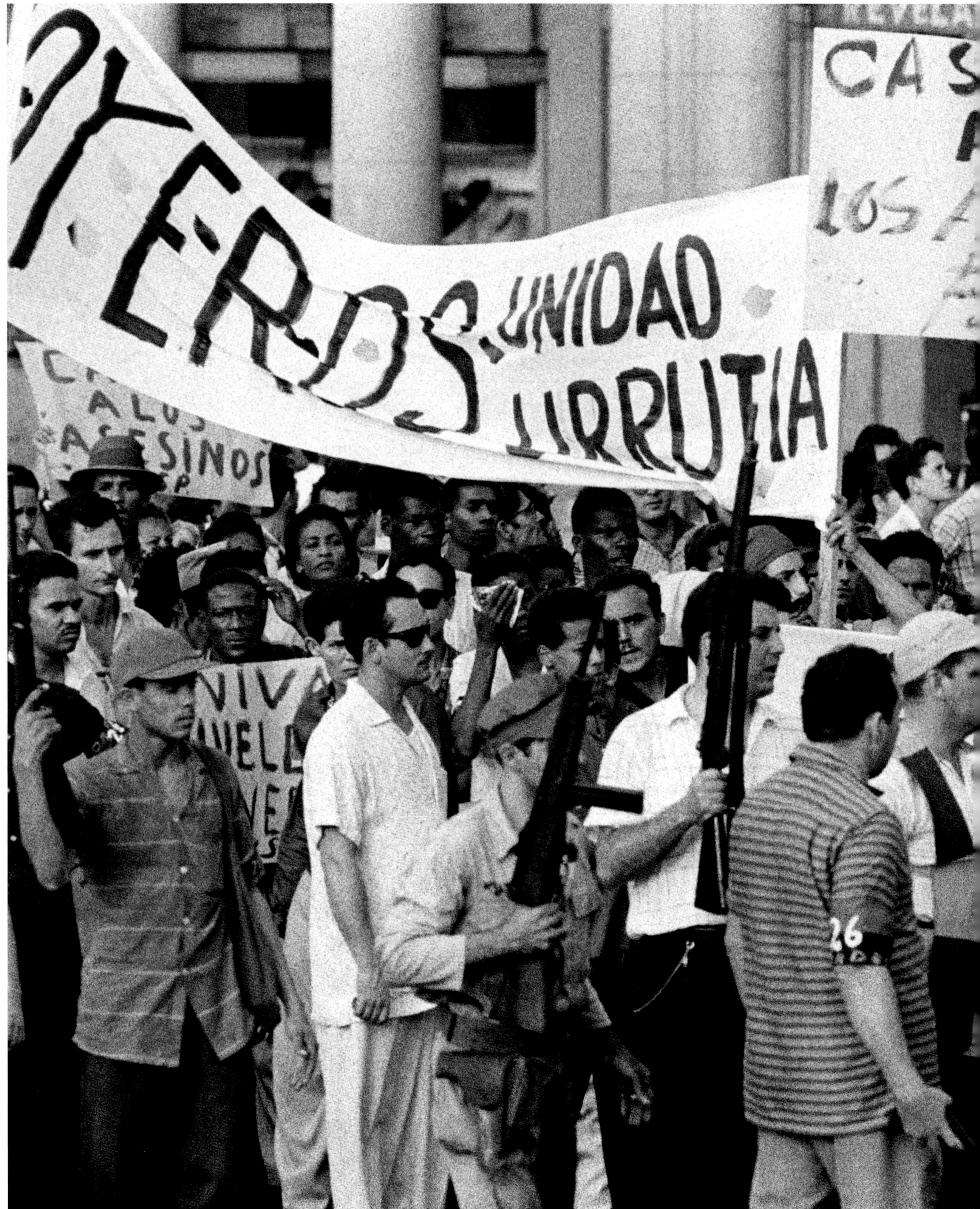
UNIDAD
URRUTIA
ASESINOS
26

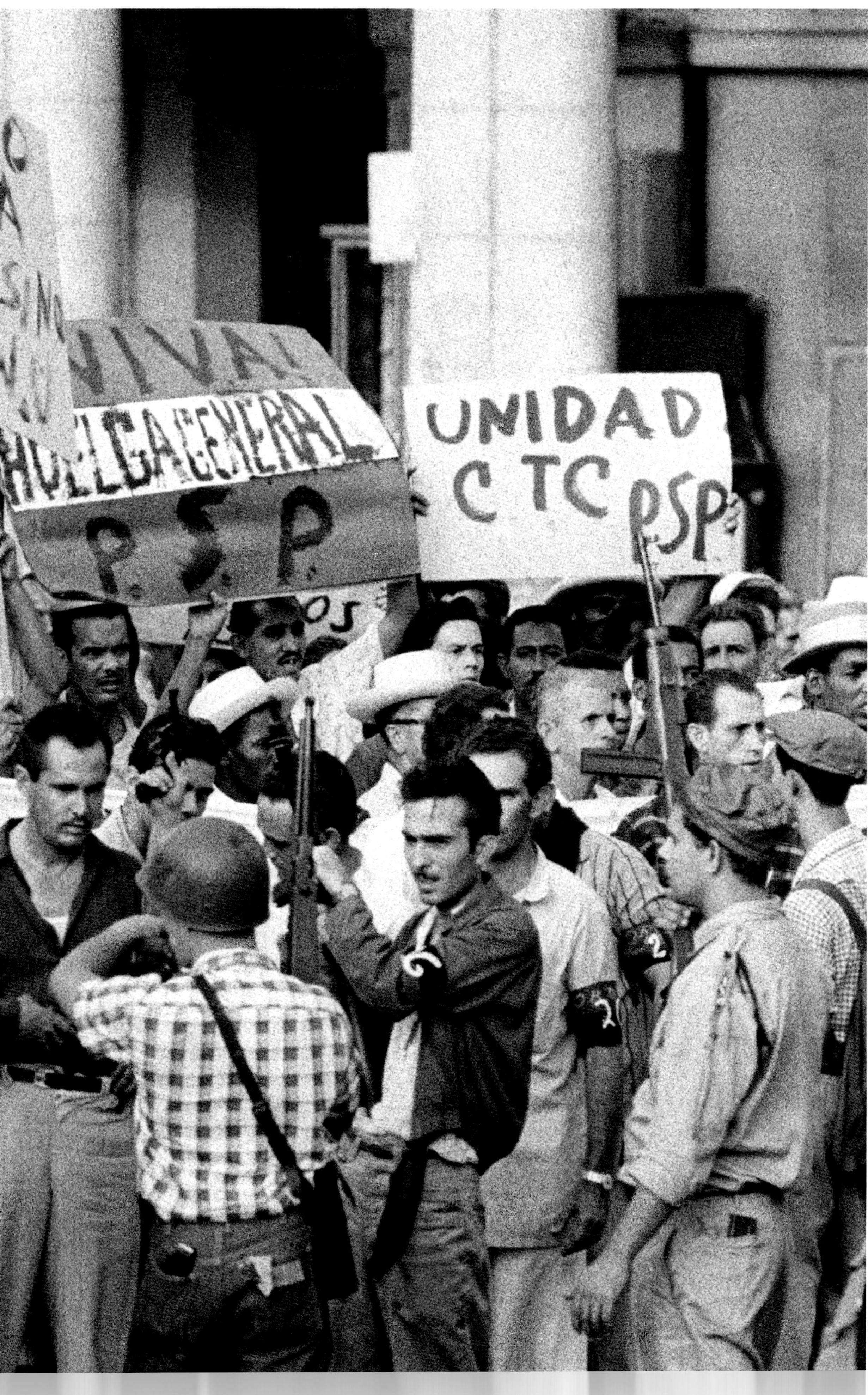
HUELGA GENERAL
P.S.P.
UNIDAD
CTC
PSP

Early celebrations have begun on the streets of Havana.

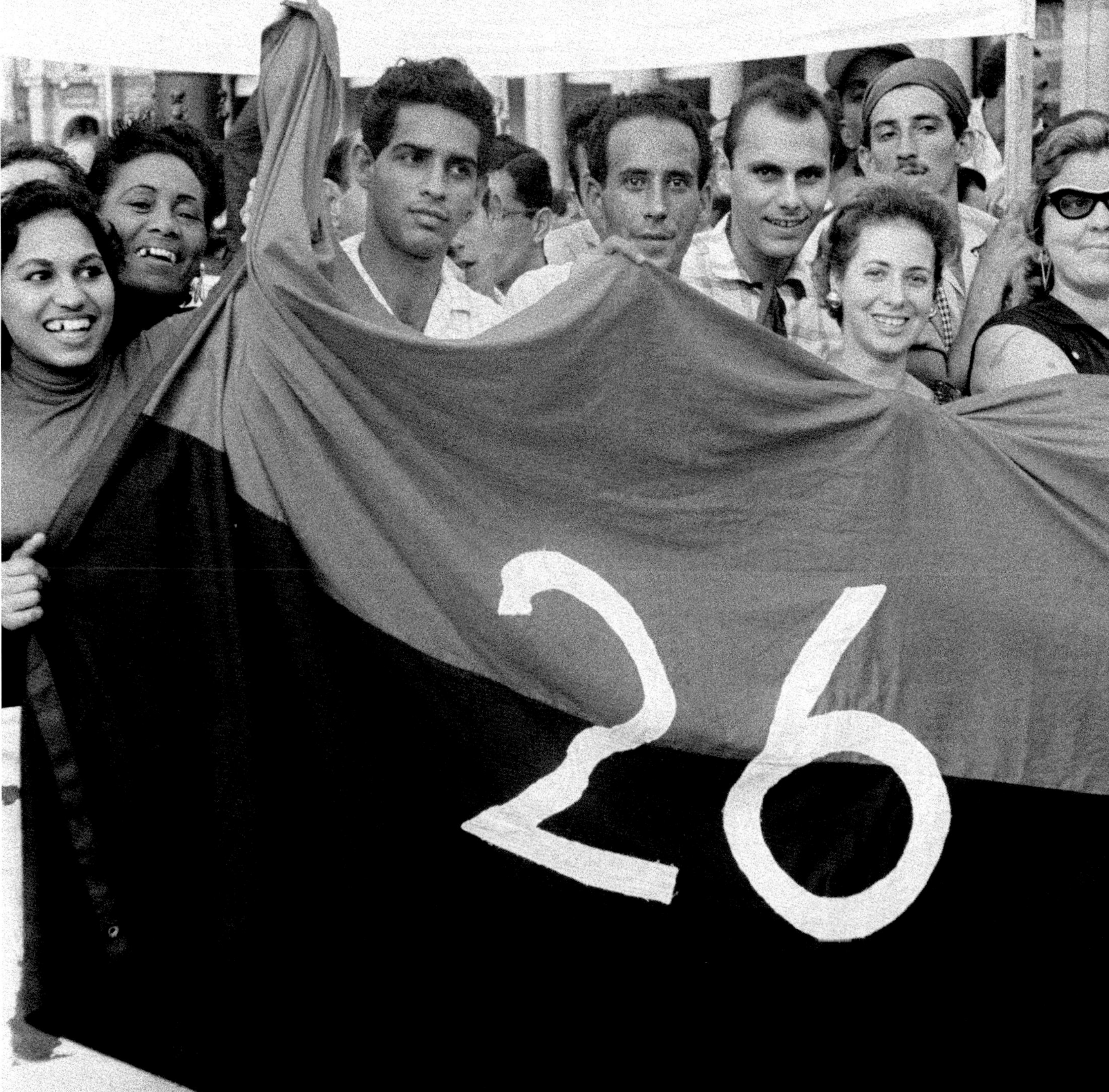
UNIDAD
URRUTIA
26

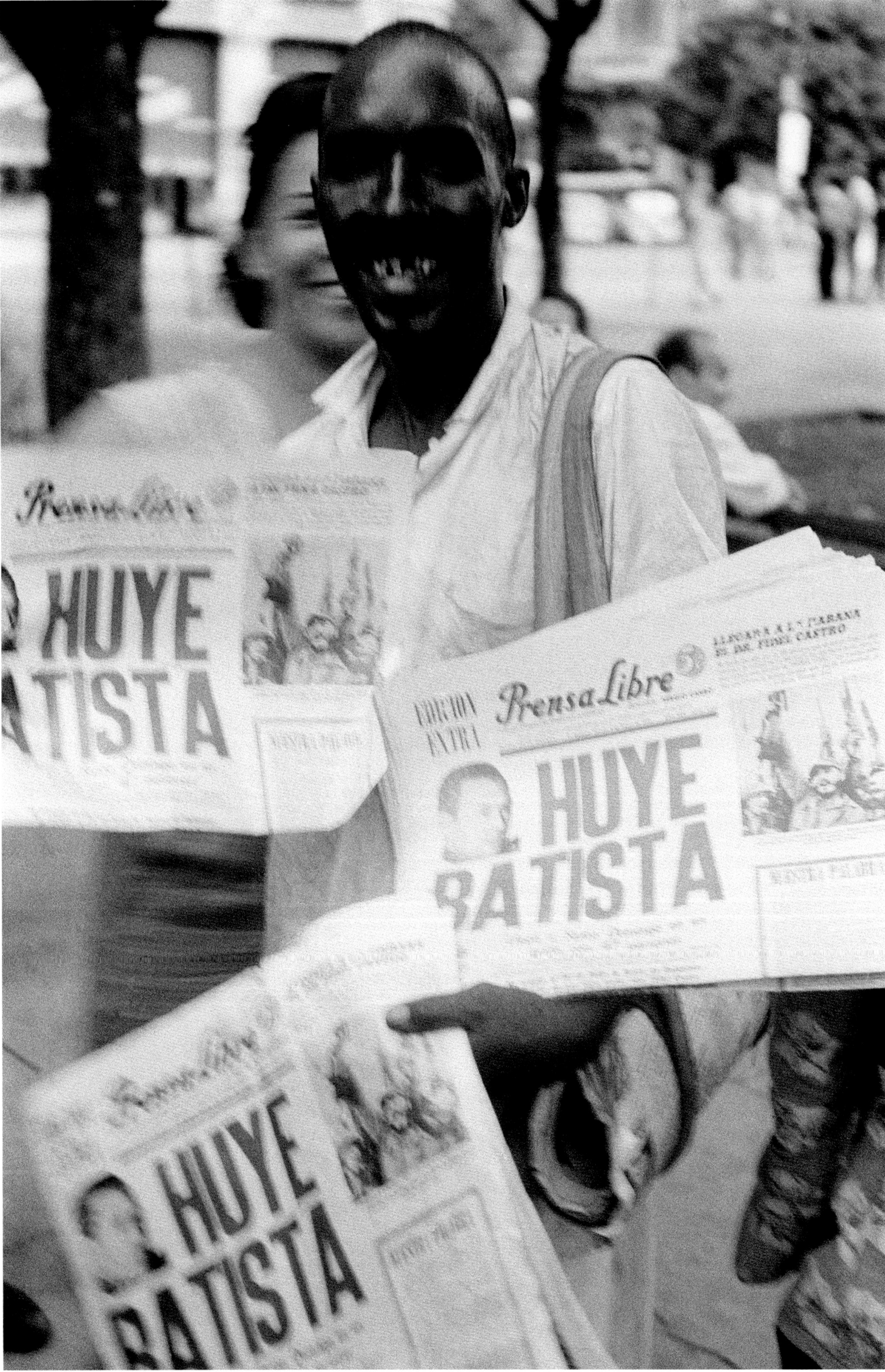
Prensa Libre
EDICION EXTRA
LLEGARA A LA HABANA EL DR. FIDEL CASTRO
HUYE
BATISTA

The news of the departure of Batista spreads through the city. Havana is full of happy people.

Soldiers have moved into the Hilton Hotel. They occupy the lobby and talk to the civilians outside. Some of them are asleep on couches—probably their first sleep on upholstery since they joined the revolution over a year ago. I don't know if they are down from the hills as they are not bearded.

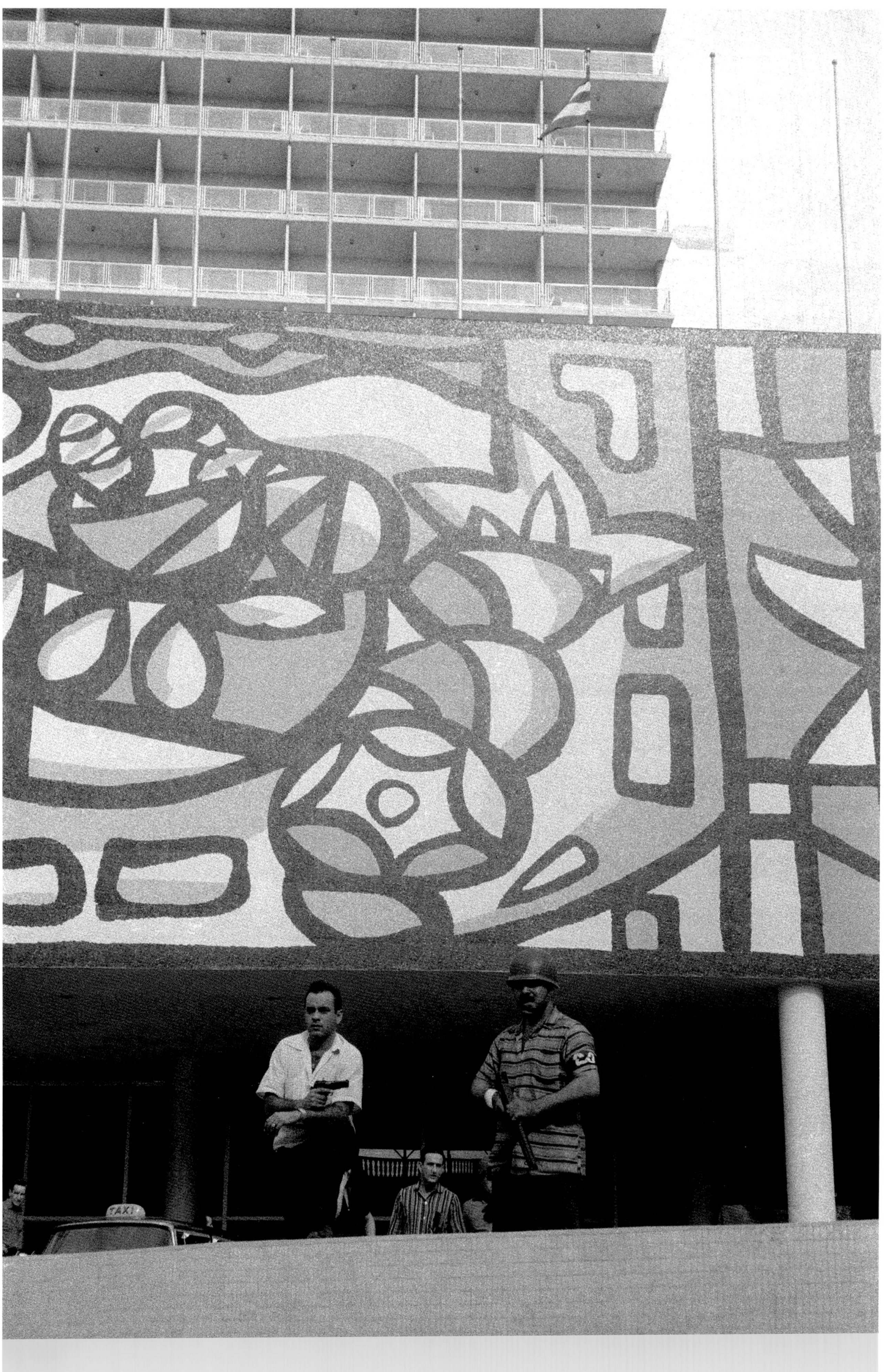
TAXI

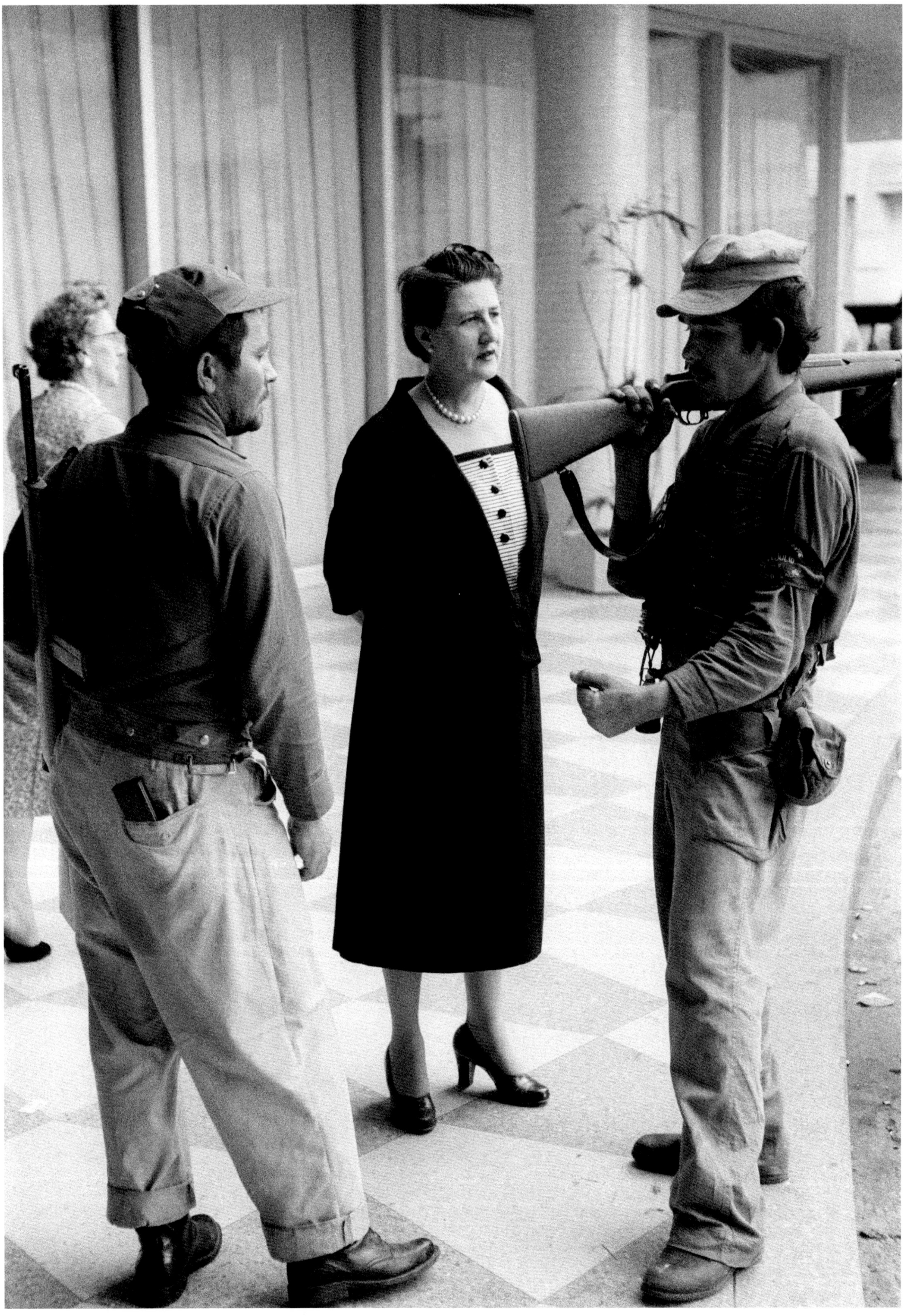

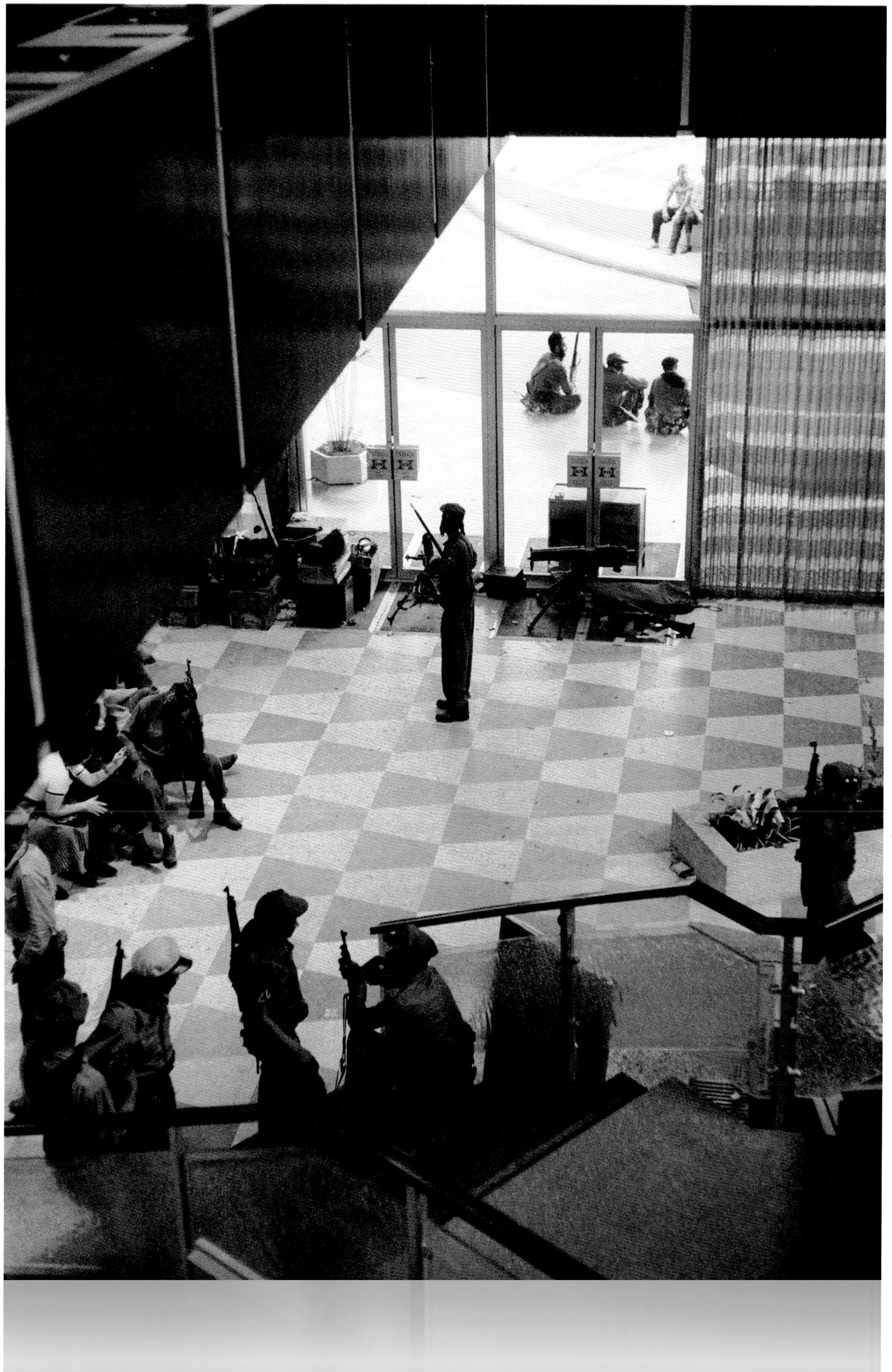

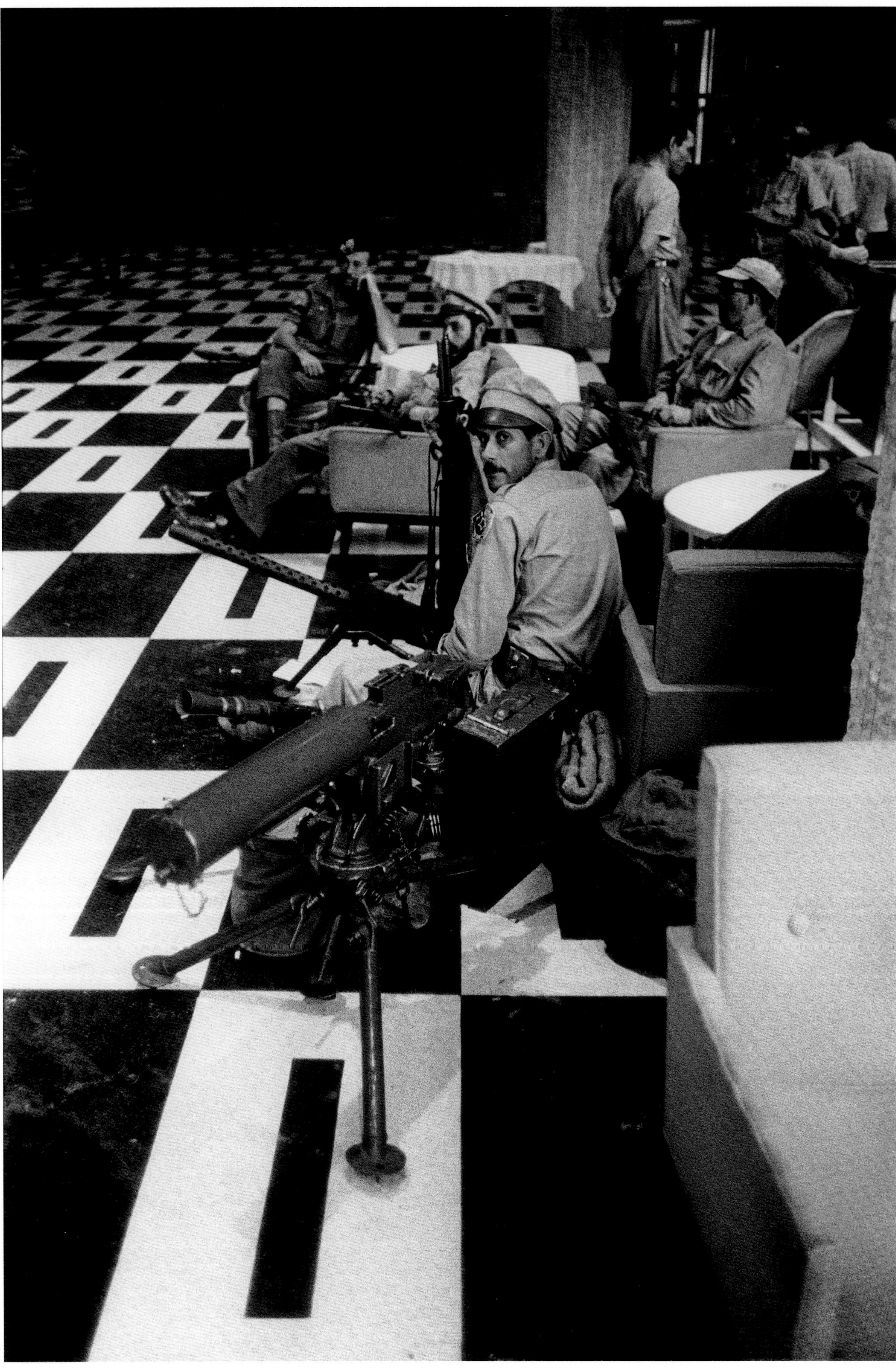

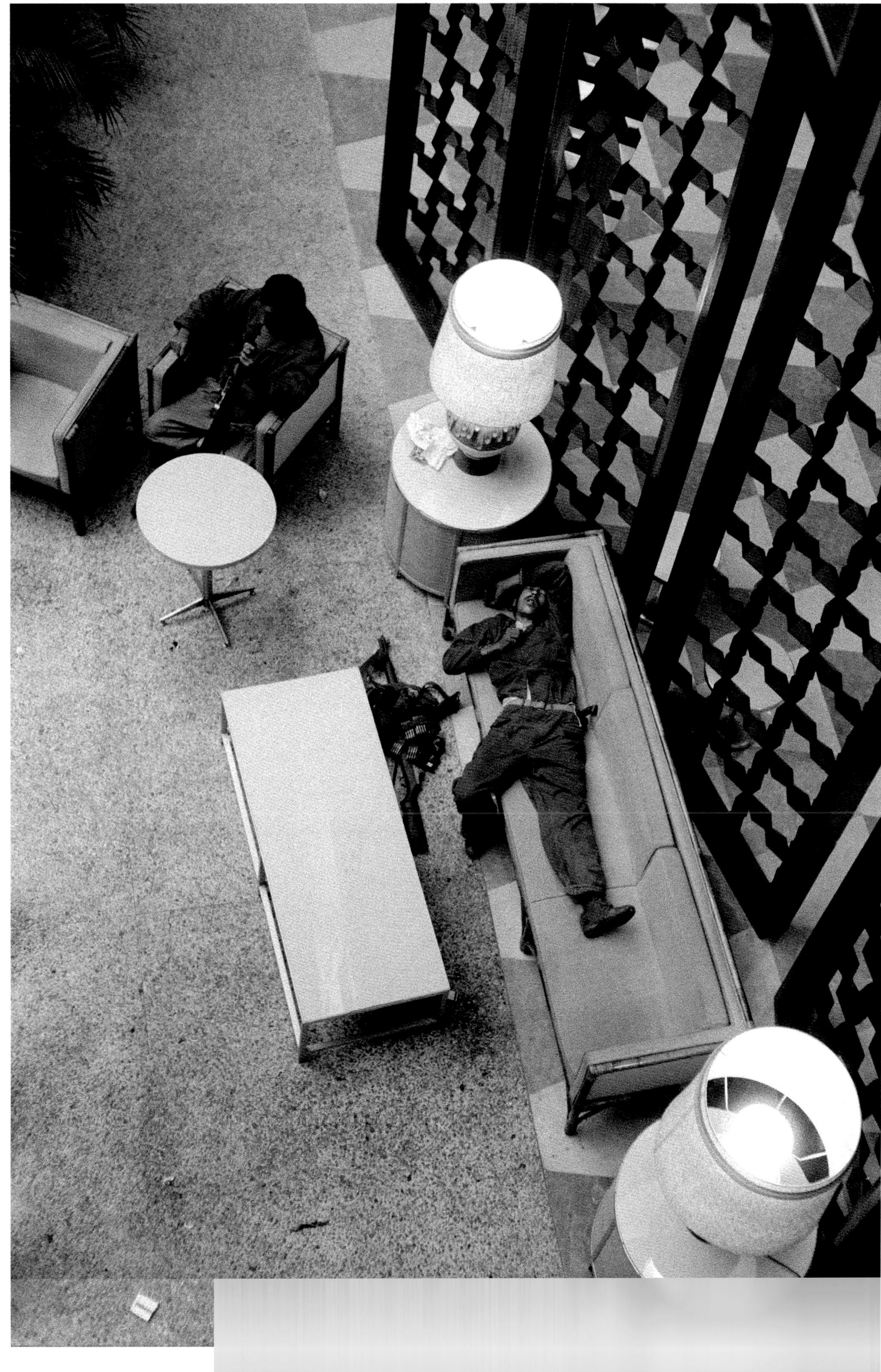

The first rallies took place at the university—the center of Castro's activity in Havana. Young women students have joined Castro.

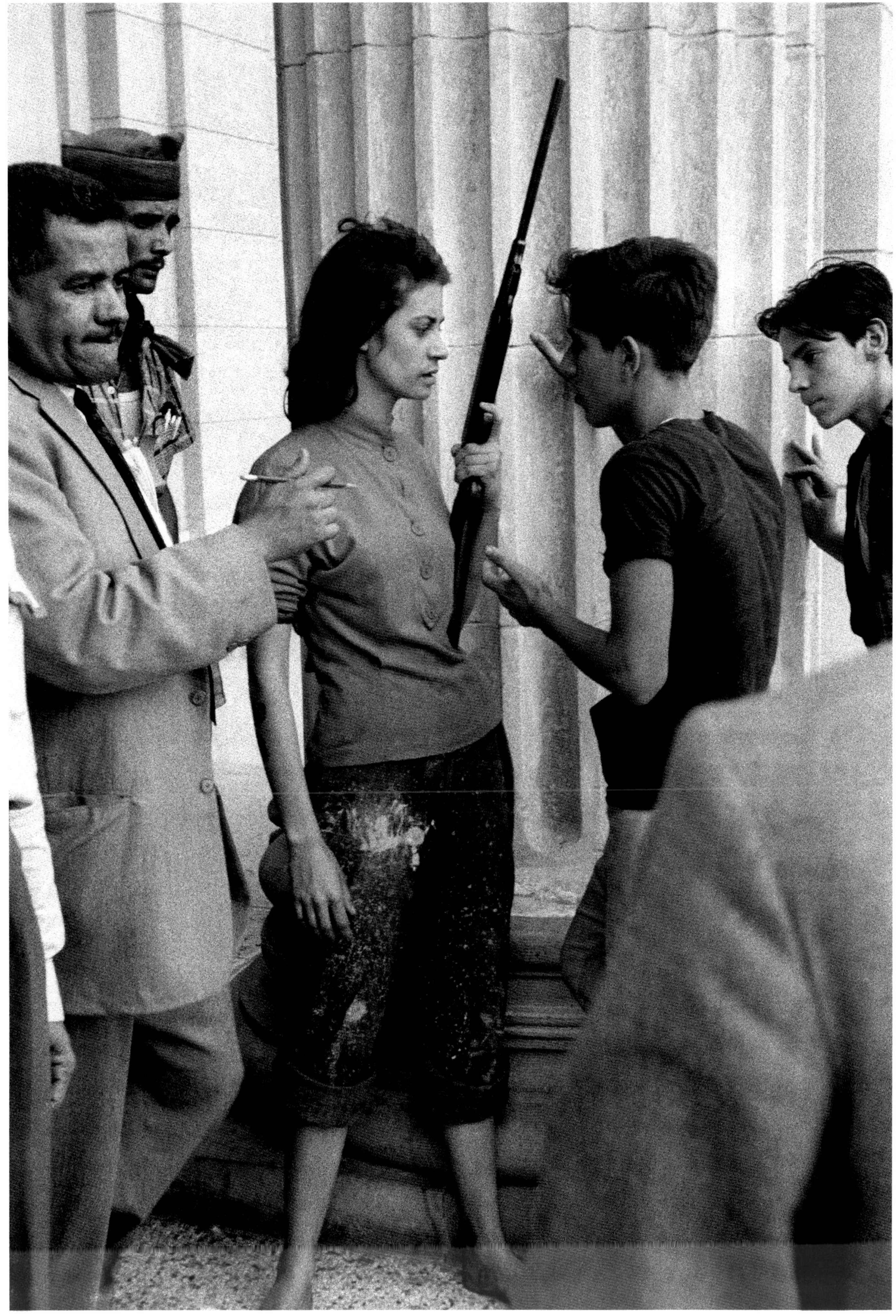

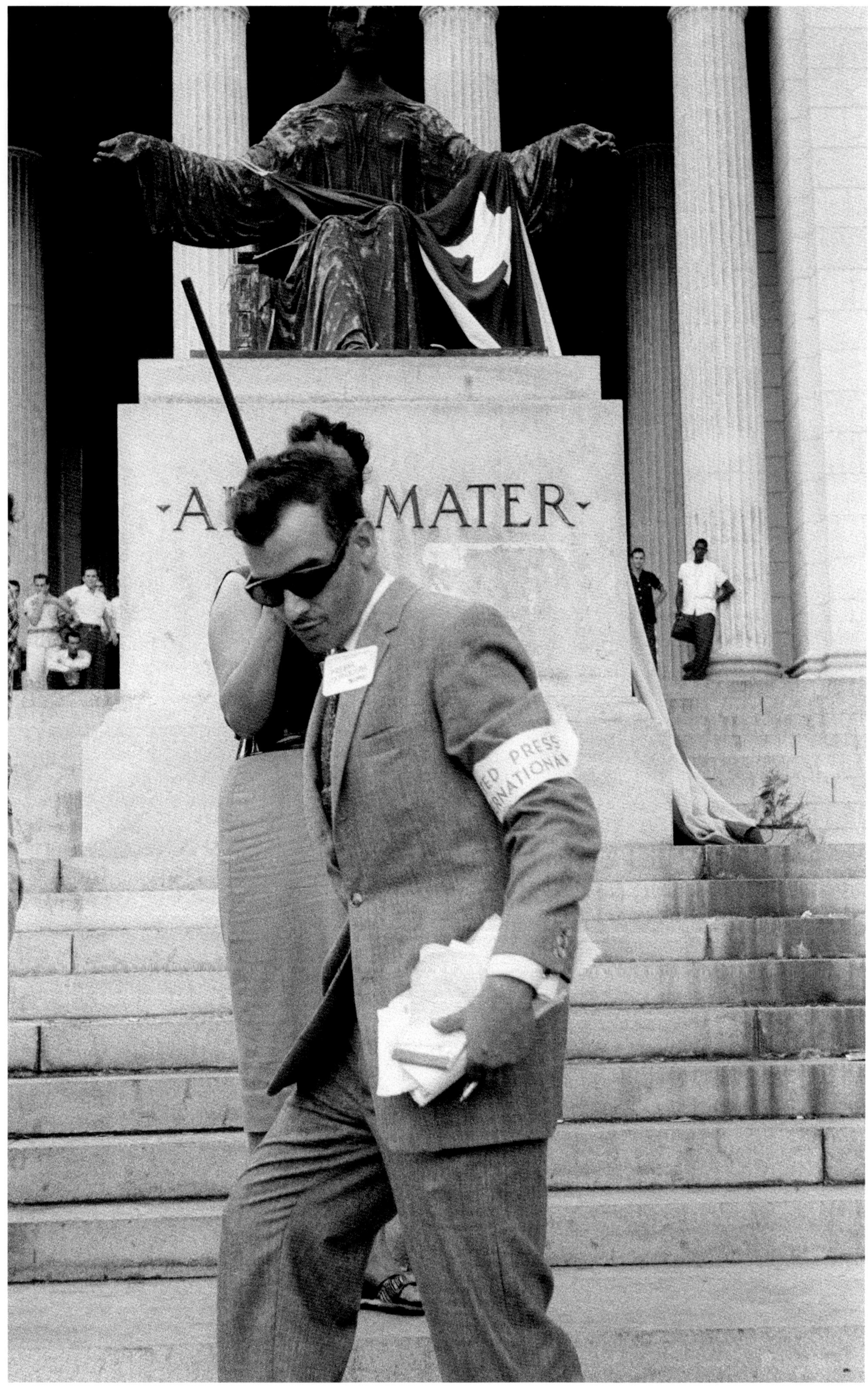
MATER
ED PRESS
RNATIONA

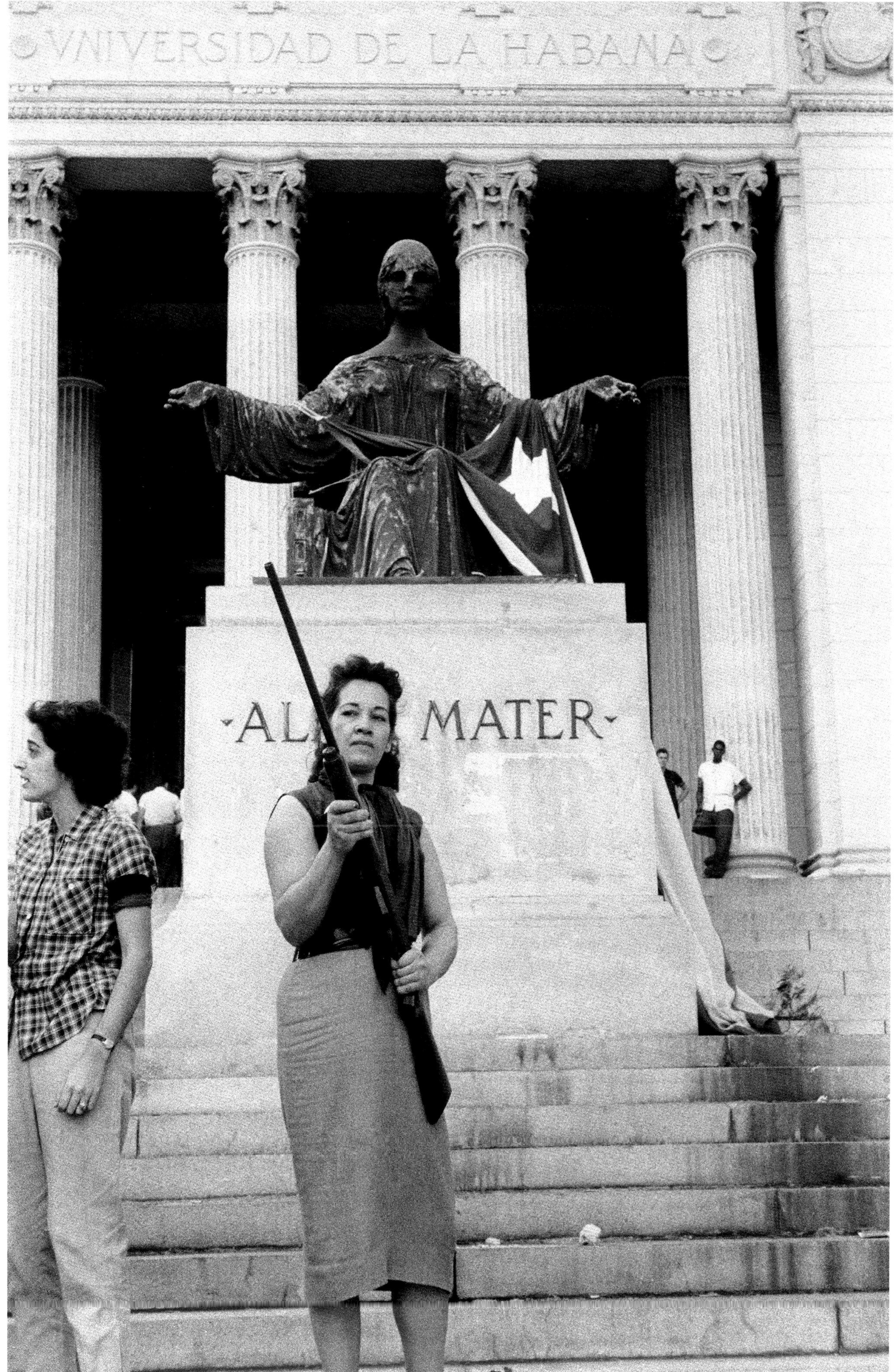
VNIVERSIDAD DE LA HABANA
ALMA MATER

A pretty, fancy Havana girl greets a young rebel soldier just after a rebel column arrives in the city. He wears his hair long after the fashion of the rebel leaders who swore not to be shorn until Batista had been ousted. Everywhere in Havana this day, authentic rebels like this one are heroes.

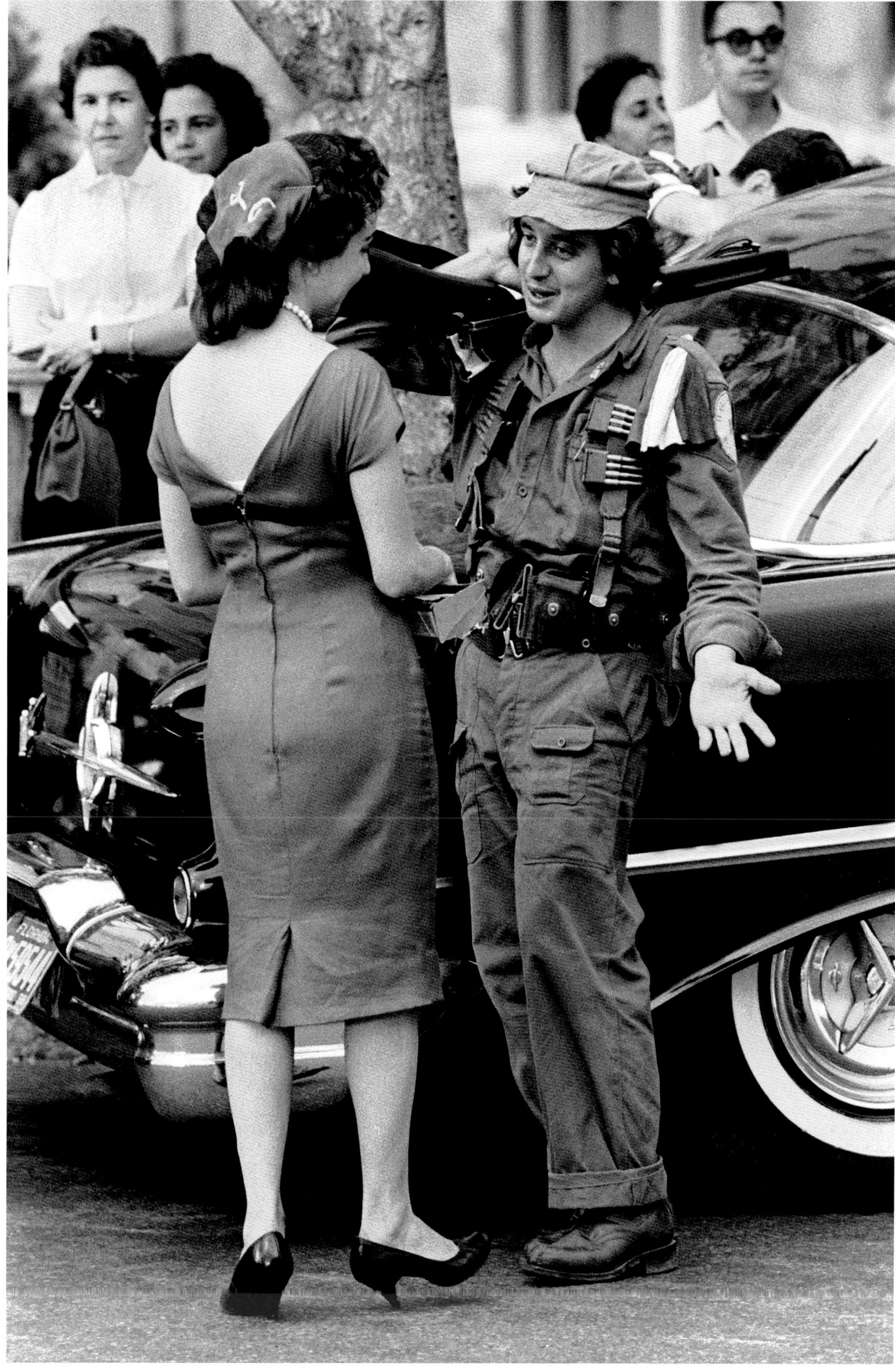

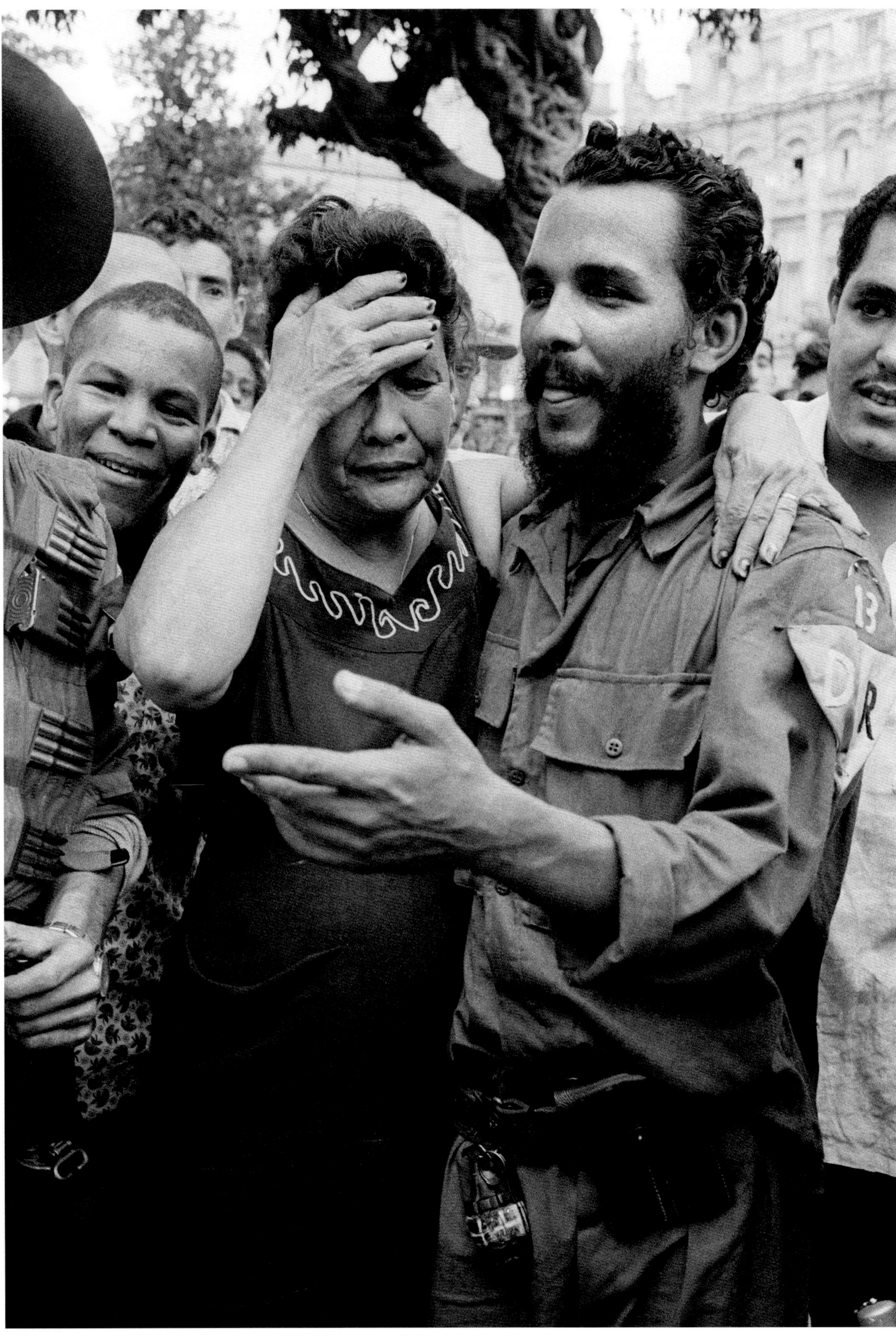
13
DR

People are finding one another after some of them have come out of hiding from Batista. A Havana mother whose rebel son had been fighting for Castro in the mountains for six months breaks into tears of joy as they are reunited.

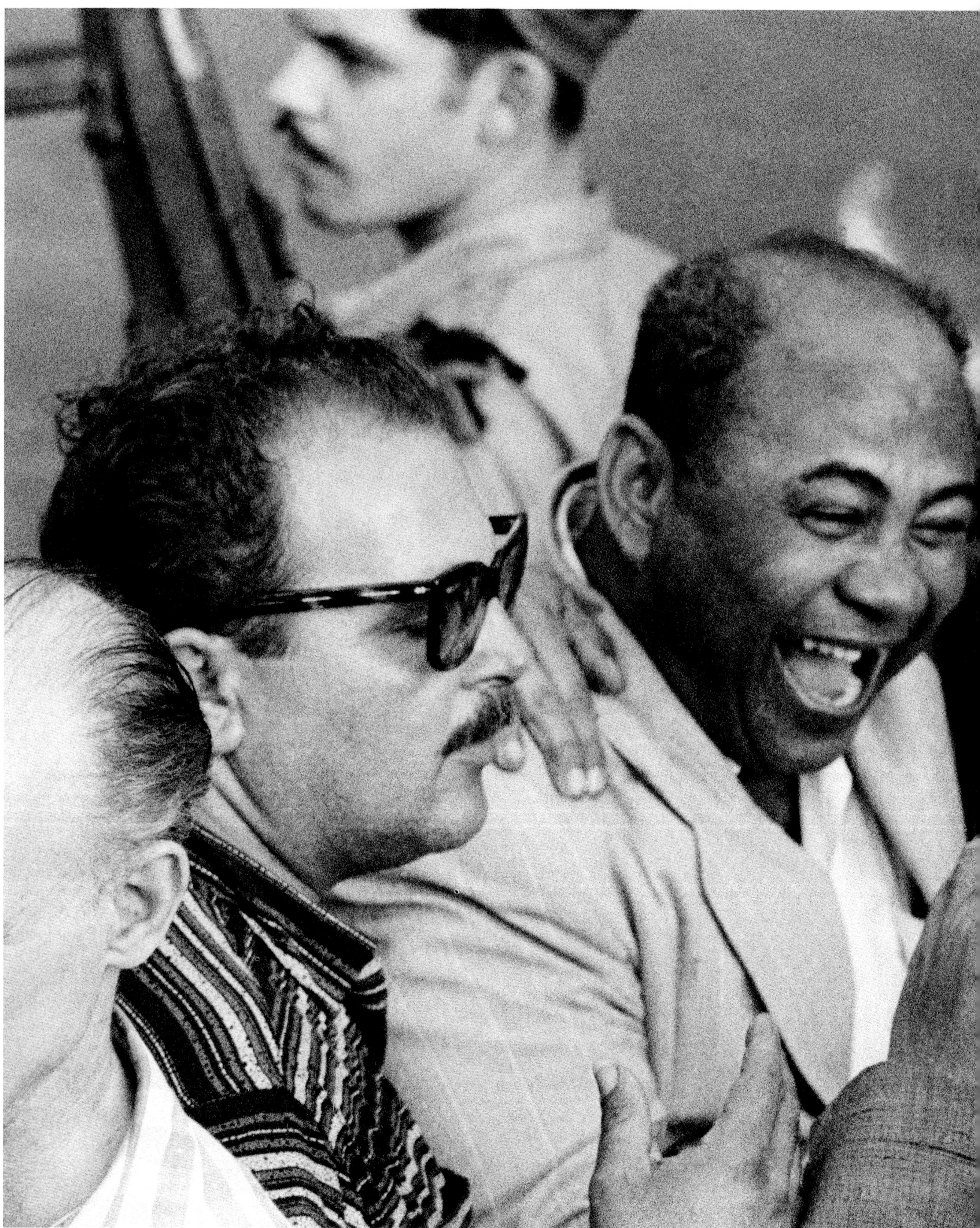

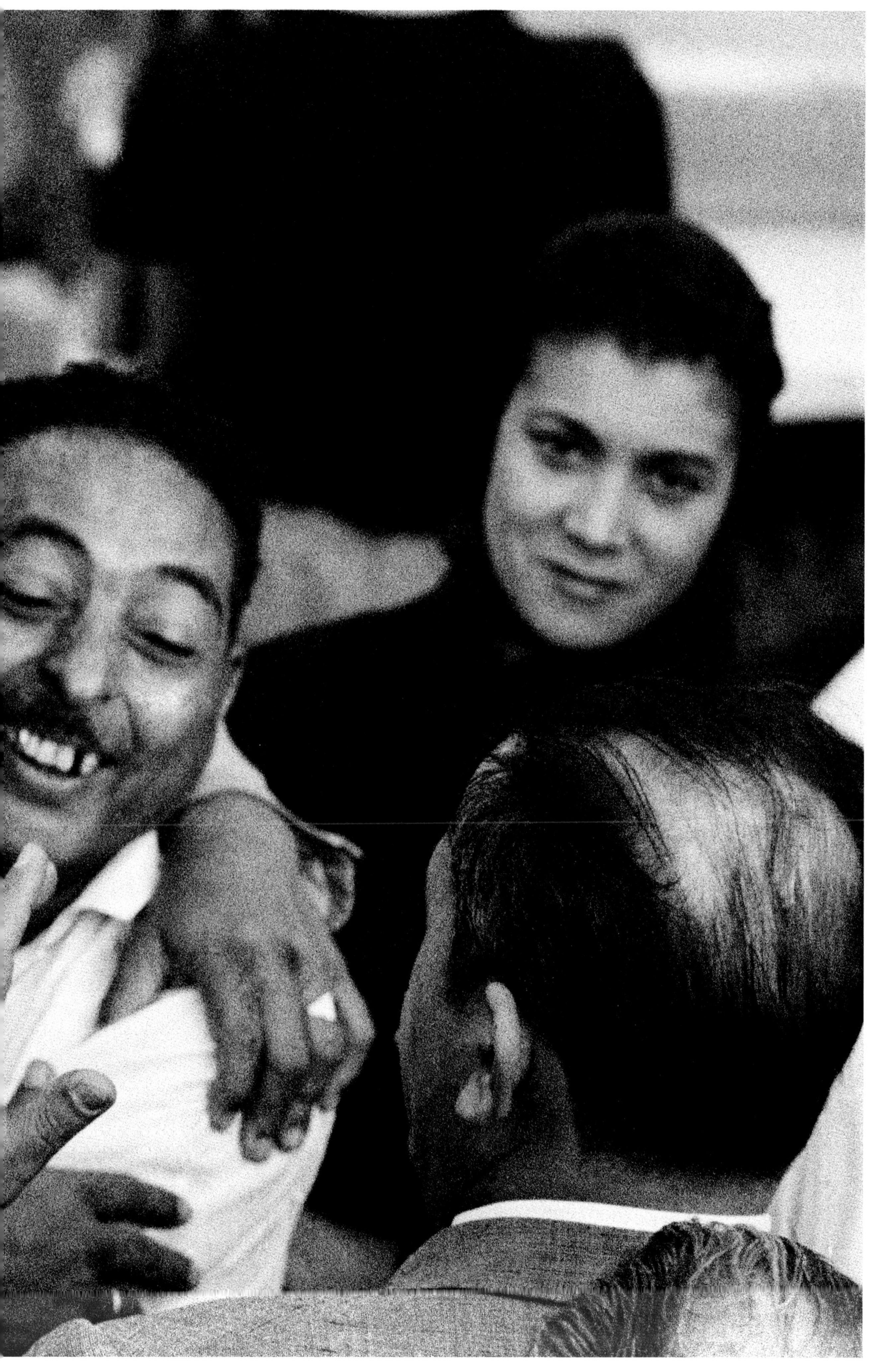

It was not clear who was the legitimate rebel and who was not until the day when some of the bearded ragged stalwarts, the "barbudos" from the mountains, came in wearing army fatigues and bandoliers of ammunition around their chests. They quickly established control of the city.

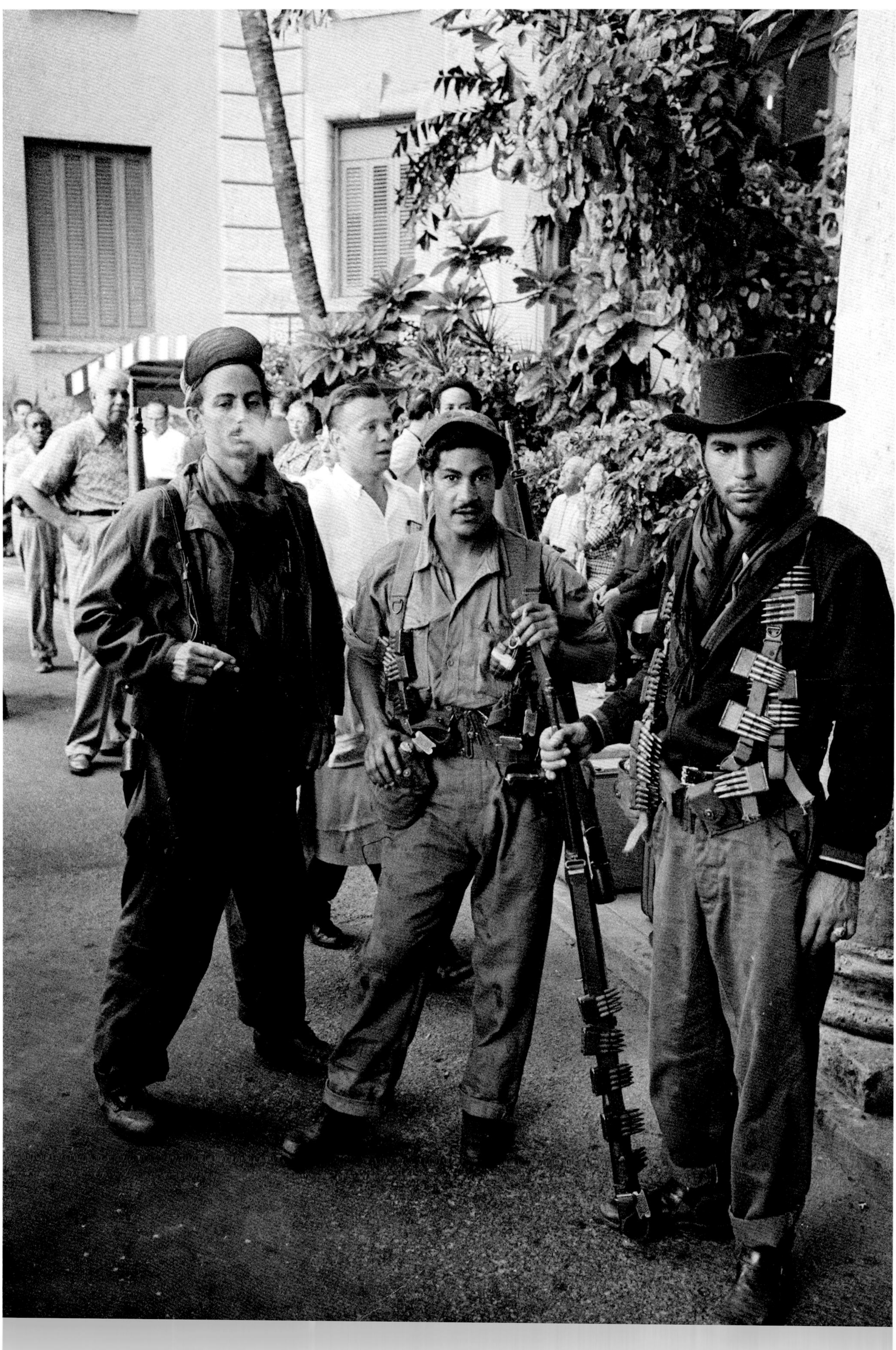

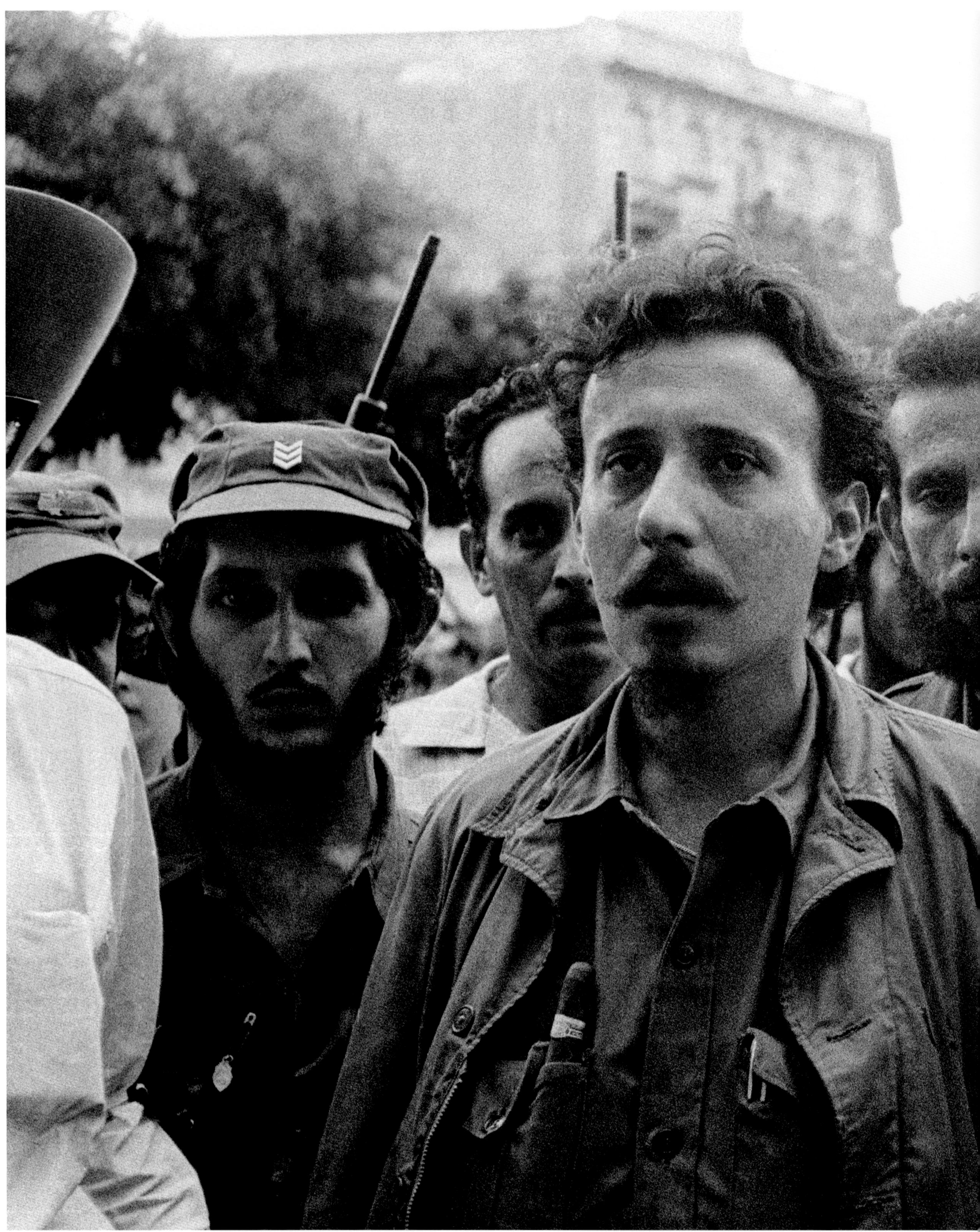

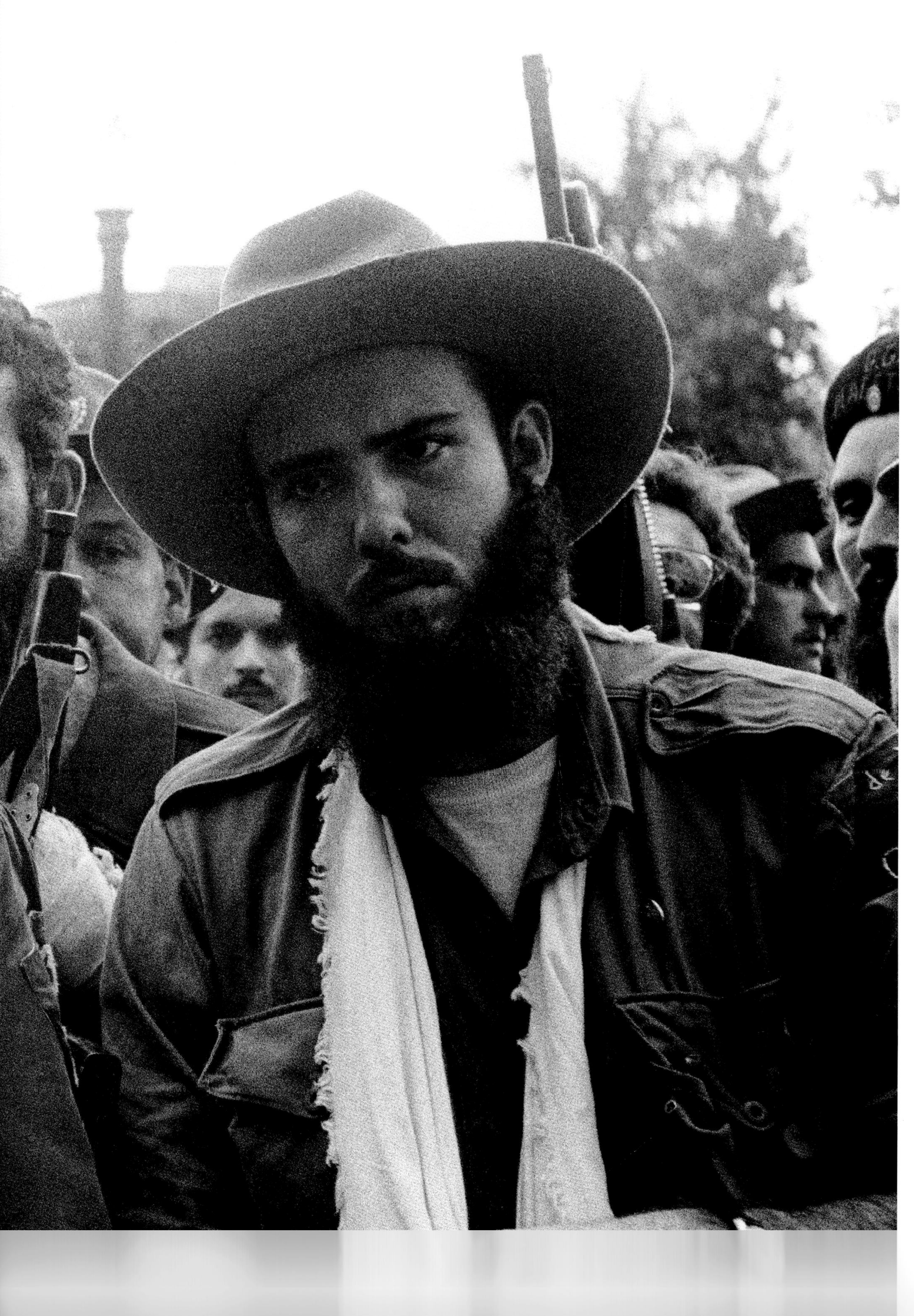

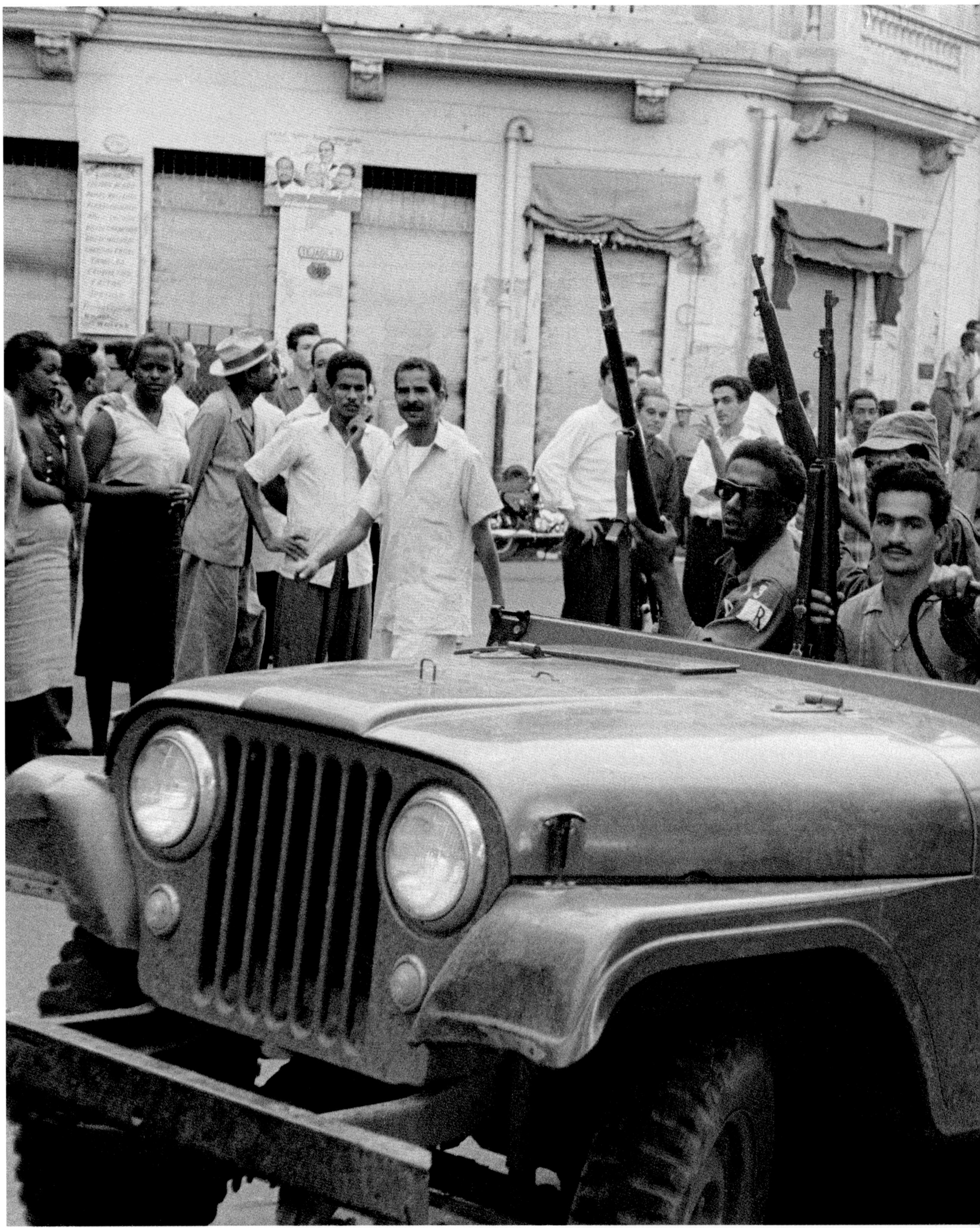

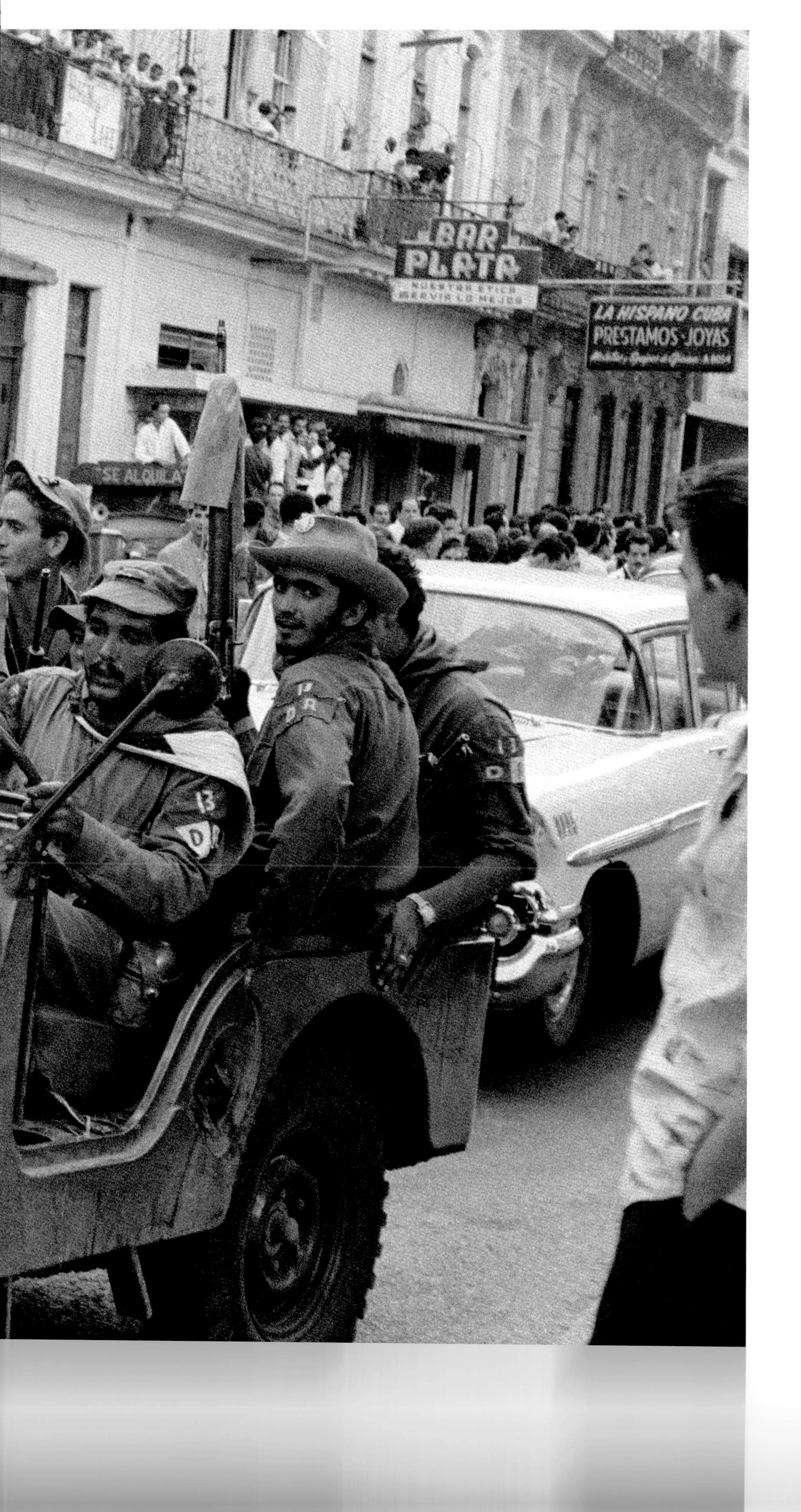
BAR
PLATA
LA HISPANO CUBA
PRESTAMOS - JOYAS
SE ALQUILA

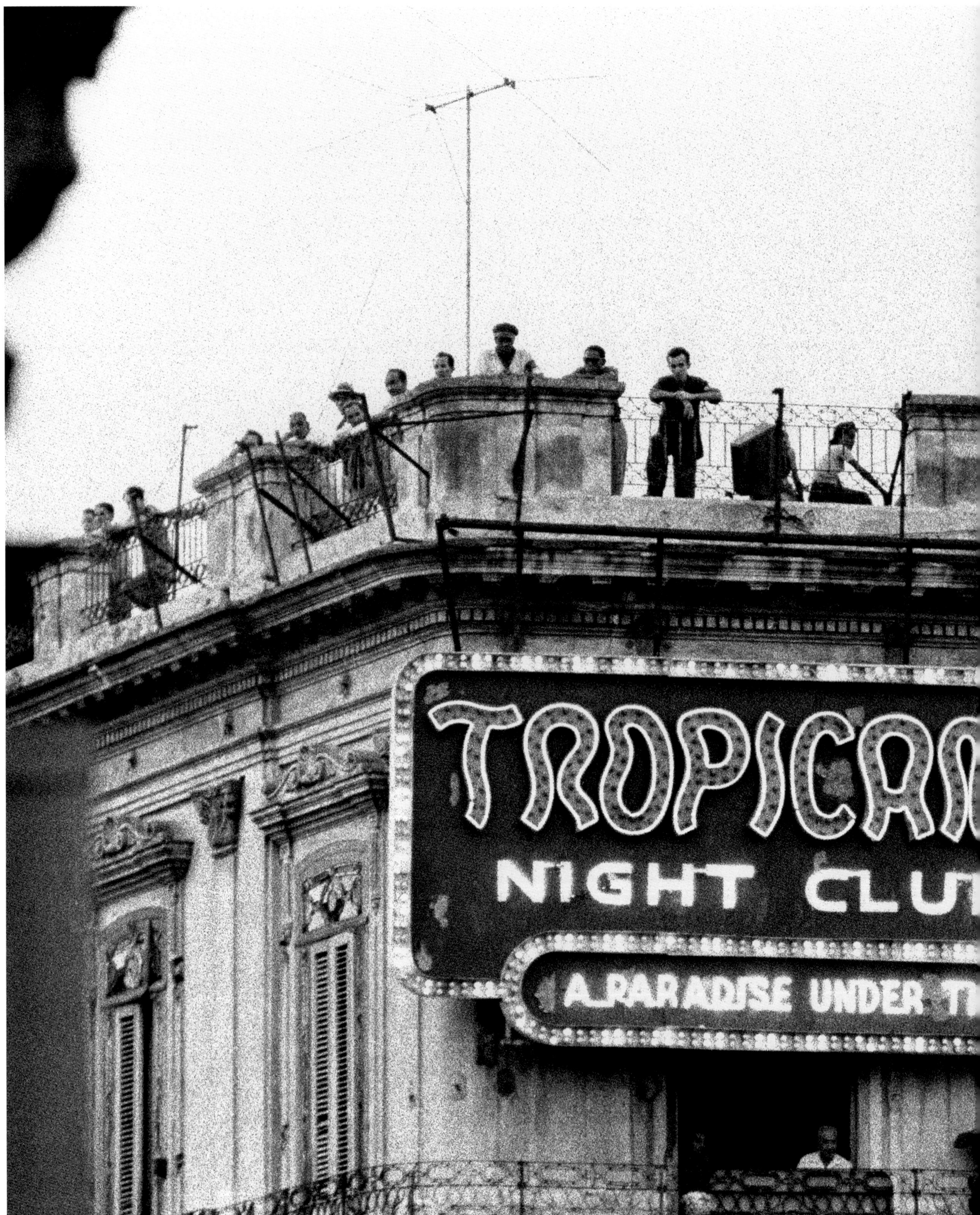
NIGHT CLU
A PARADISE UNDER T

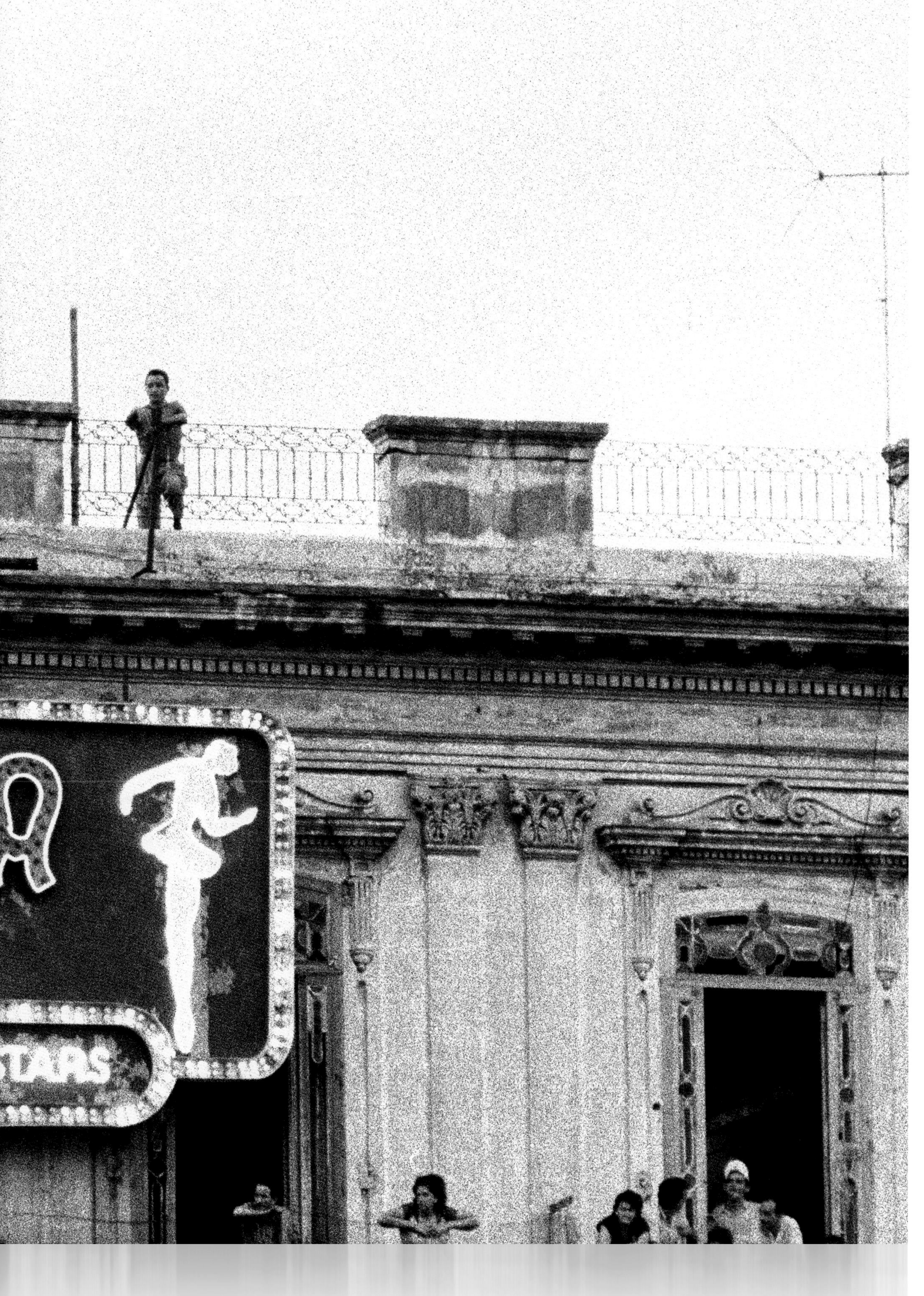
STARS

Anticipating his arrival in Santa Clara, people wait for Castro to appear. Santa Clara was the one big battle of the revolution. Che Guevara had captured the city. That was the signal to the army that they were finished and they asked Batista to leave. Although the city had been in rebel hands, the column with Castro arriving was greeted almost like the liberation of Paris. This was the first sight that I had gotten of Castro.

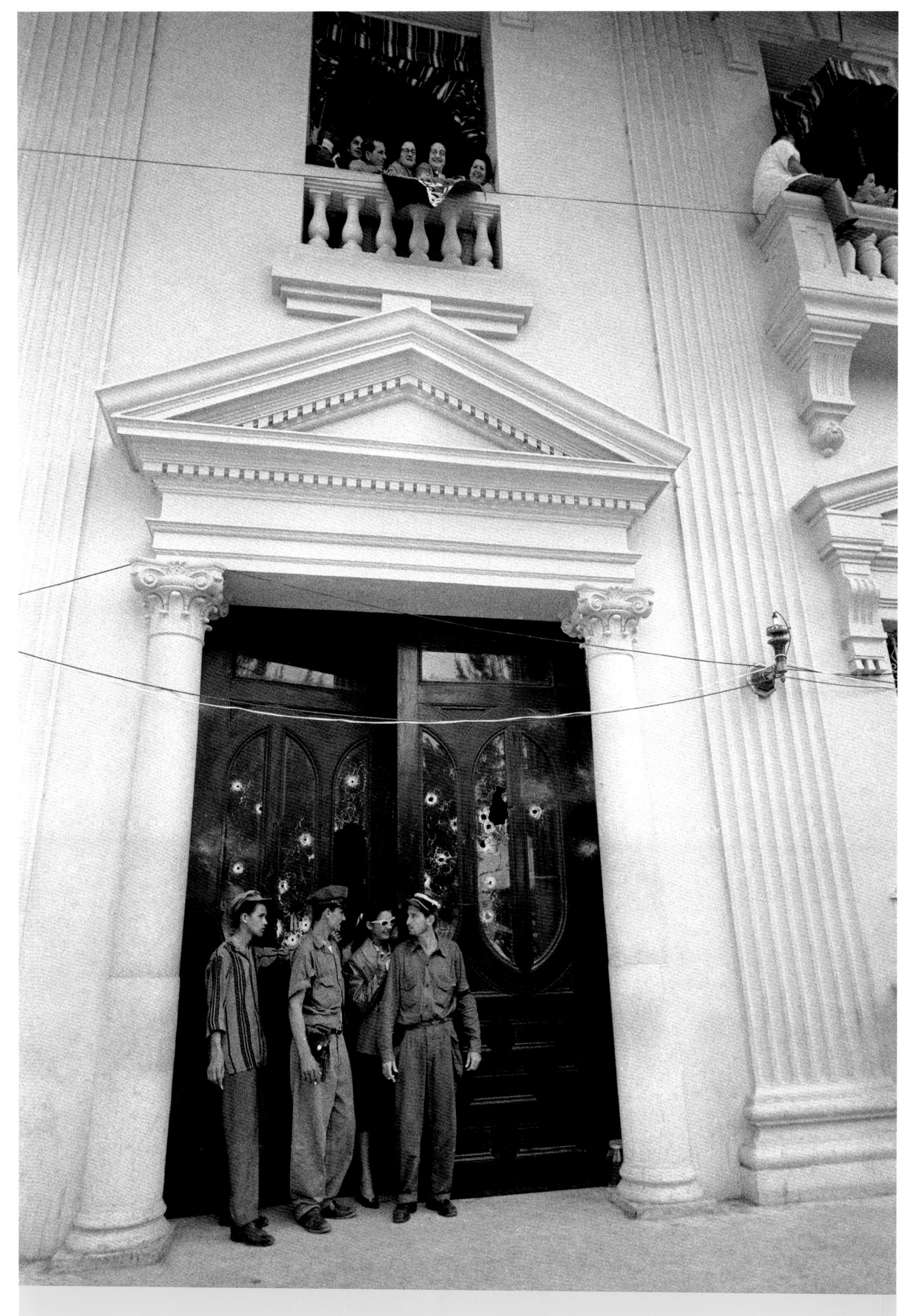

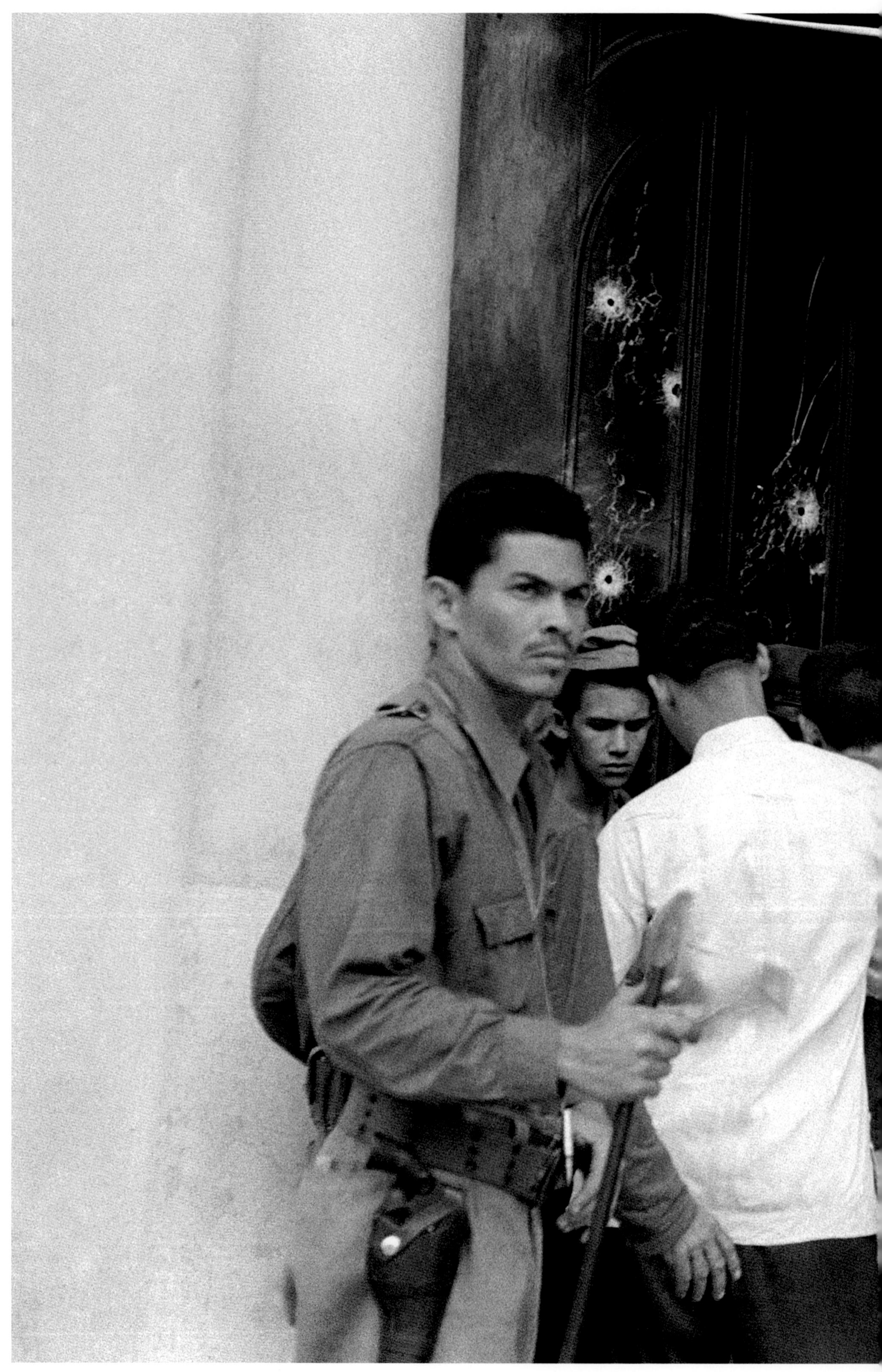

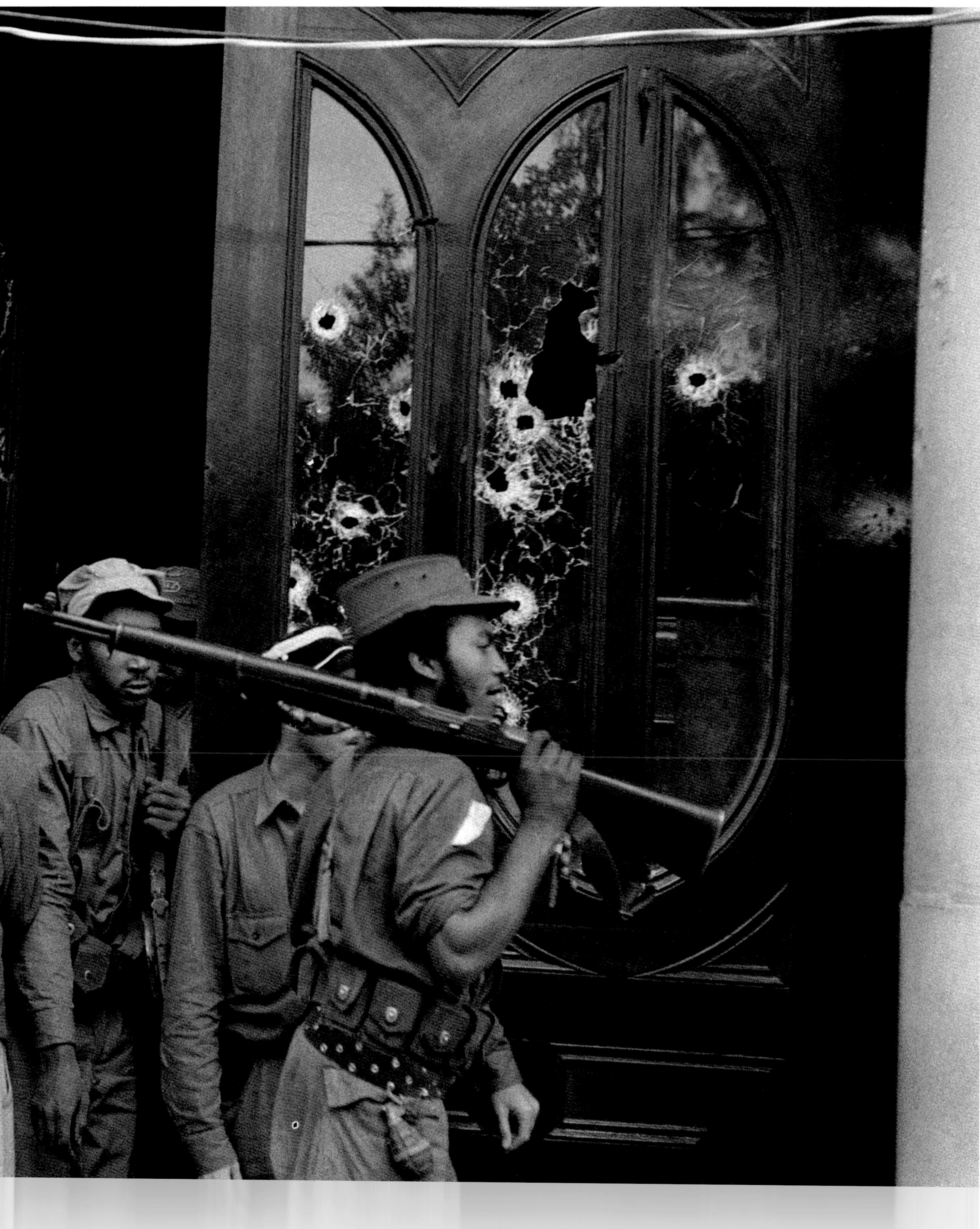

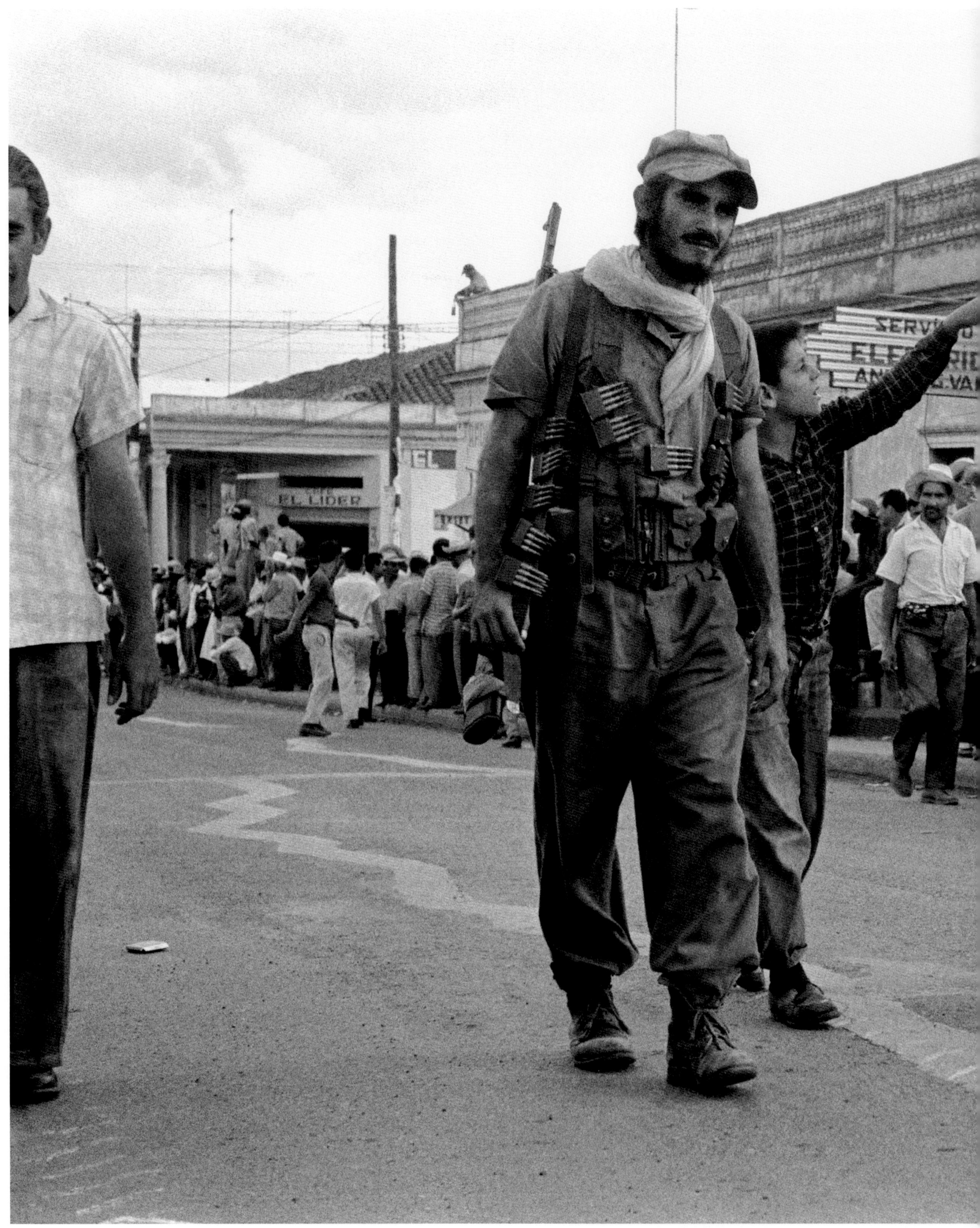
EL LIDER

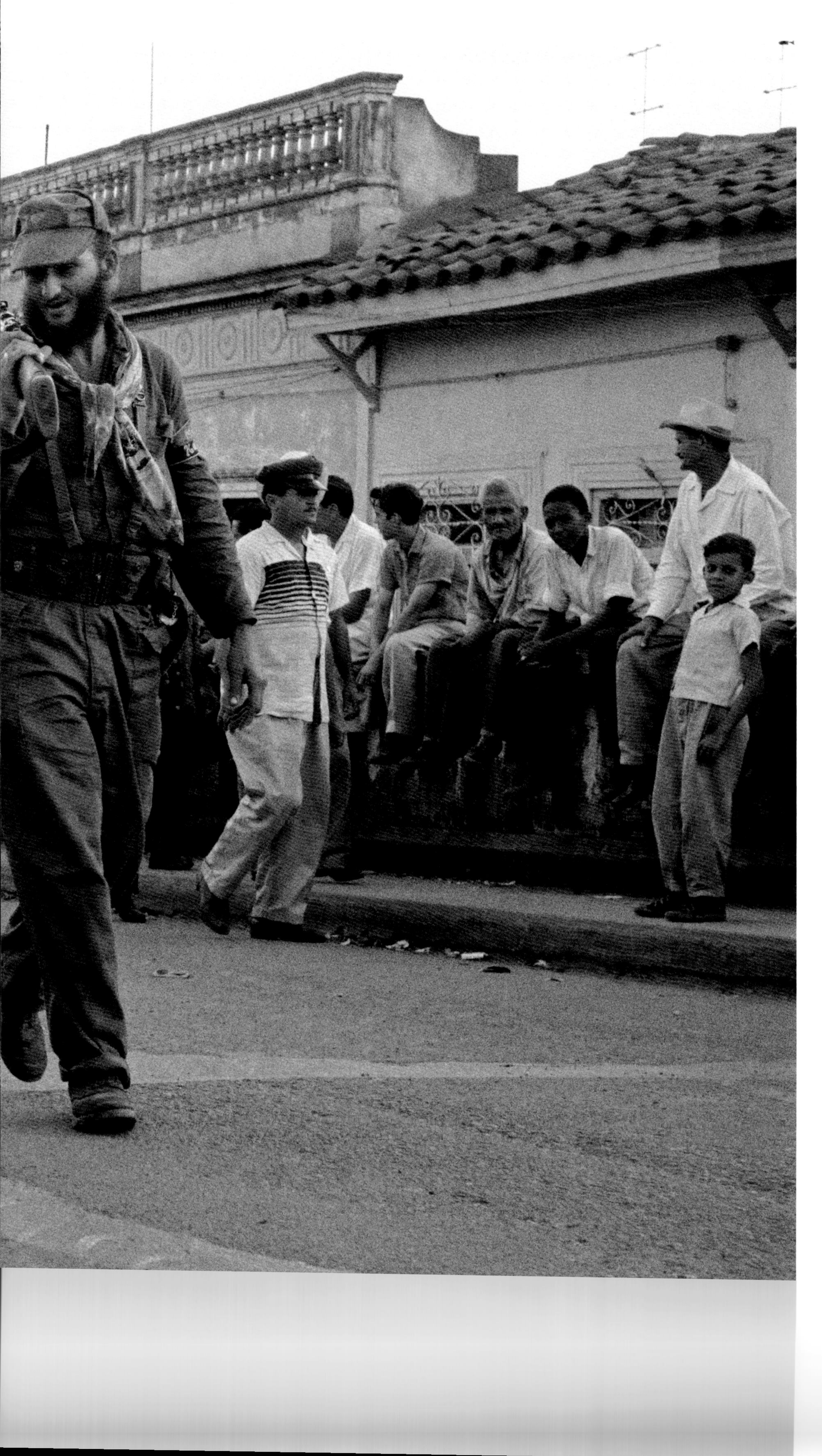

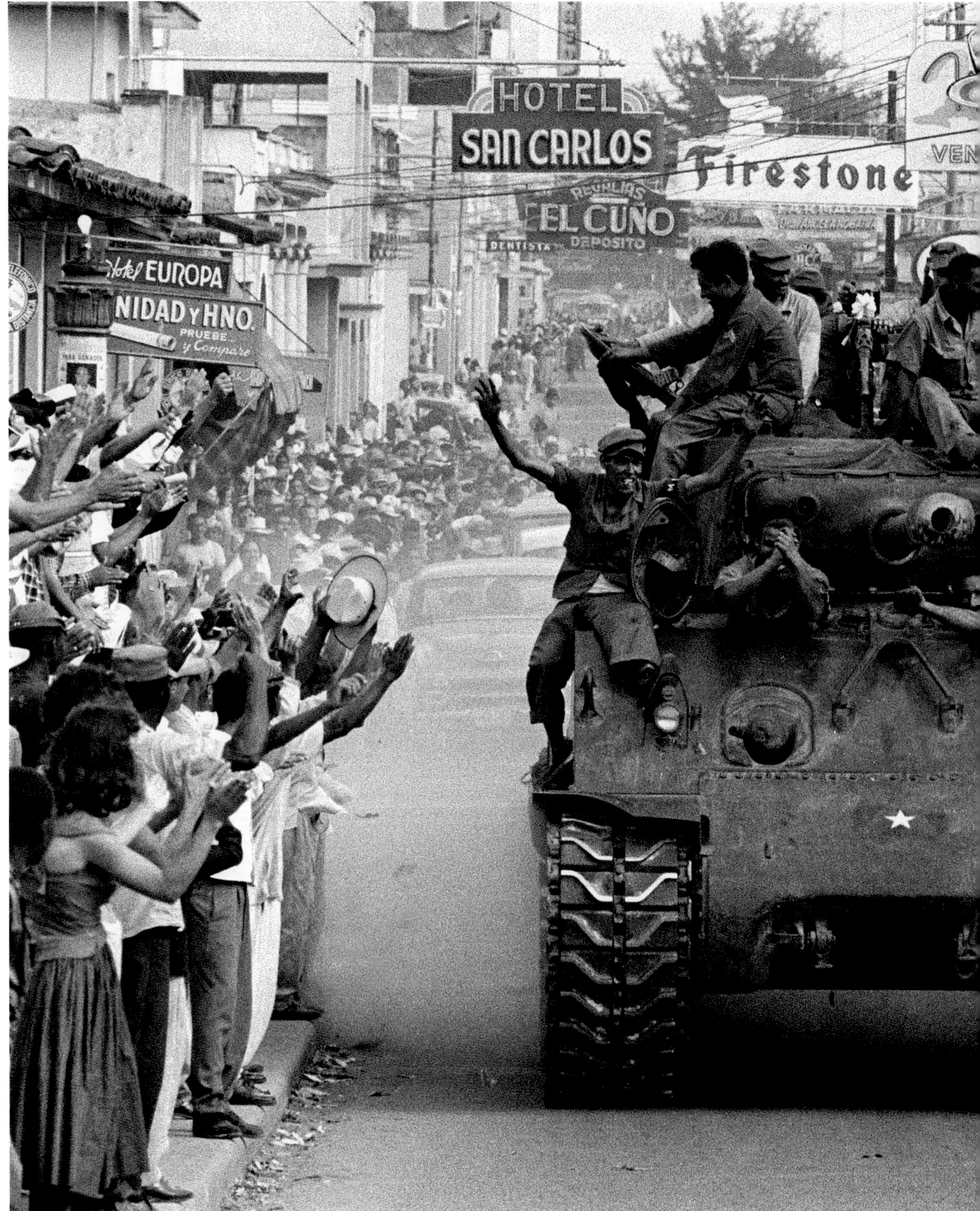
HOTEL
SAN CARLOS
Firestone
EL CUÑO
DEPOSITO
DENTISTA
Hotel EUROPA
NIDAD Y HNO.
PRUEBE...
y Compare

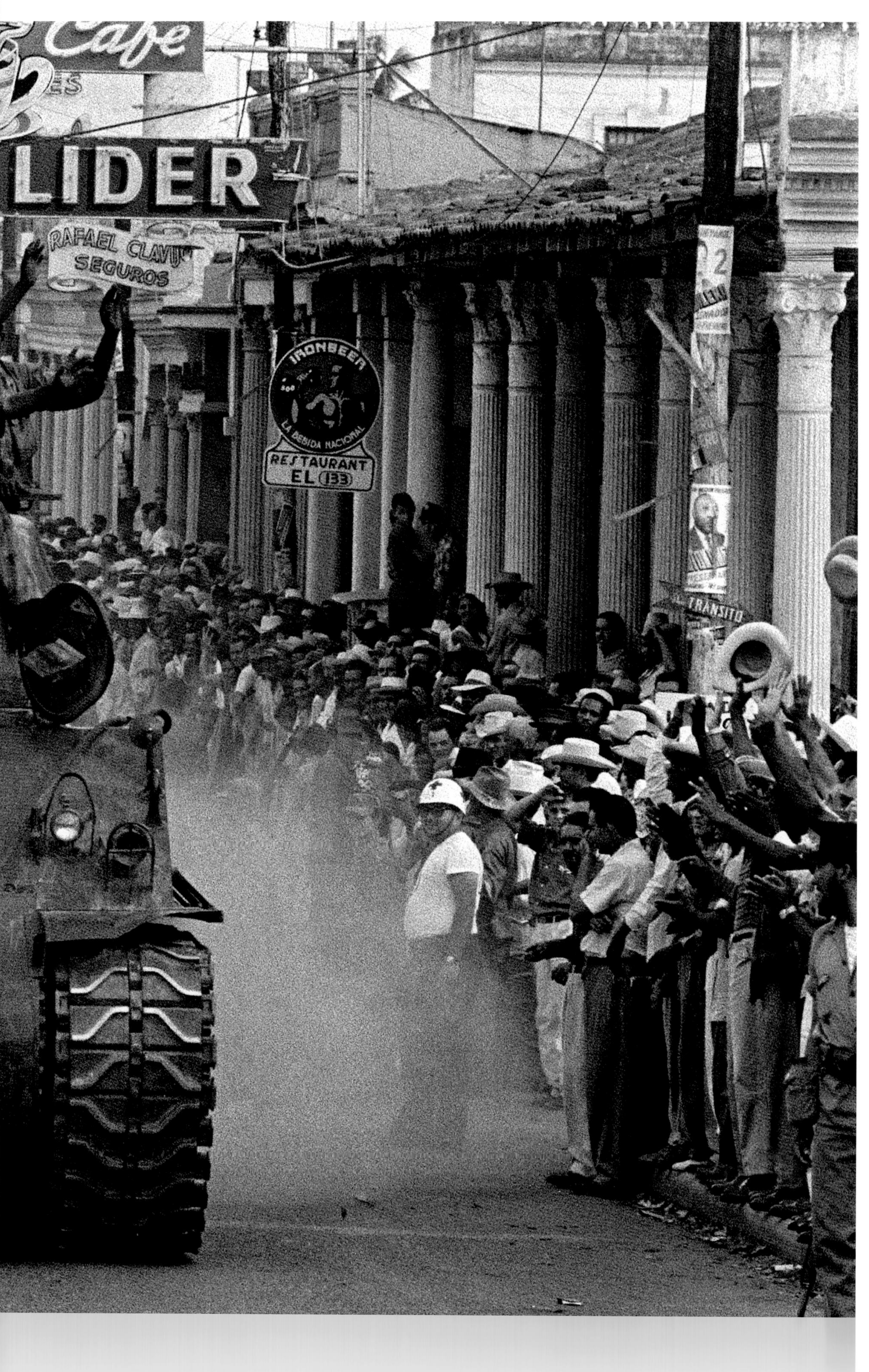
Cafe
LIDER
RAFAEL
SEGUROS
IRONBEER
LA BEBIDA NACIONAL
RESTAURANT
EL 133
TRANSITO

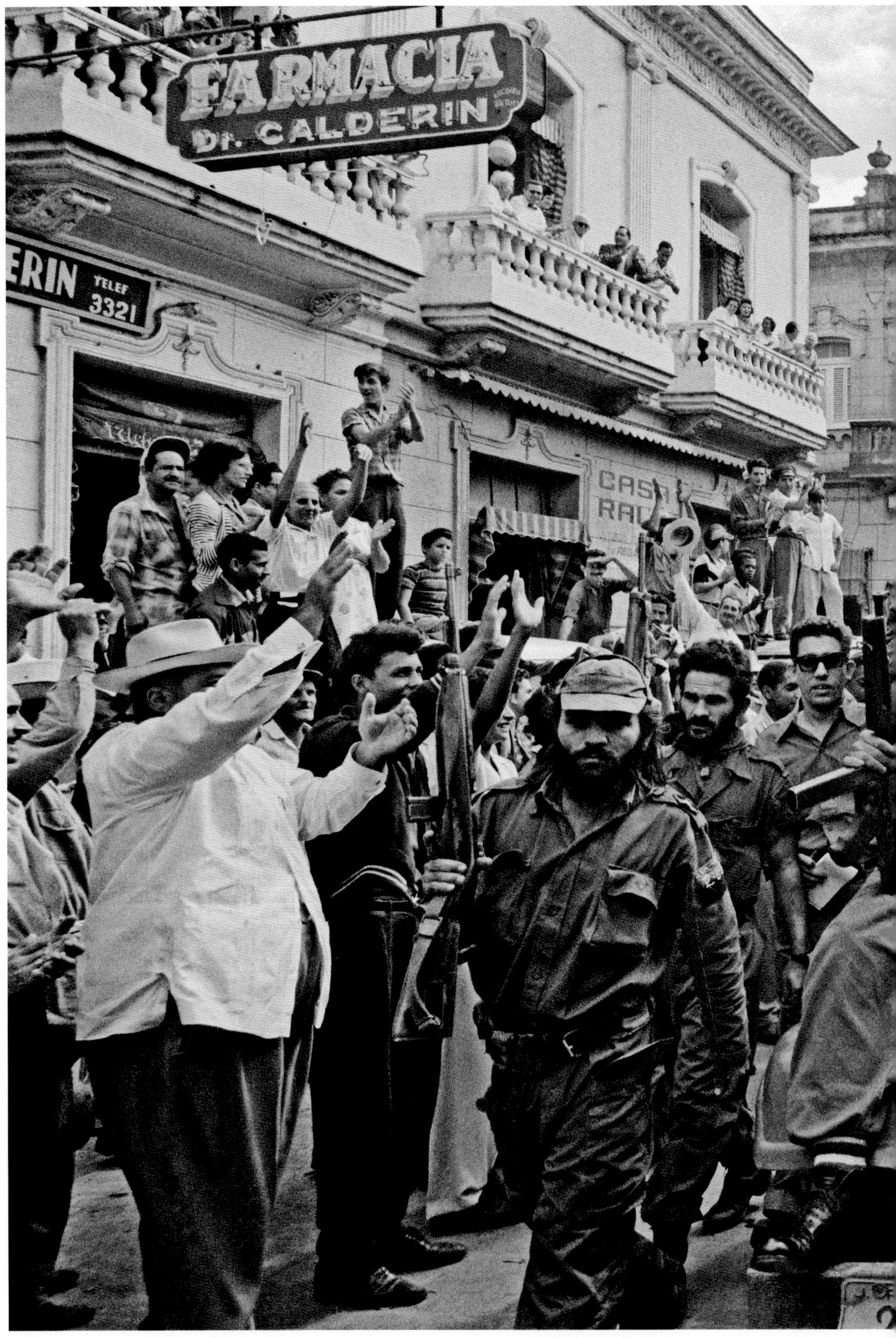
FARMACIA
Dr. CALDERIN
ERIN TELEF 3321
CASA

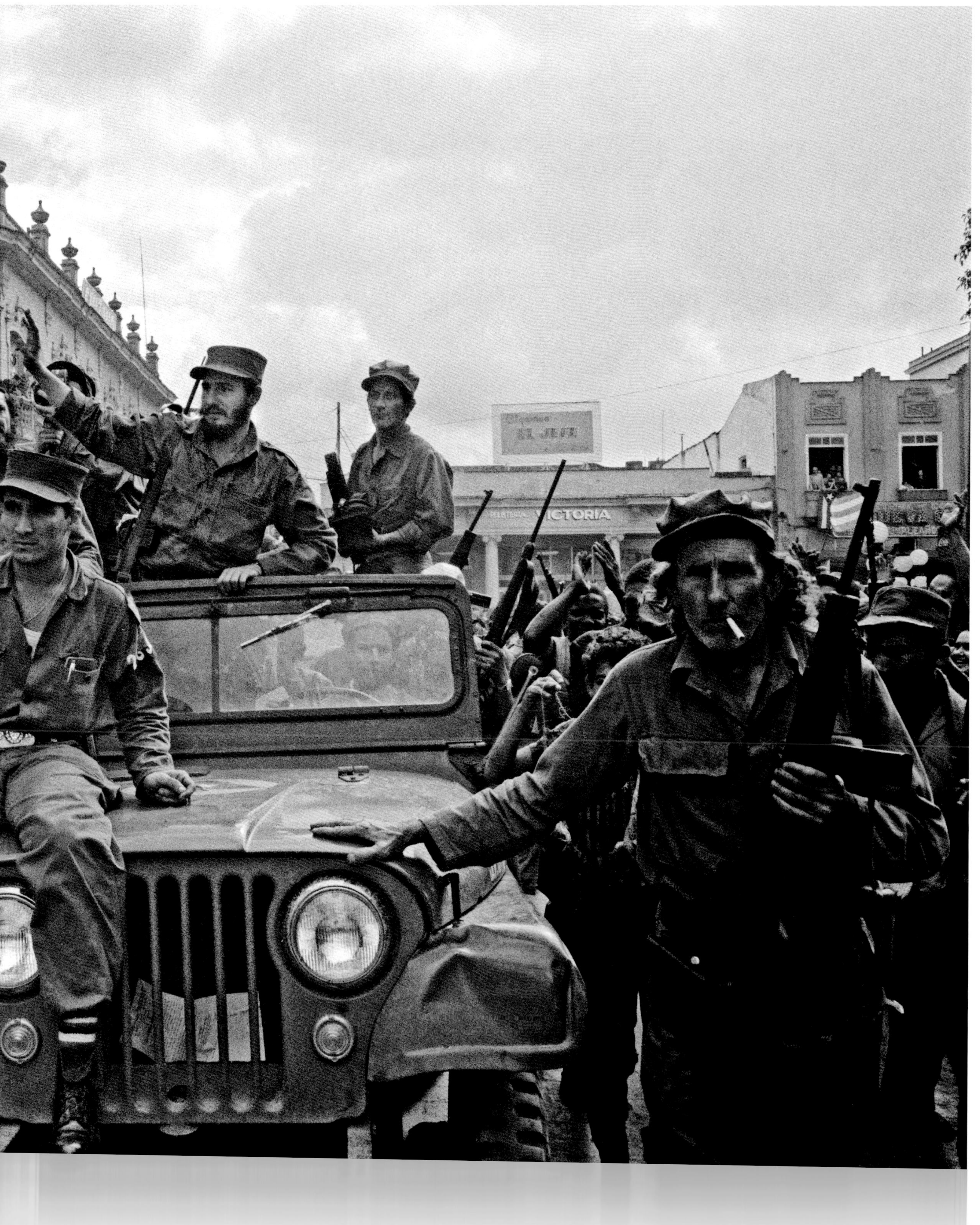
VICTORIA

Shots rang out as Castro entered the town.

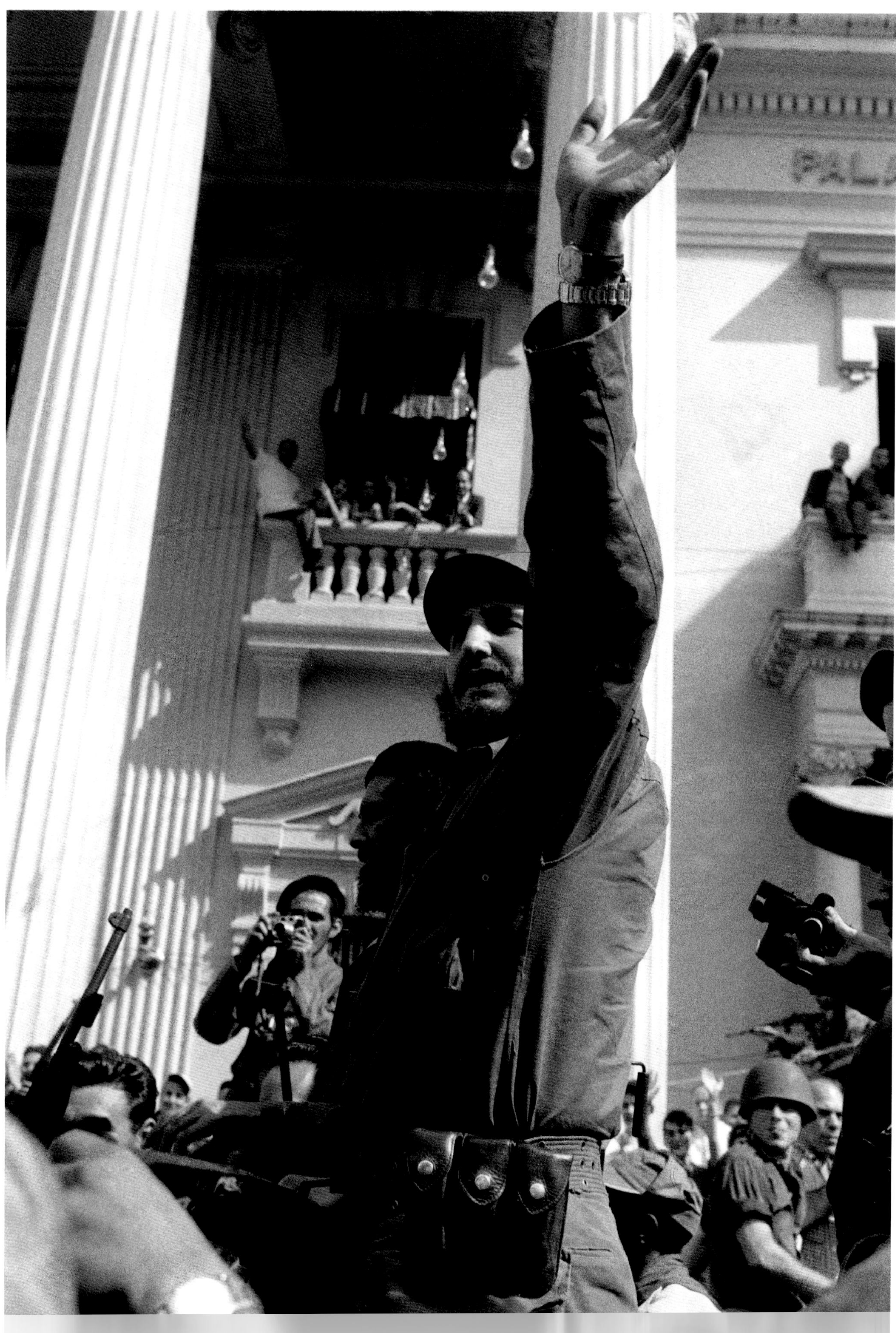

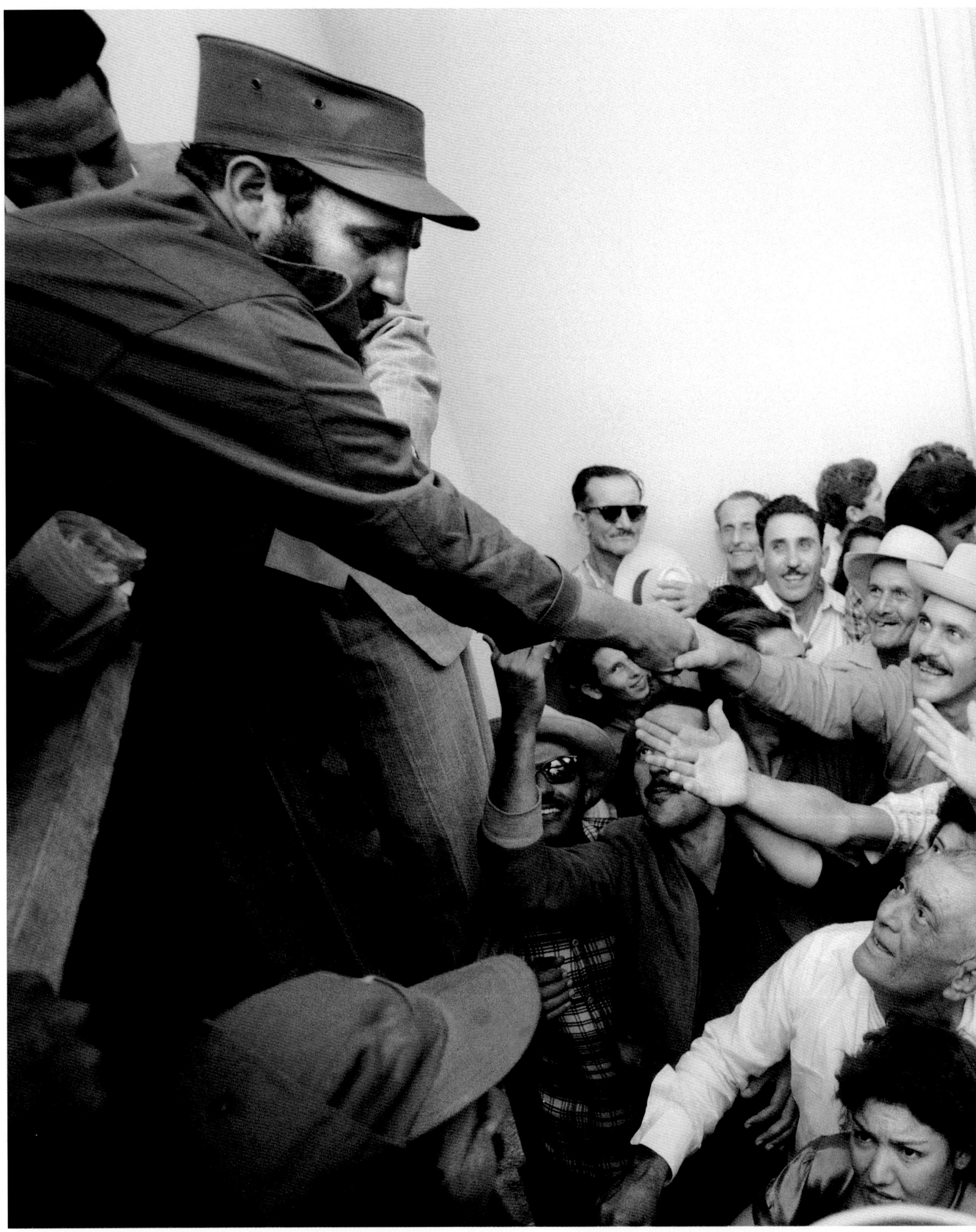

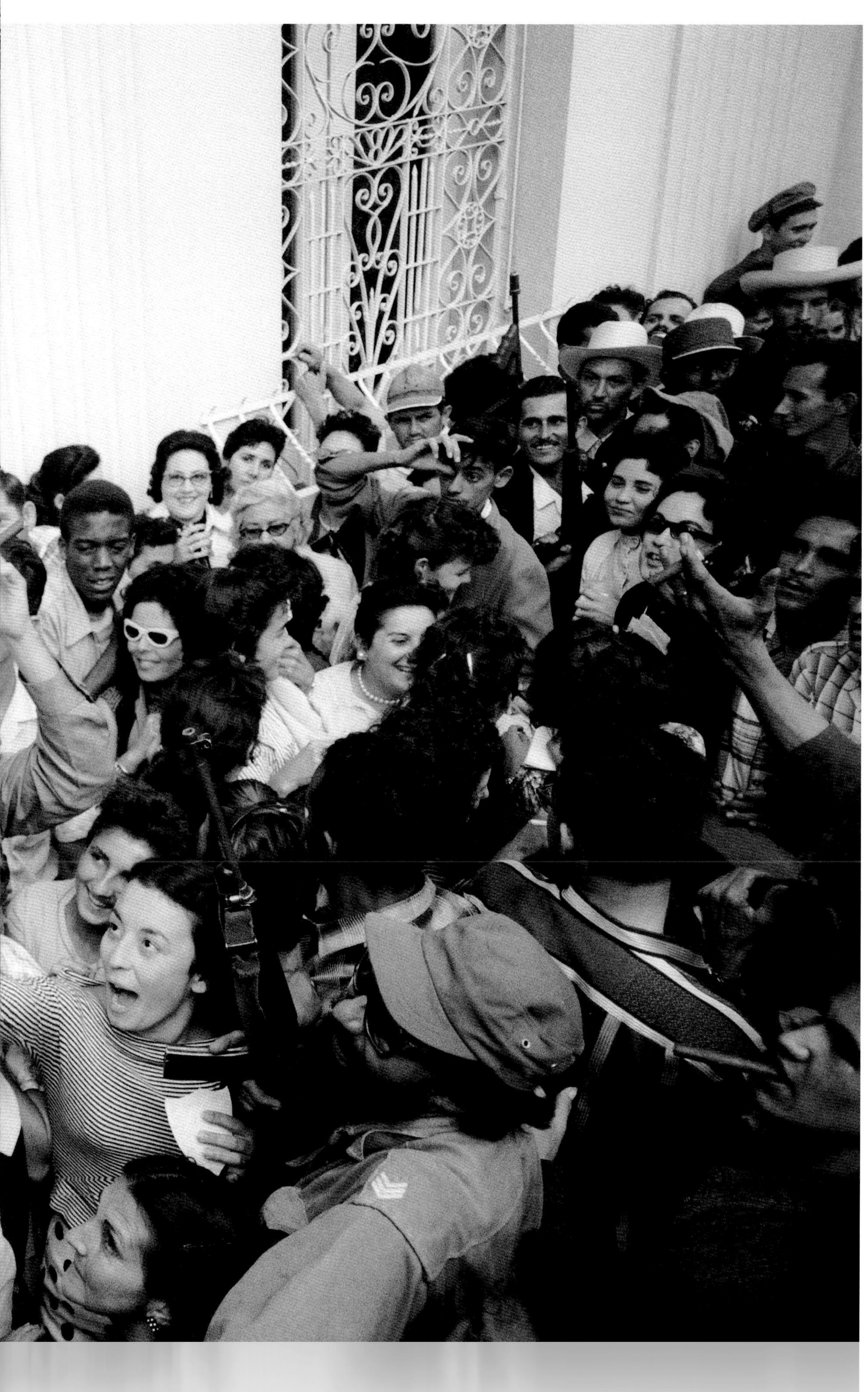

Castro arrives on the speaker's platform. In Cuba's history, the people have never before governed, Castro said. It has been a democracy without honesty. To survive, a monarchy needs honor, a democracy needs honesty—and a tyrant needs fear.

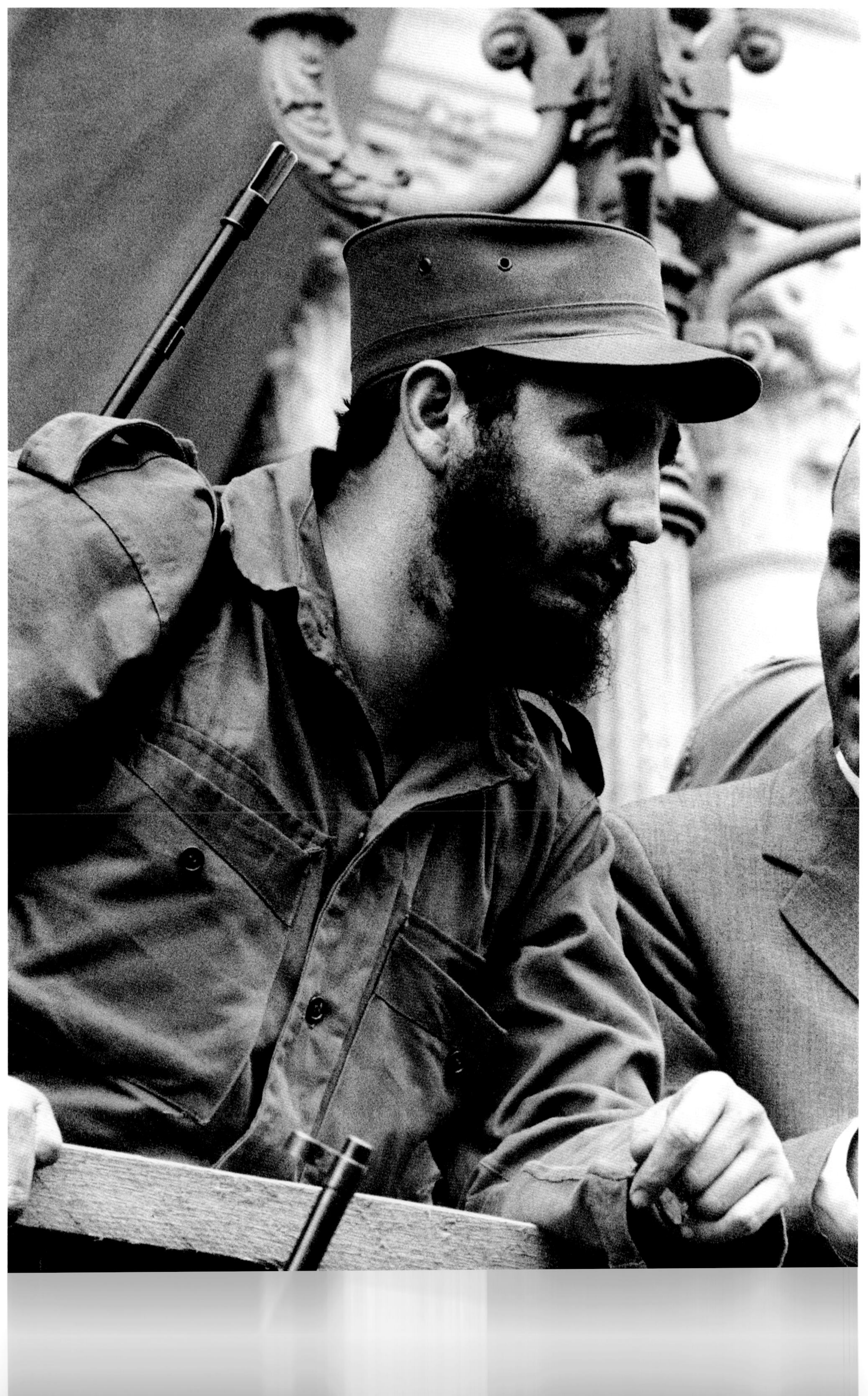

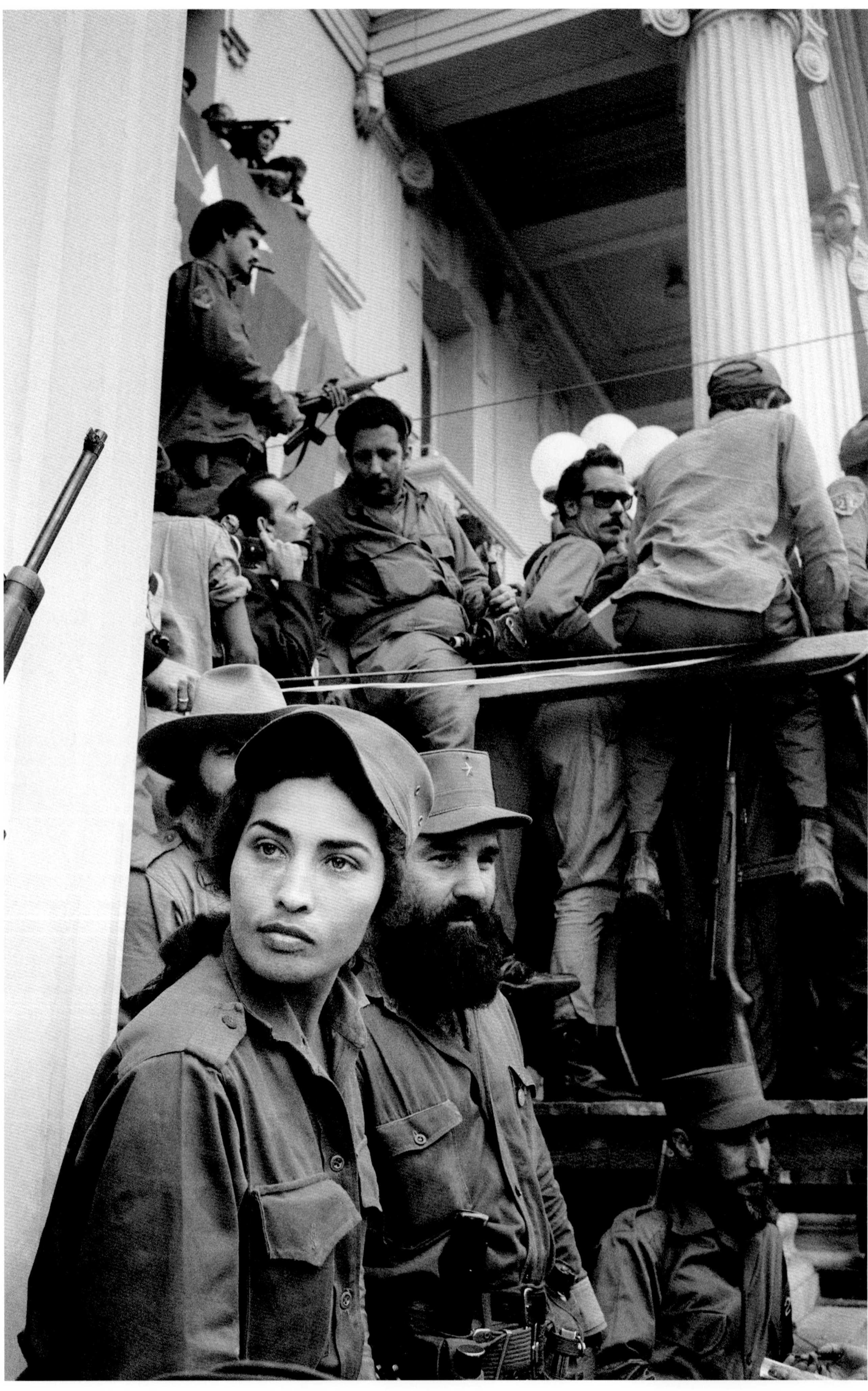

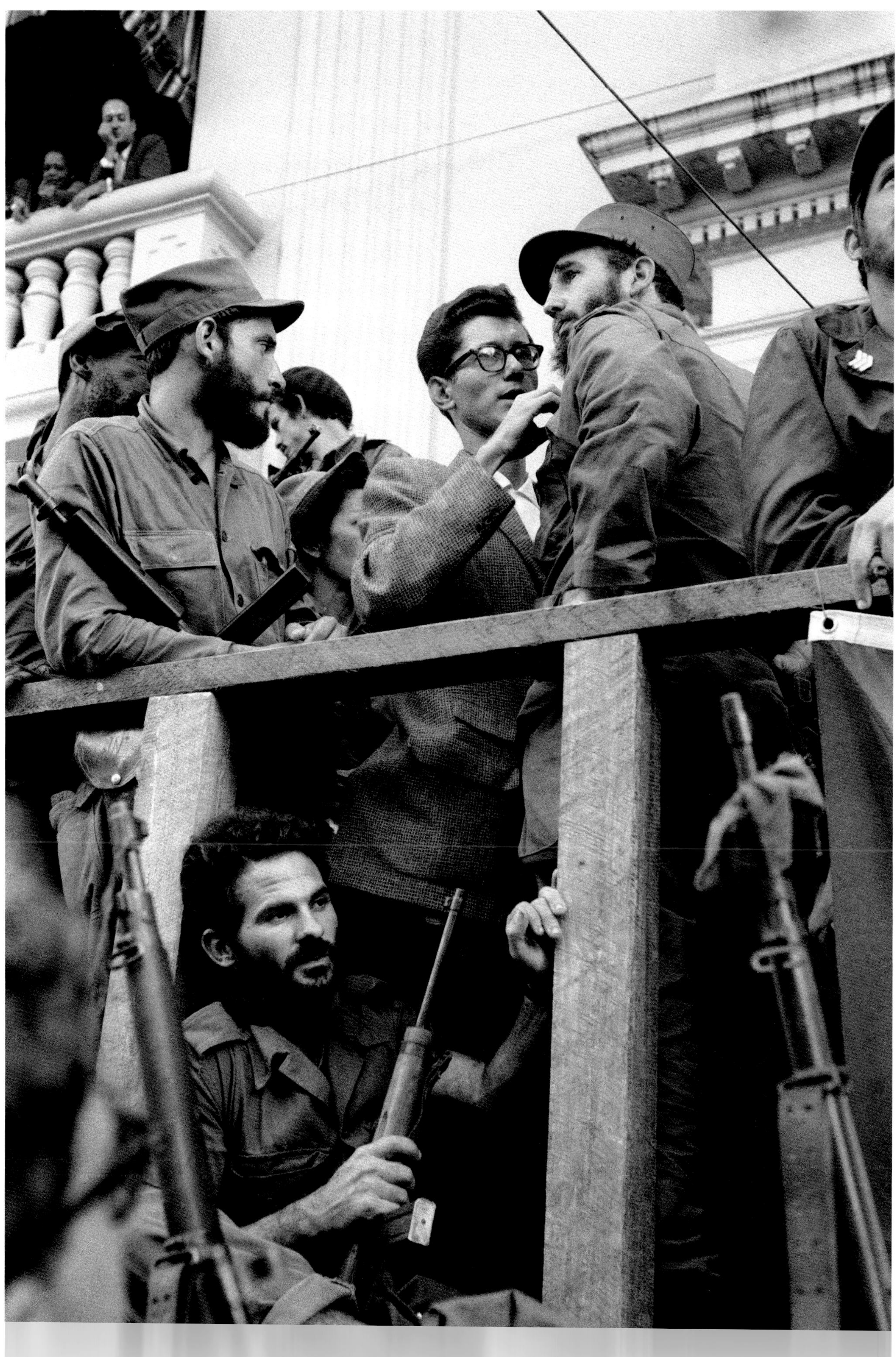

Castro's speech in Santa Clara went on for quite some time. Notice all the guns and the fact he is surrounded by the soldiers who had come down from the hills with him.

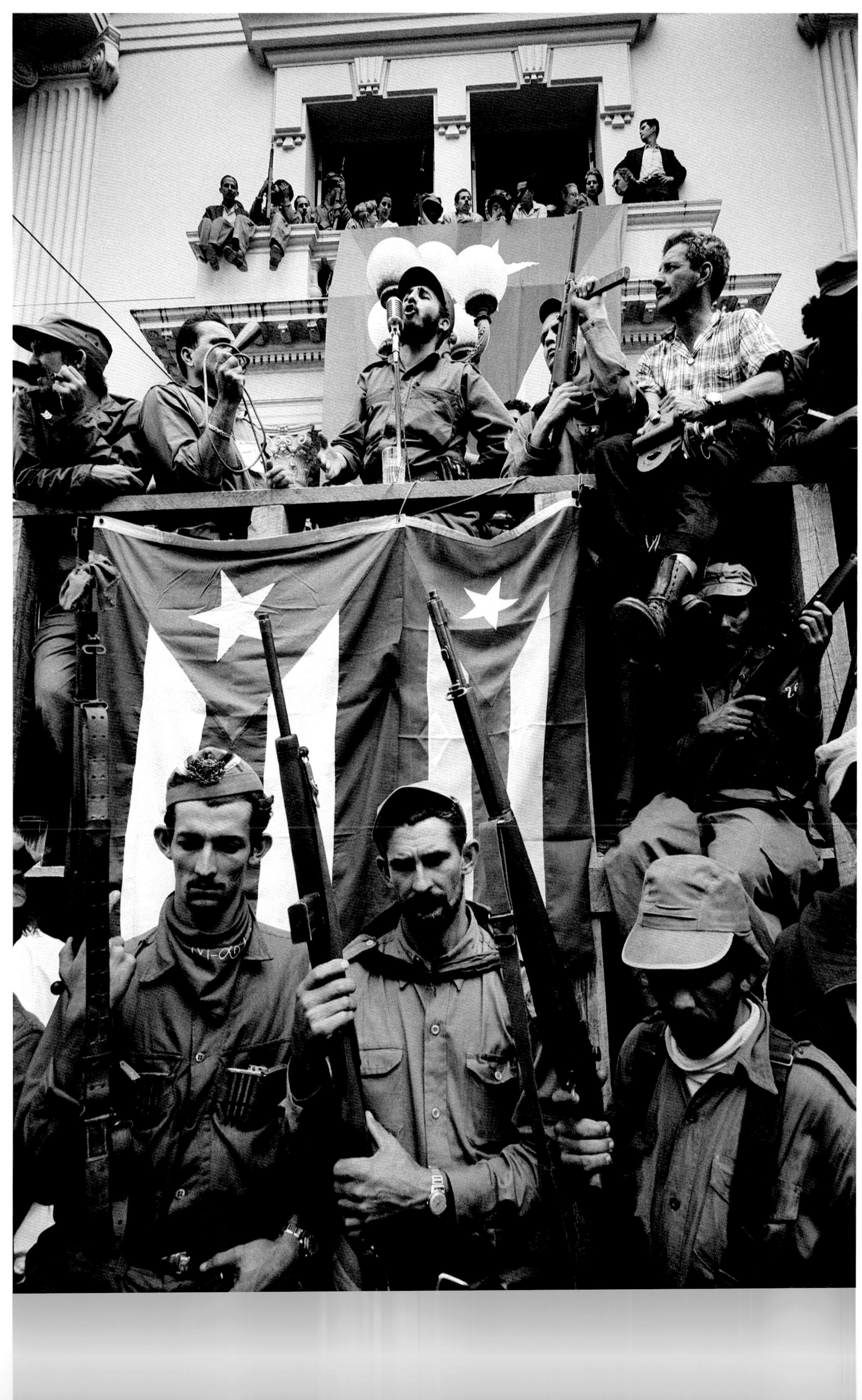

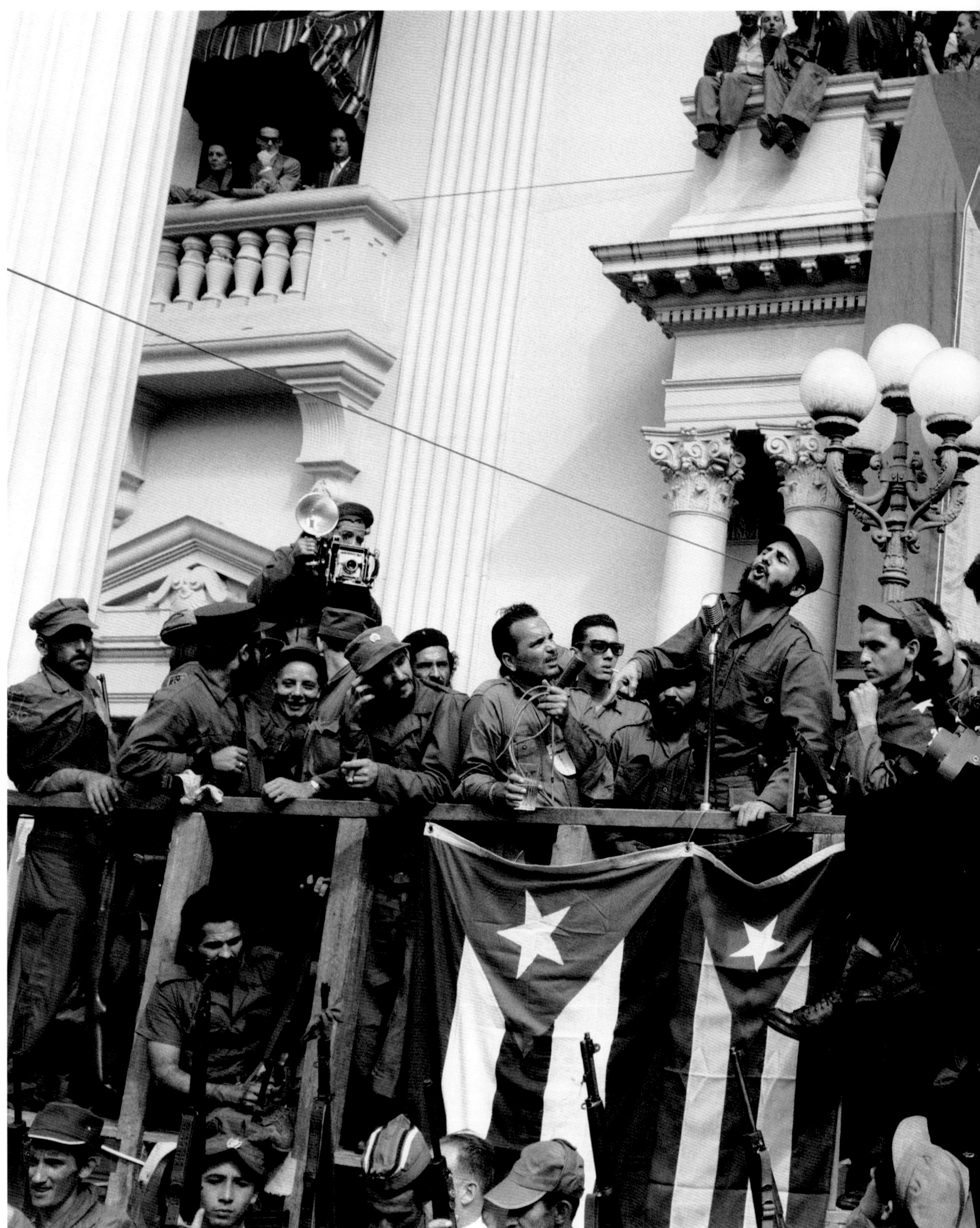

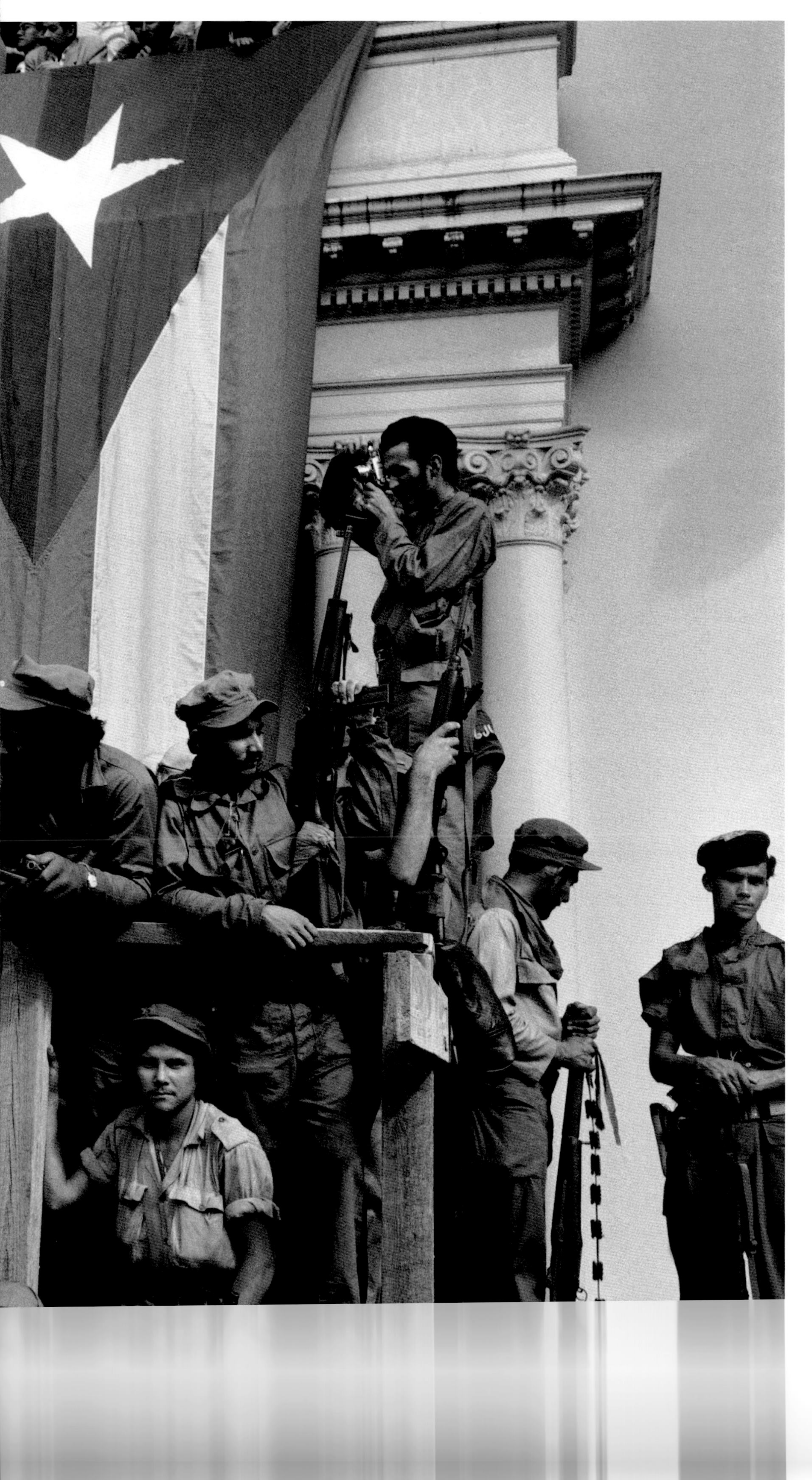

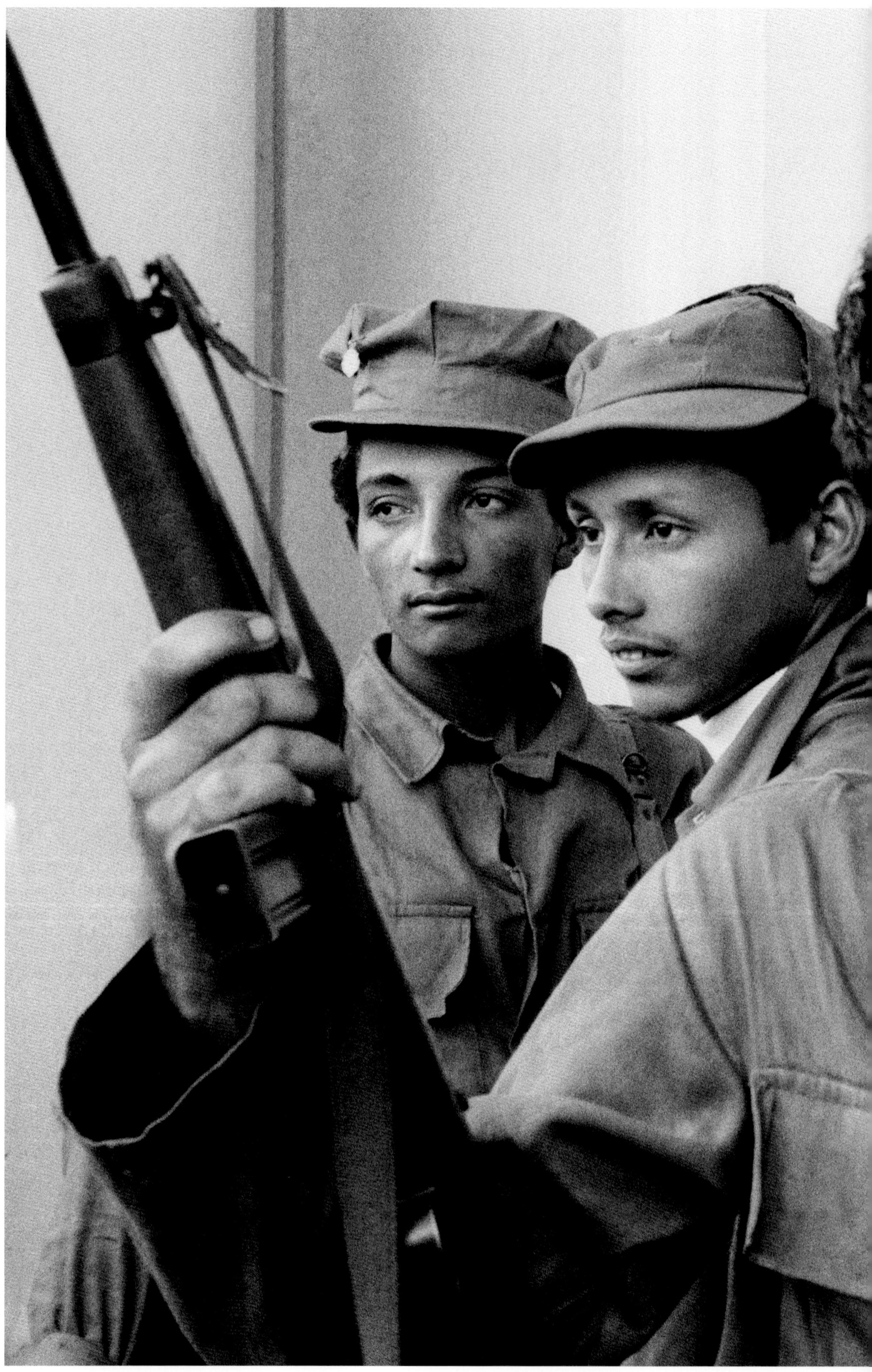

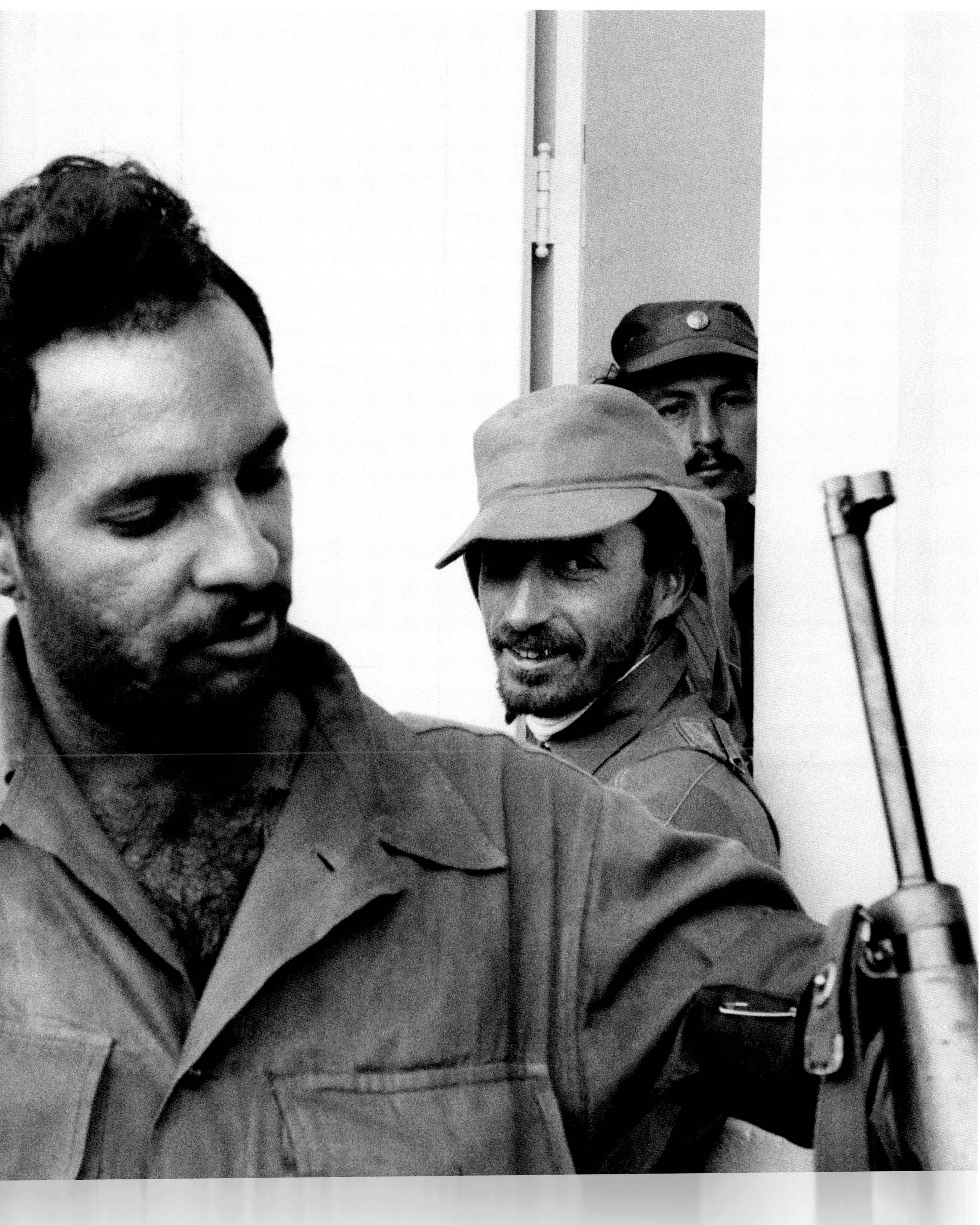

Triumphal column on the move through the countryside. They went by bus, truck, commandeered automobiles, tanks. Some people were even pedaling bicycles as they came through the streets.

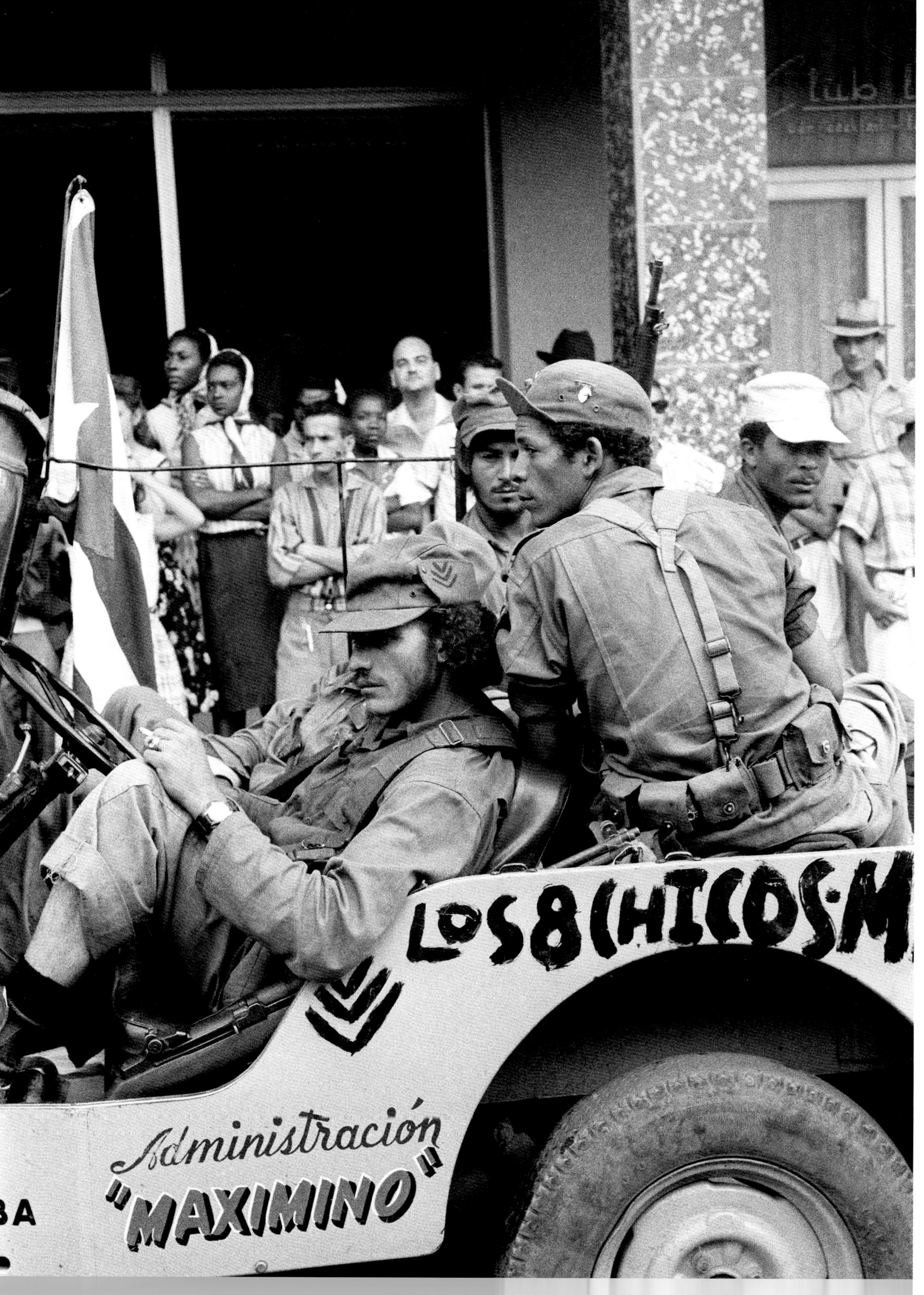
LOS 8 CHICOS-M
Administración
"MAXIMINO"
BA

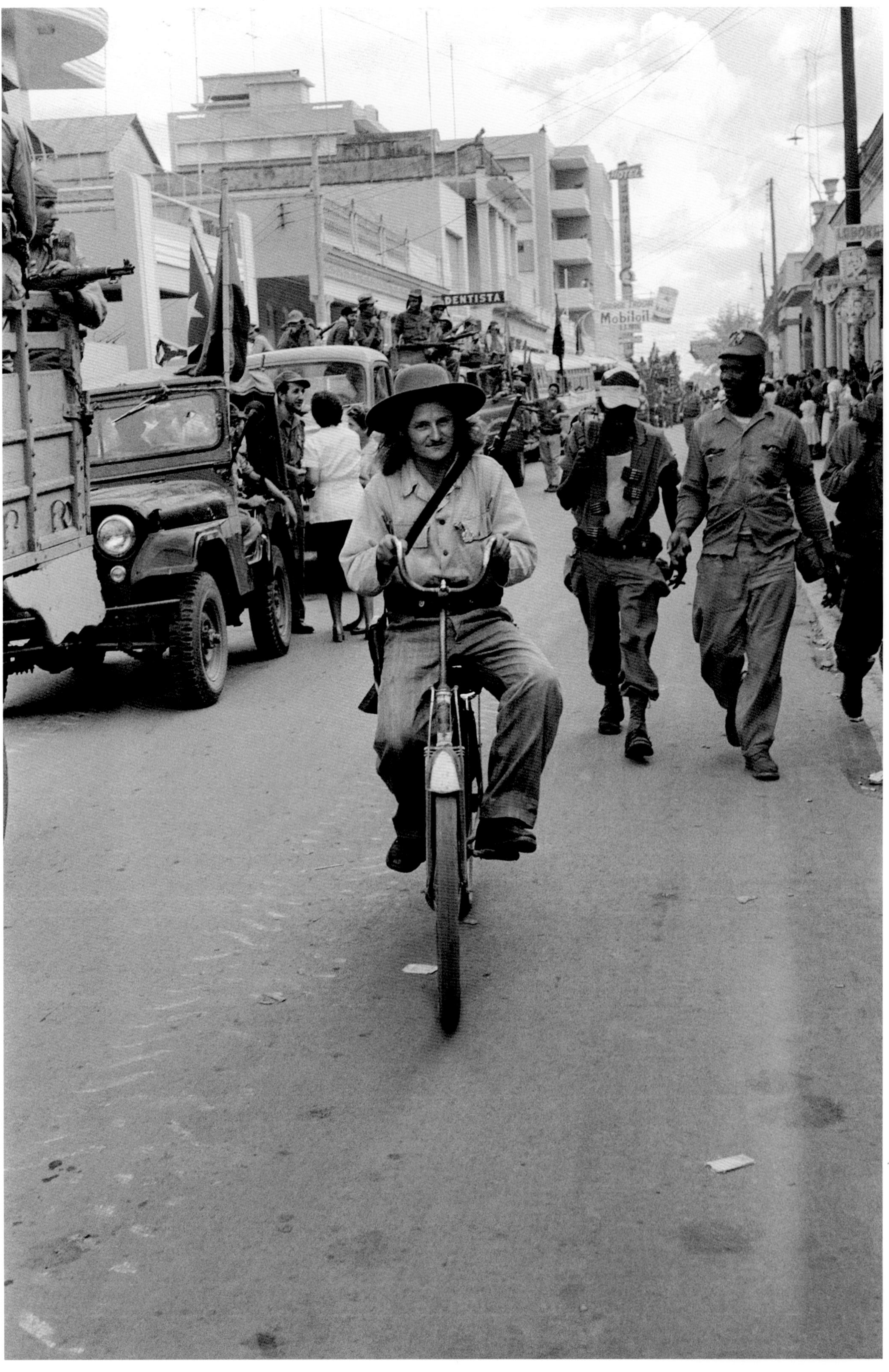
DENTISTA
Mobiloil

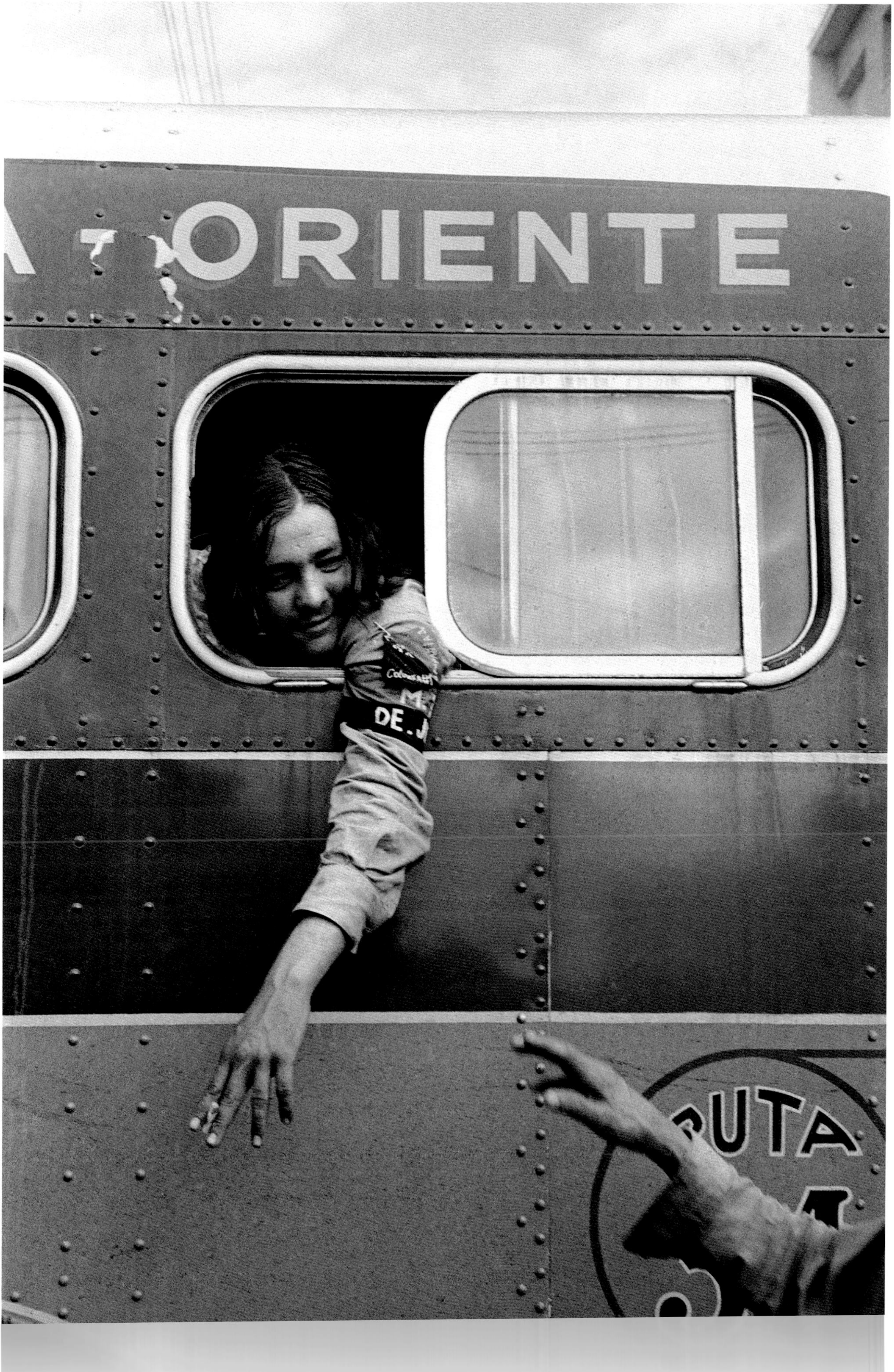

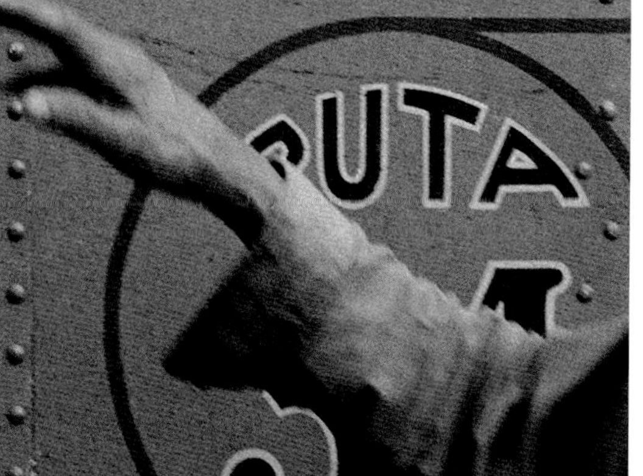
ORIENTE
RUTA

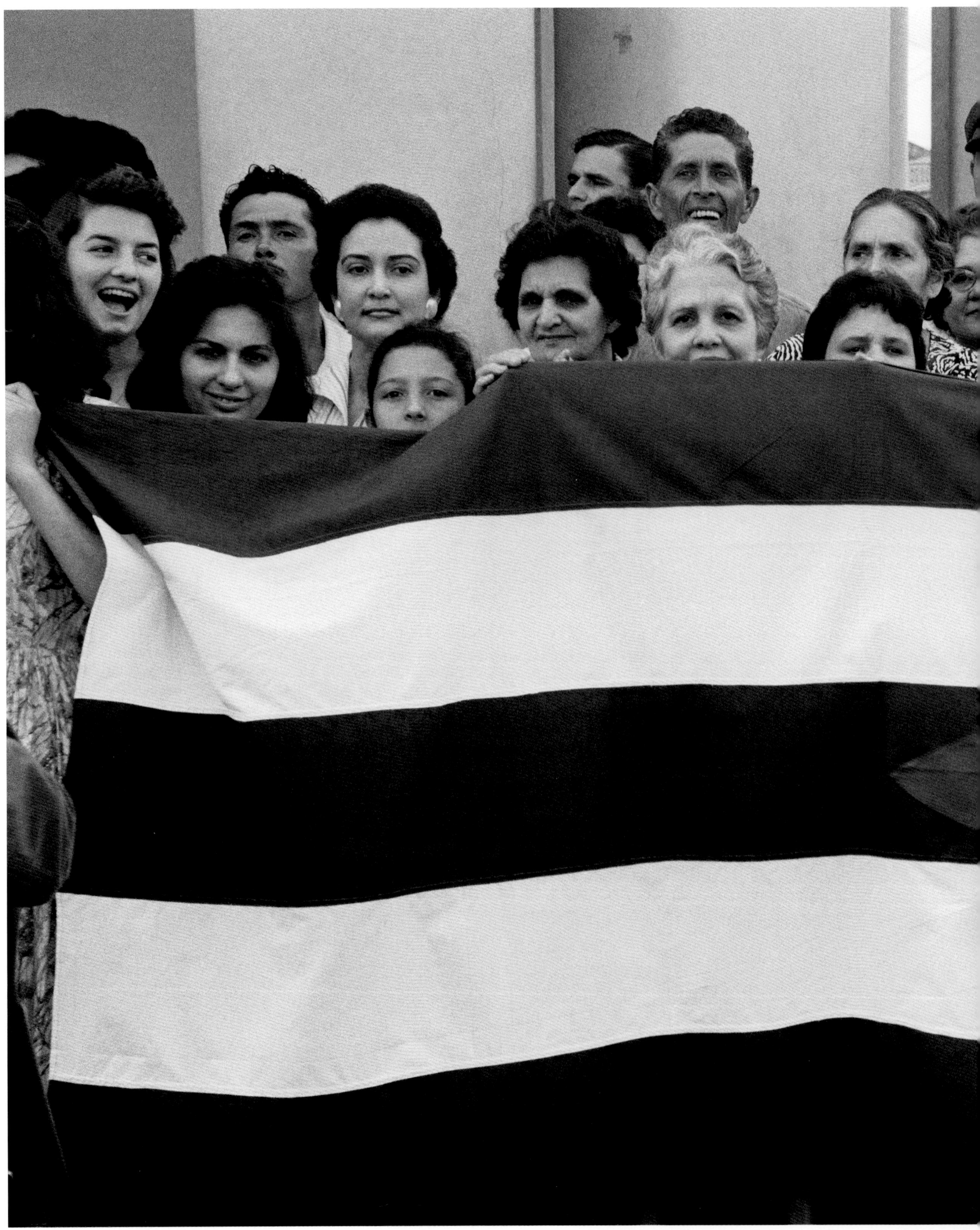

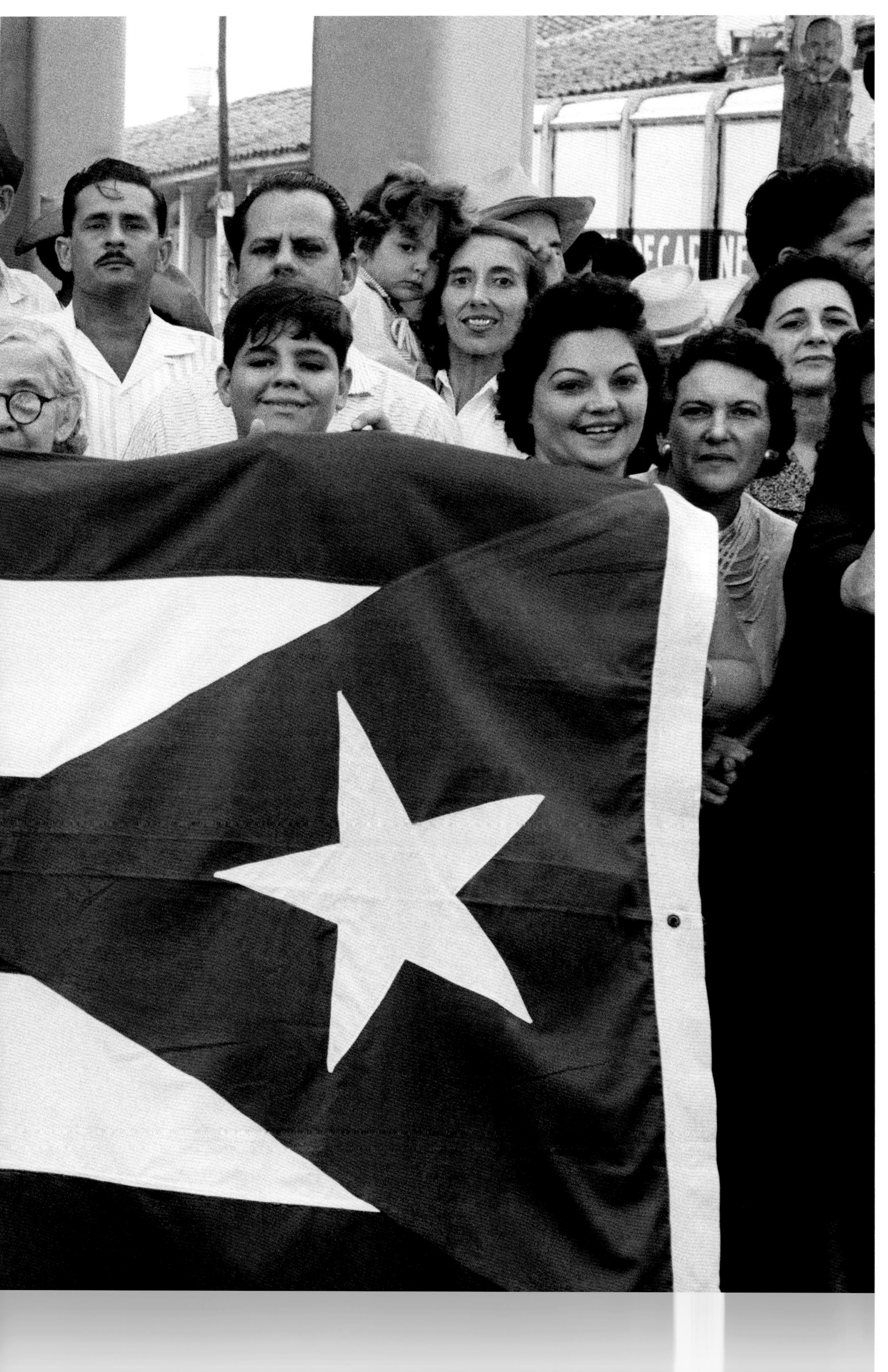

One of Castro's revolutionary soldiers, part of the group that had spent six years in the mountains in their struggle against the Batista regime.

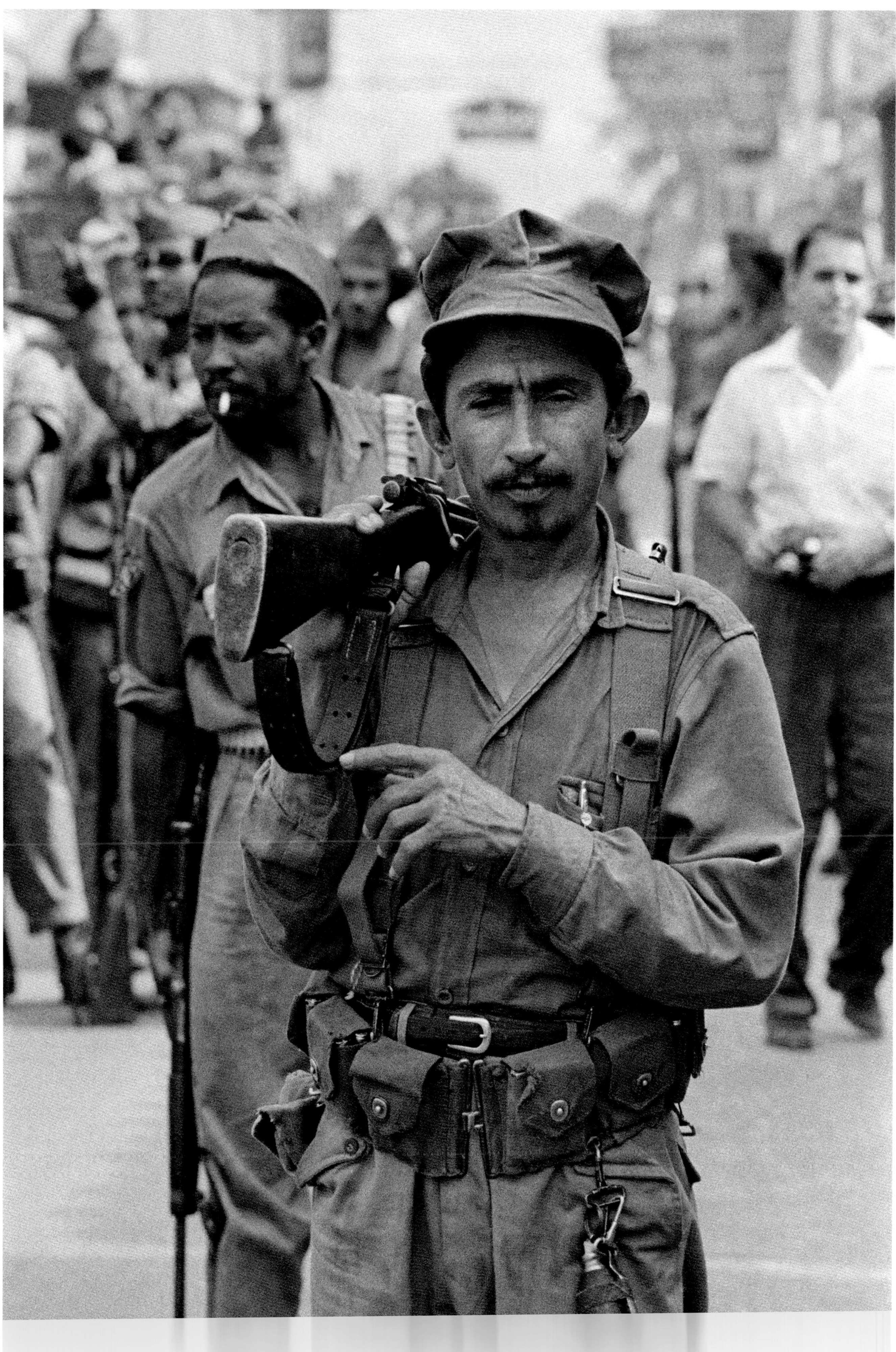

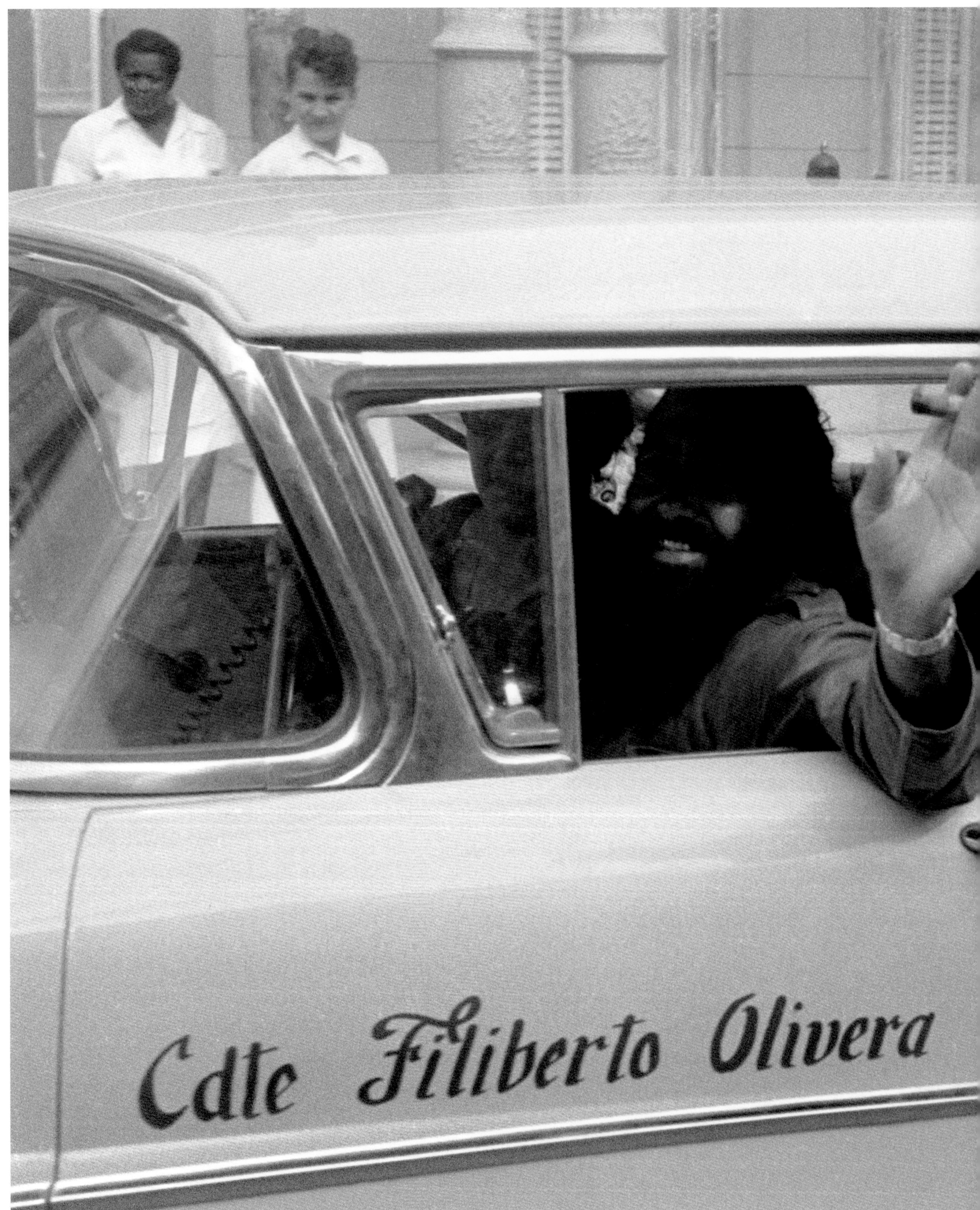
Cdte Filiberto Olivera

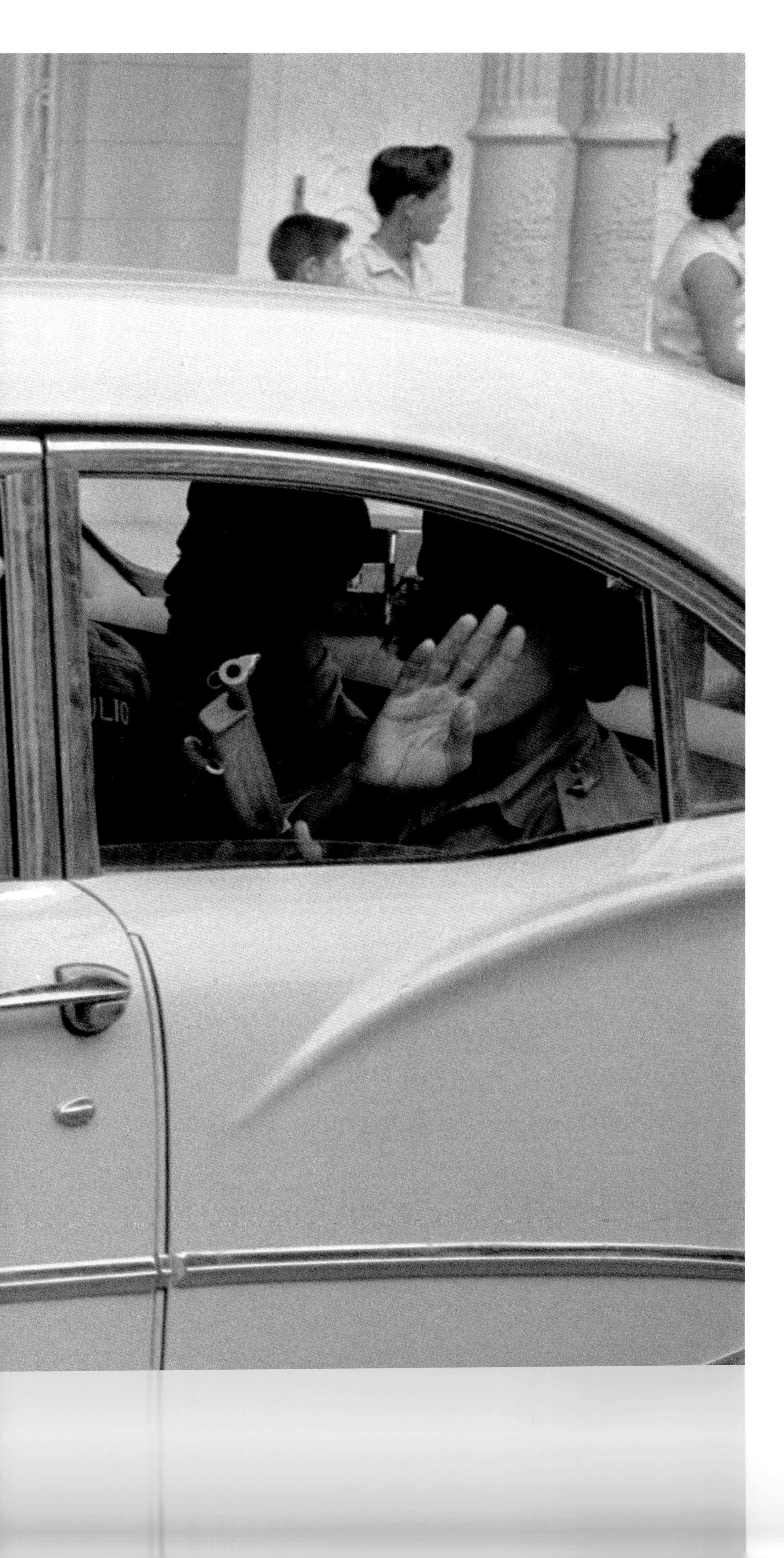
ULIO

This was one of the first times that reporters got any rest whatsoever on this trip. Along the way, Castro kept up to date with his press notices.

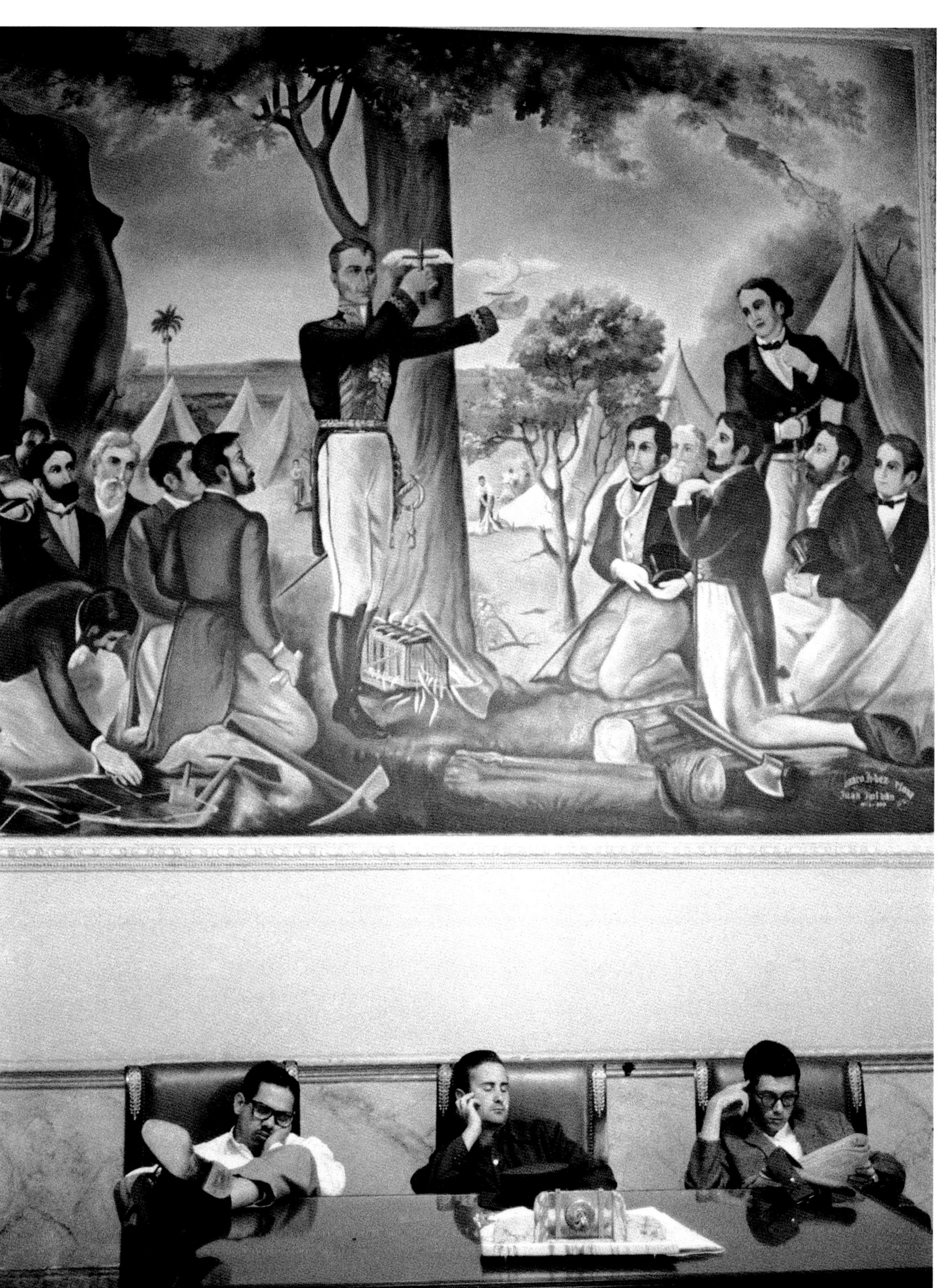

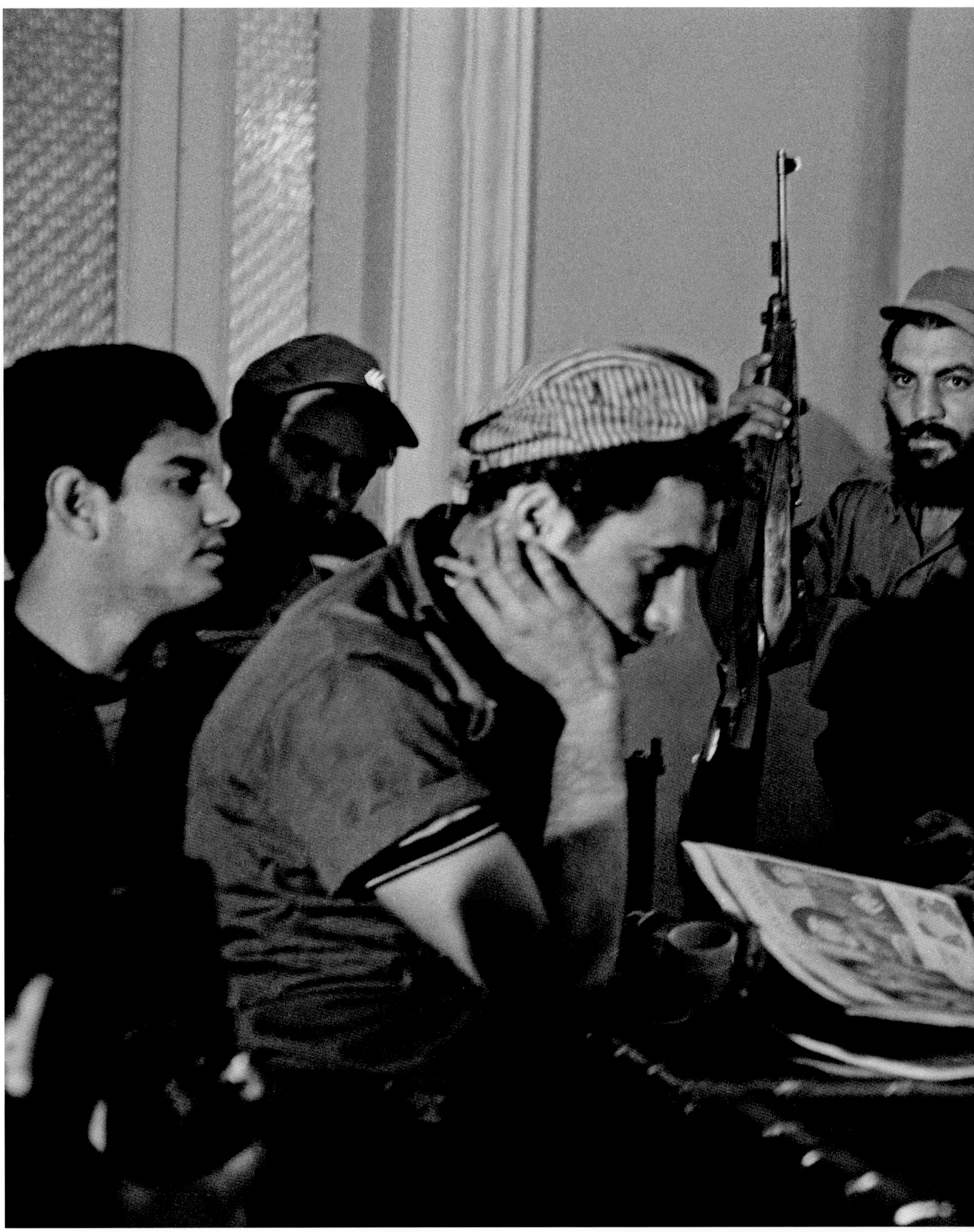

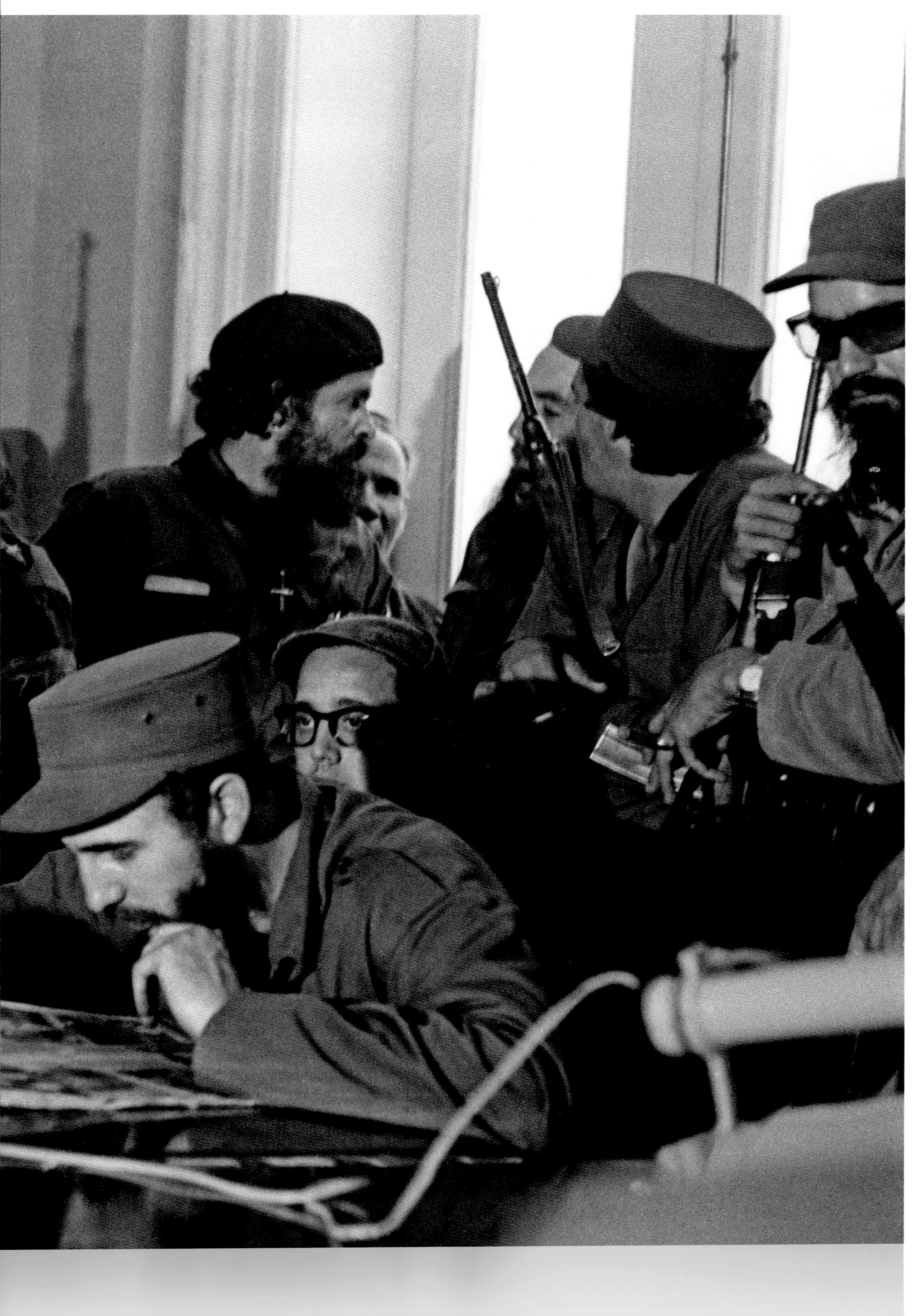

Troops rolling into Cienfuegos at night on their way to Havana.

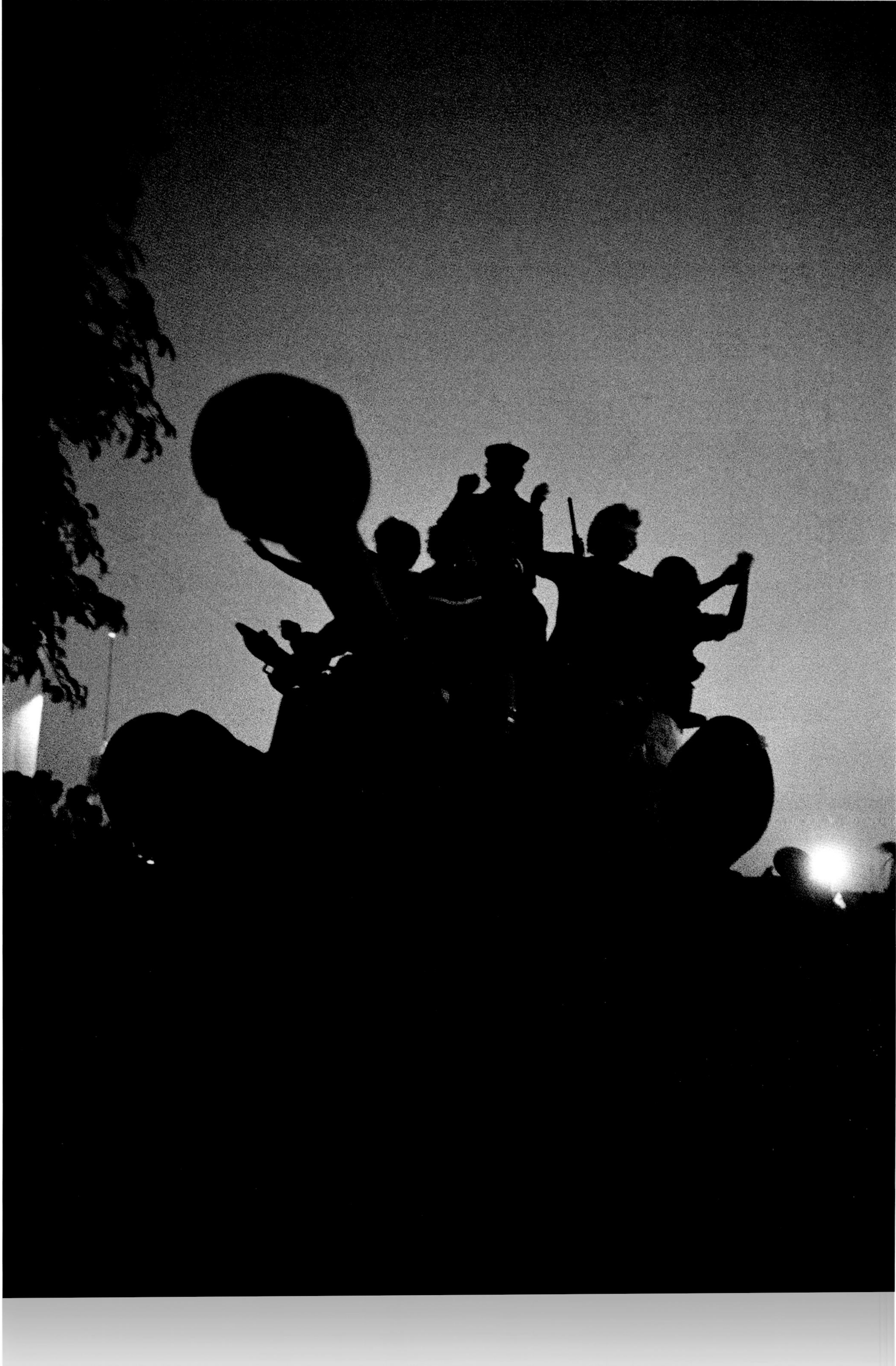

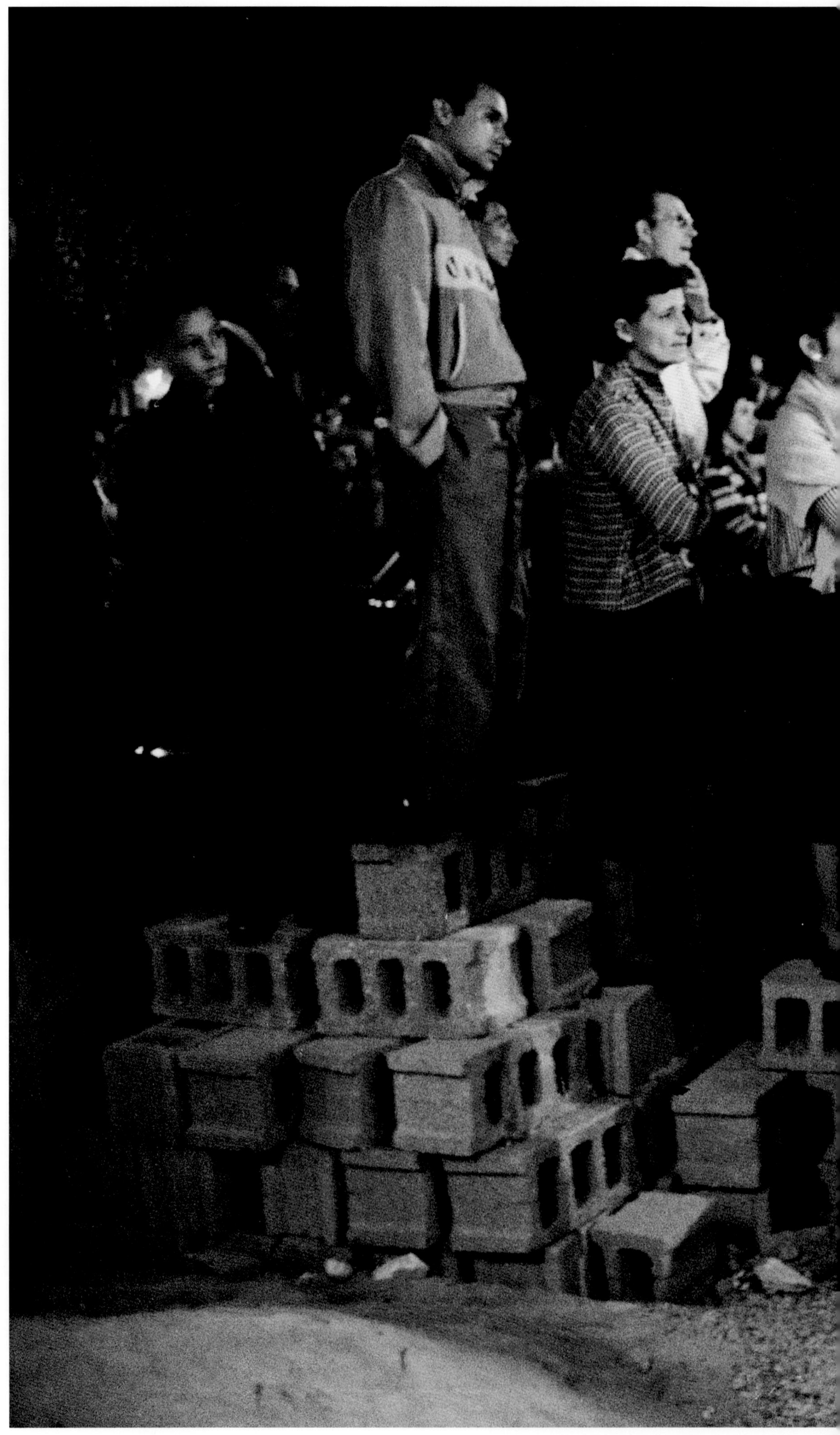

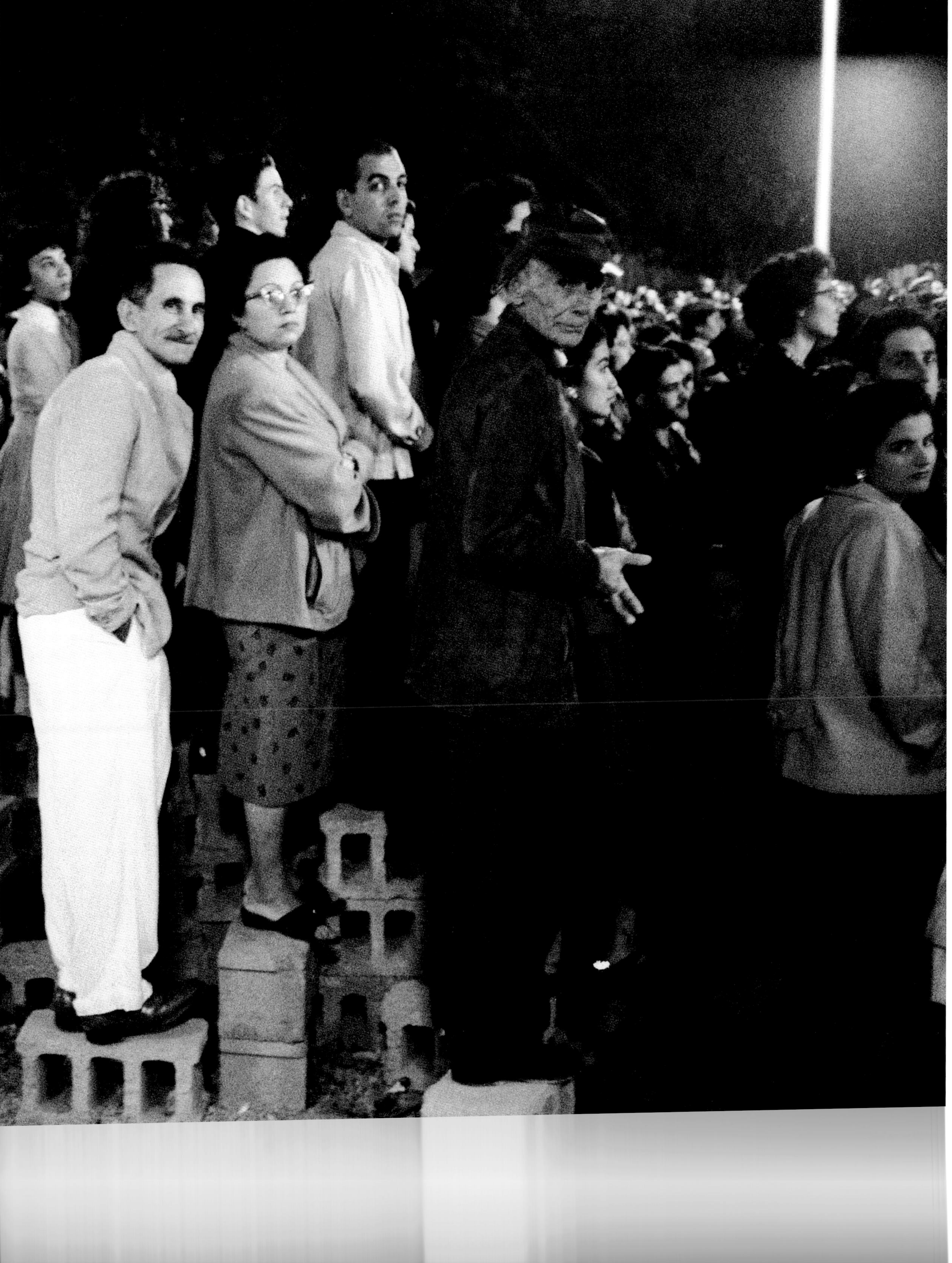

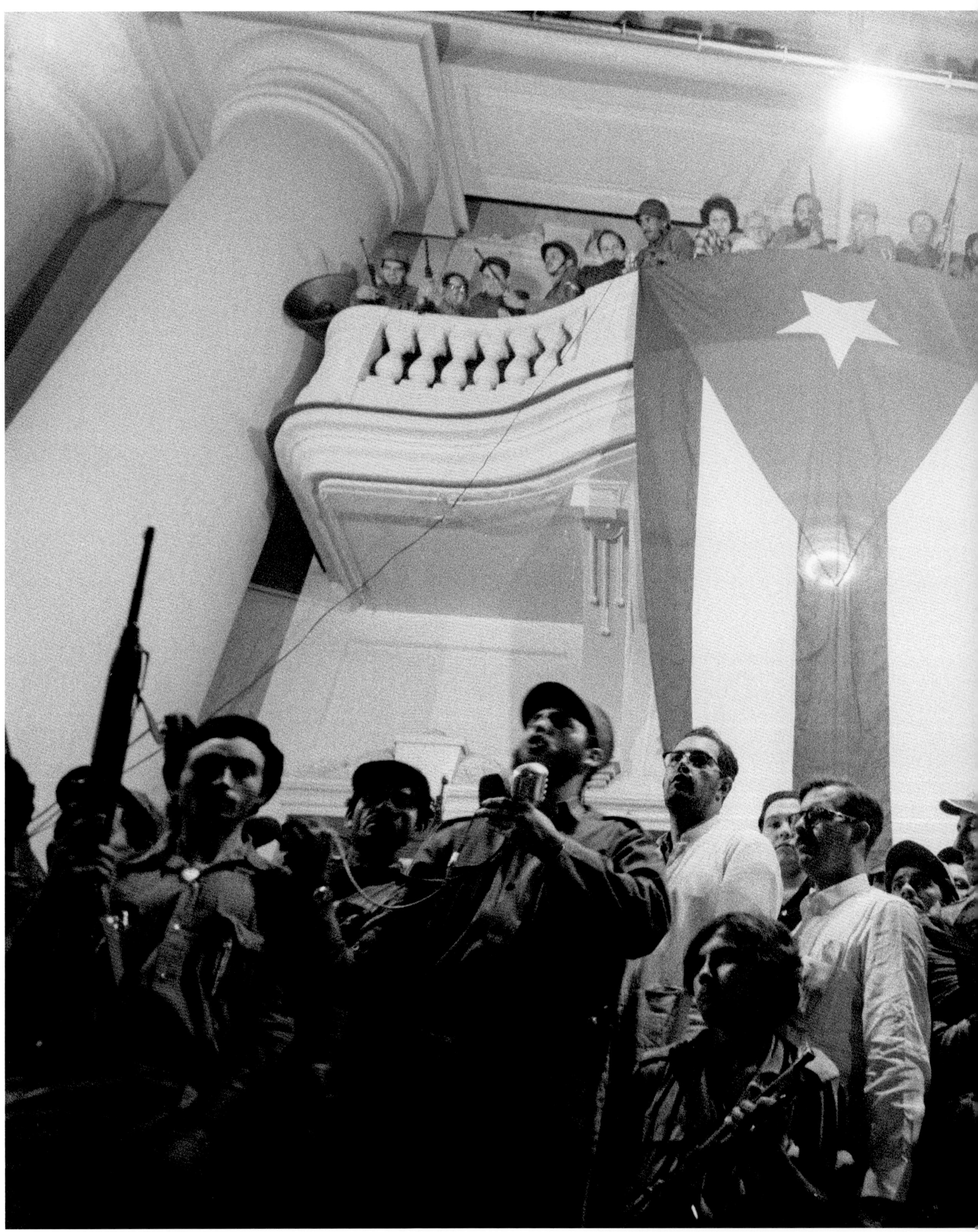

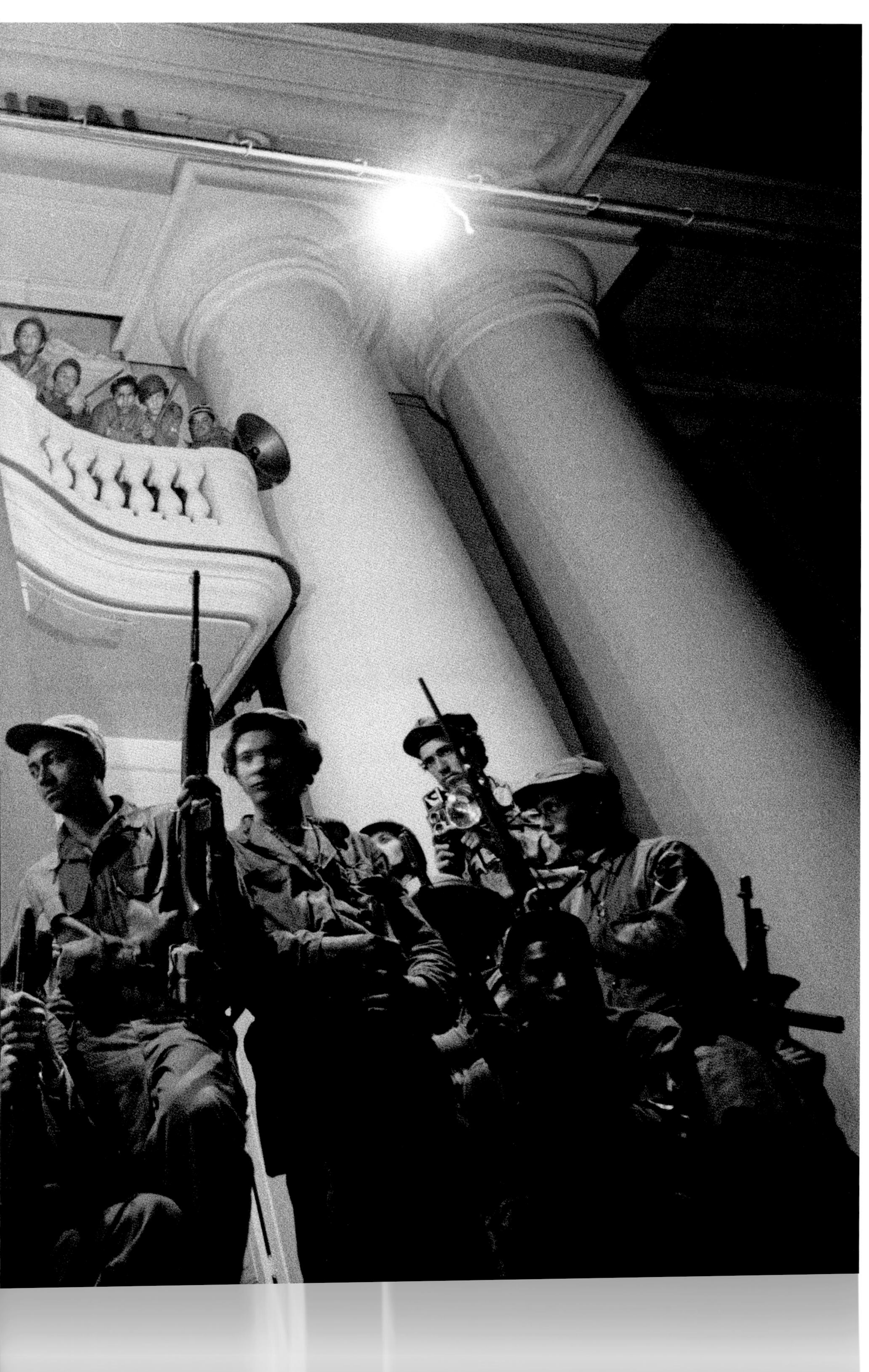

Castro is relaxed and very much in control during an interview with a reporter on the outskirts of Havana.

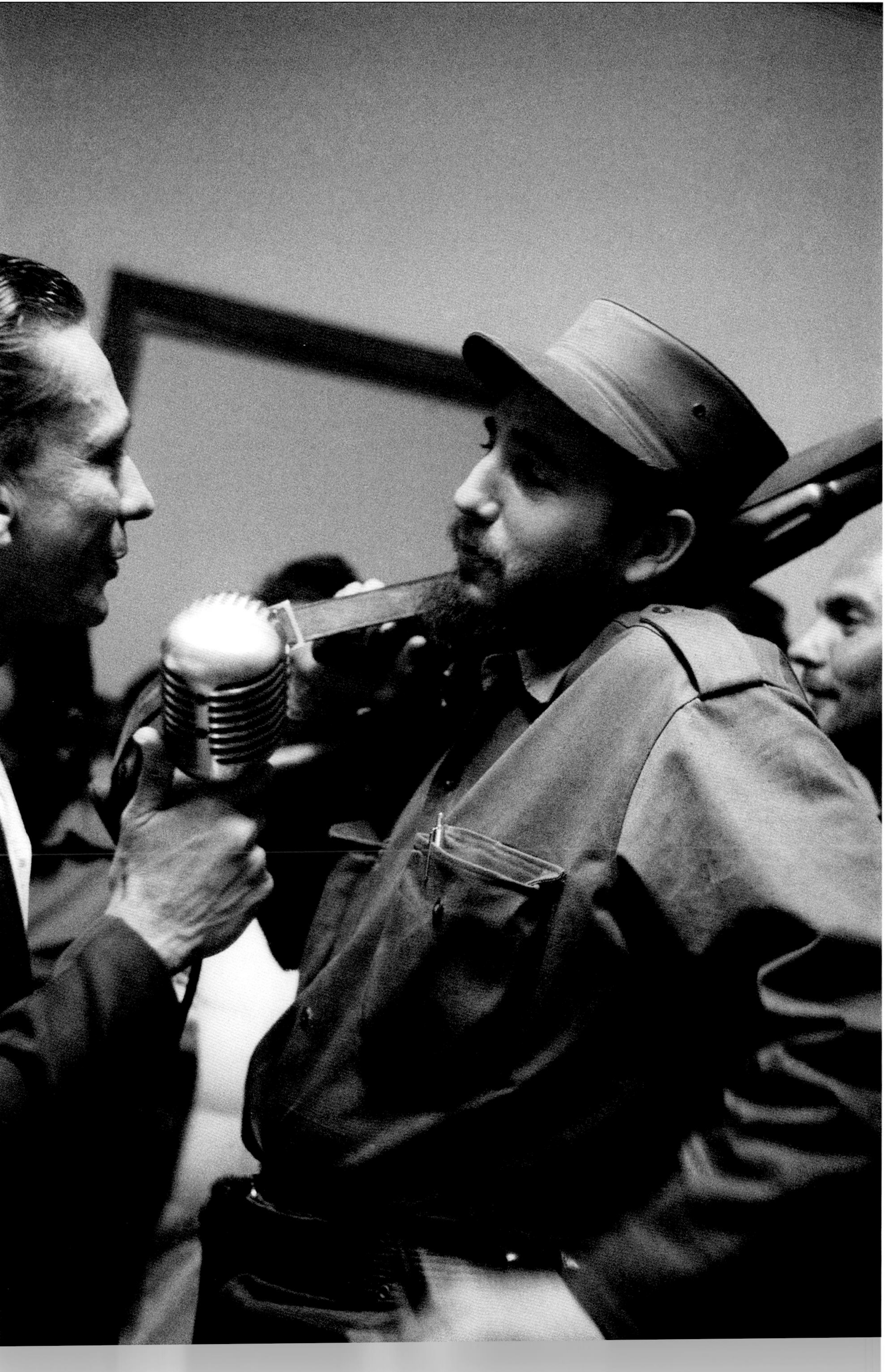

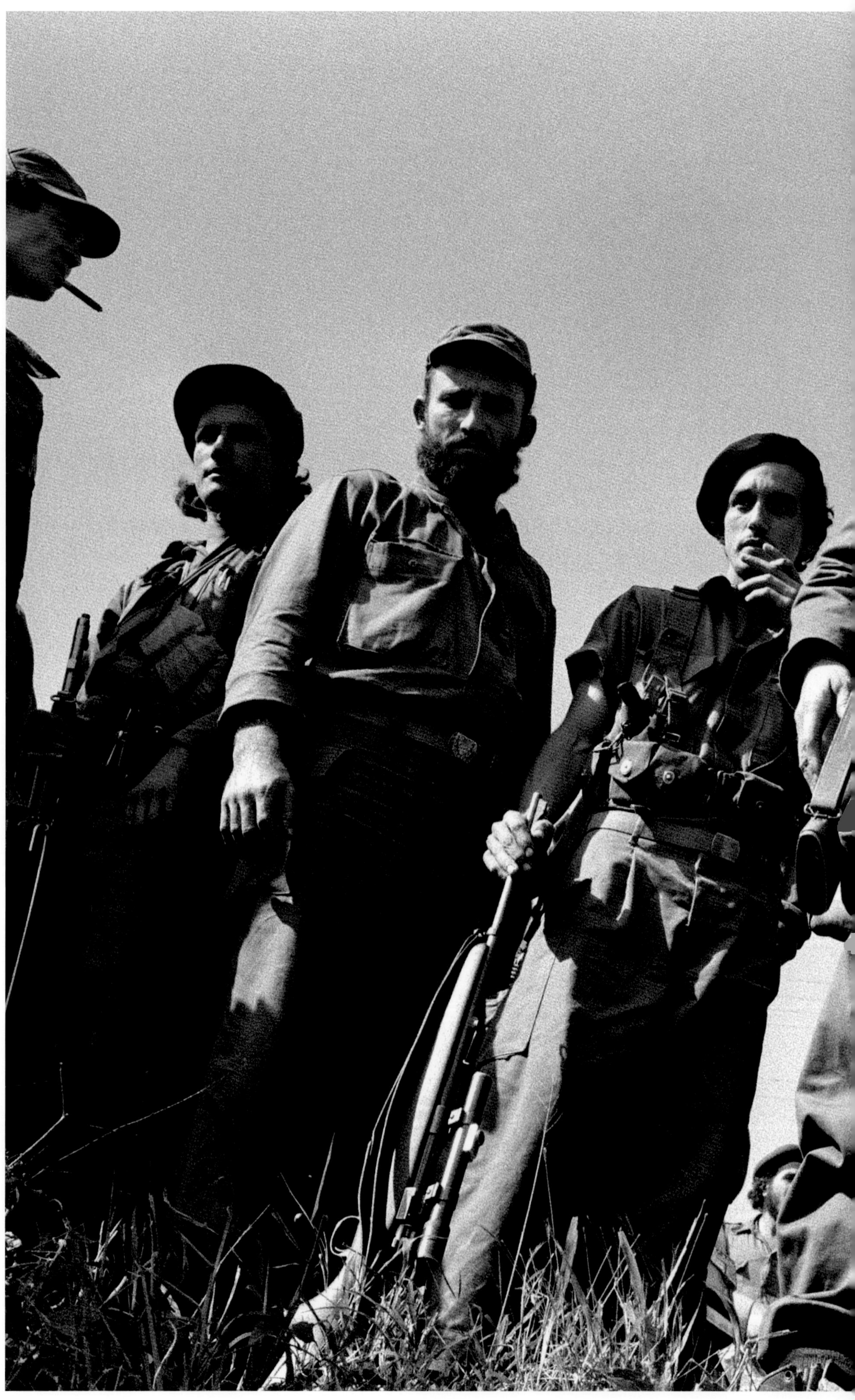

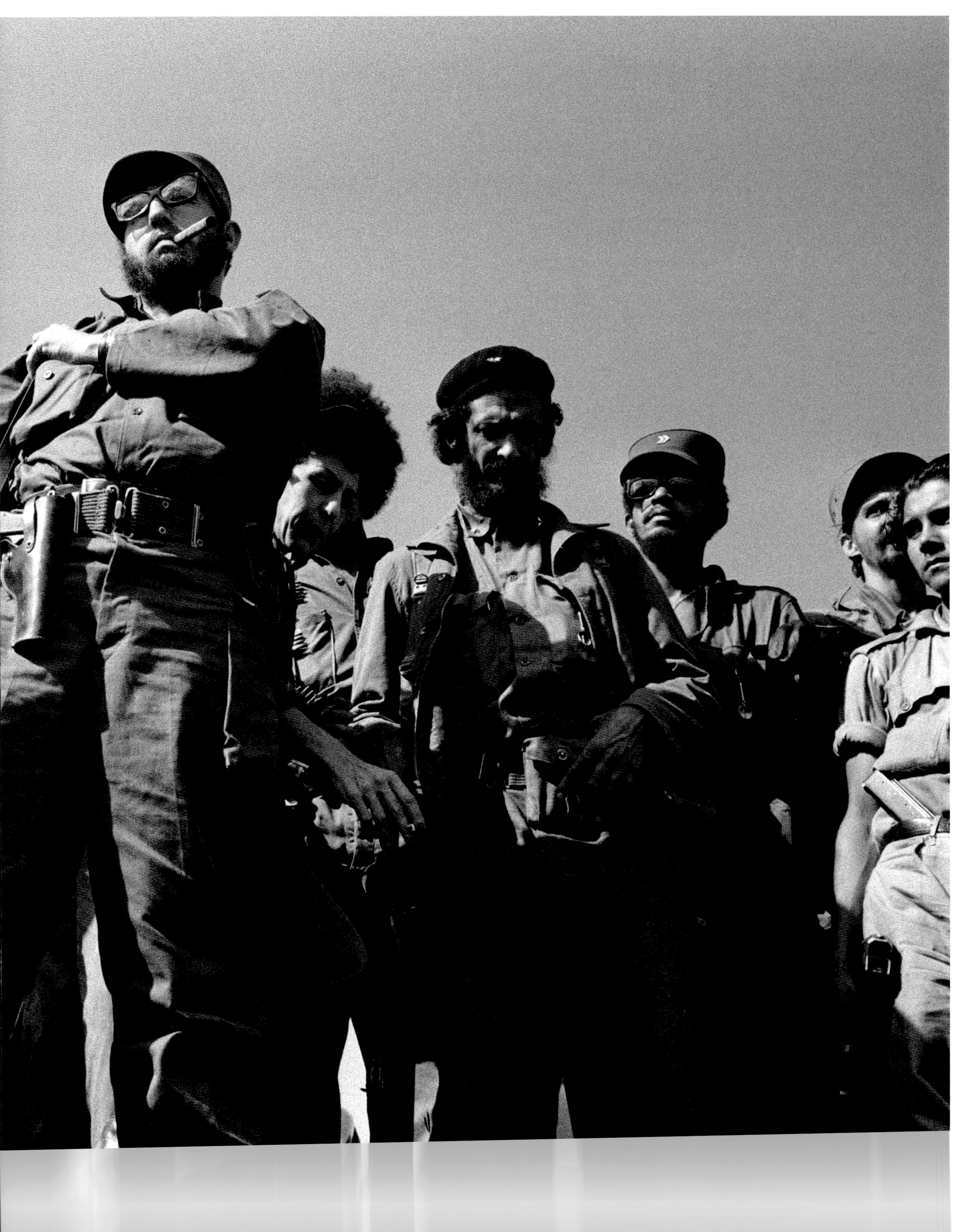

The unruly column proceeds through the countryside. Castro has made an unscheduled stop at a gas station and gotten a soda pop. The woman running the place is absolutely startled. She gives Castro advice on how to run the country.

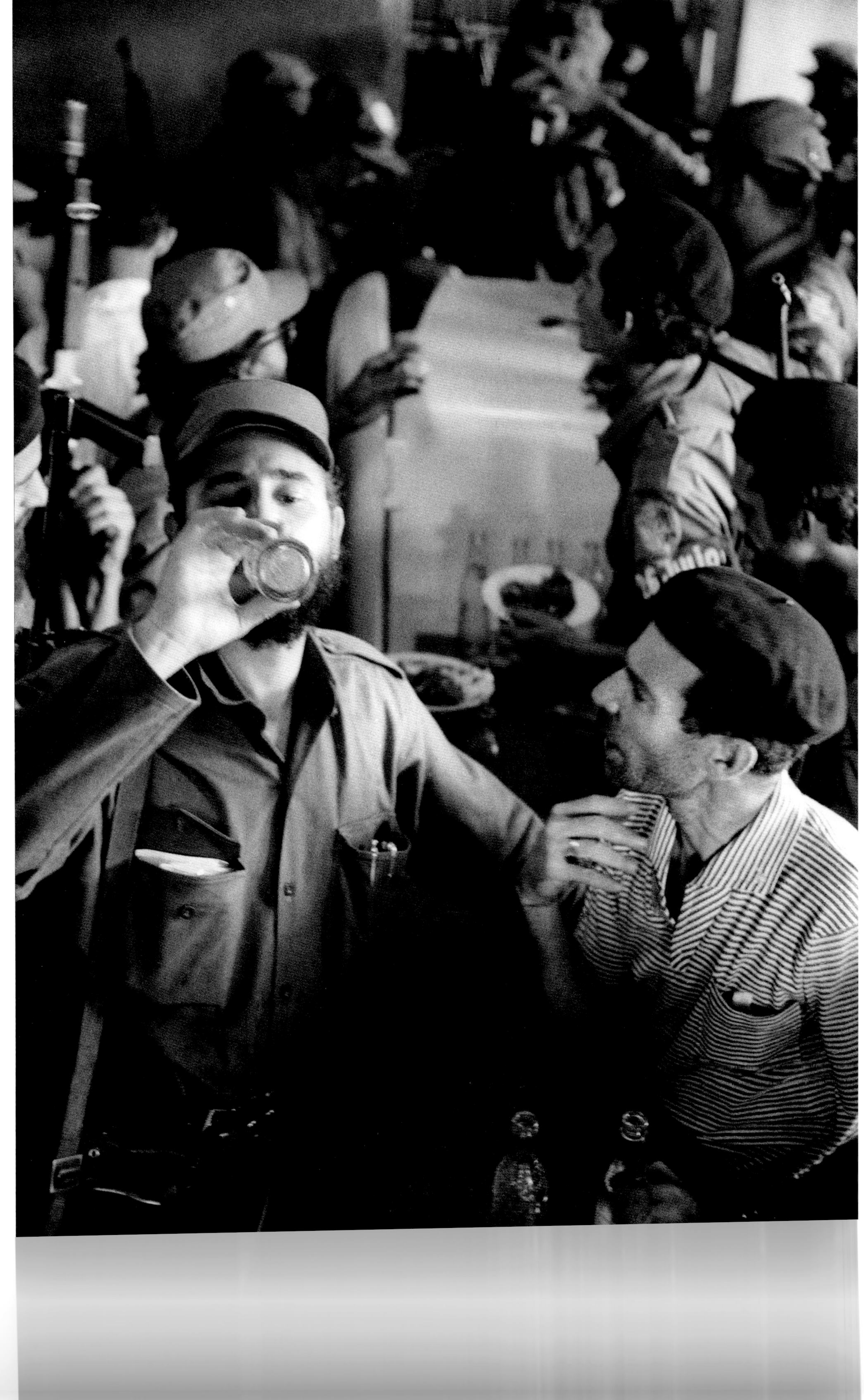

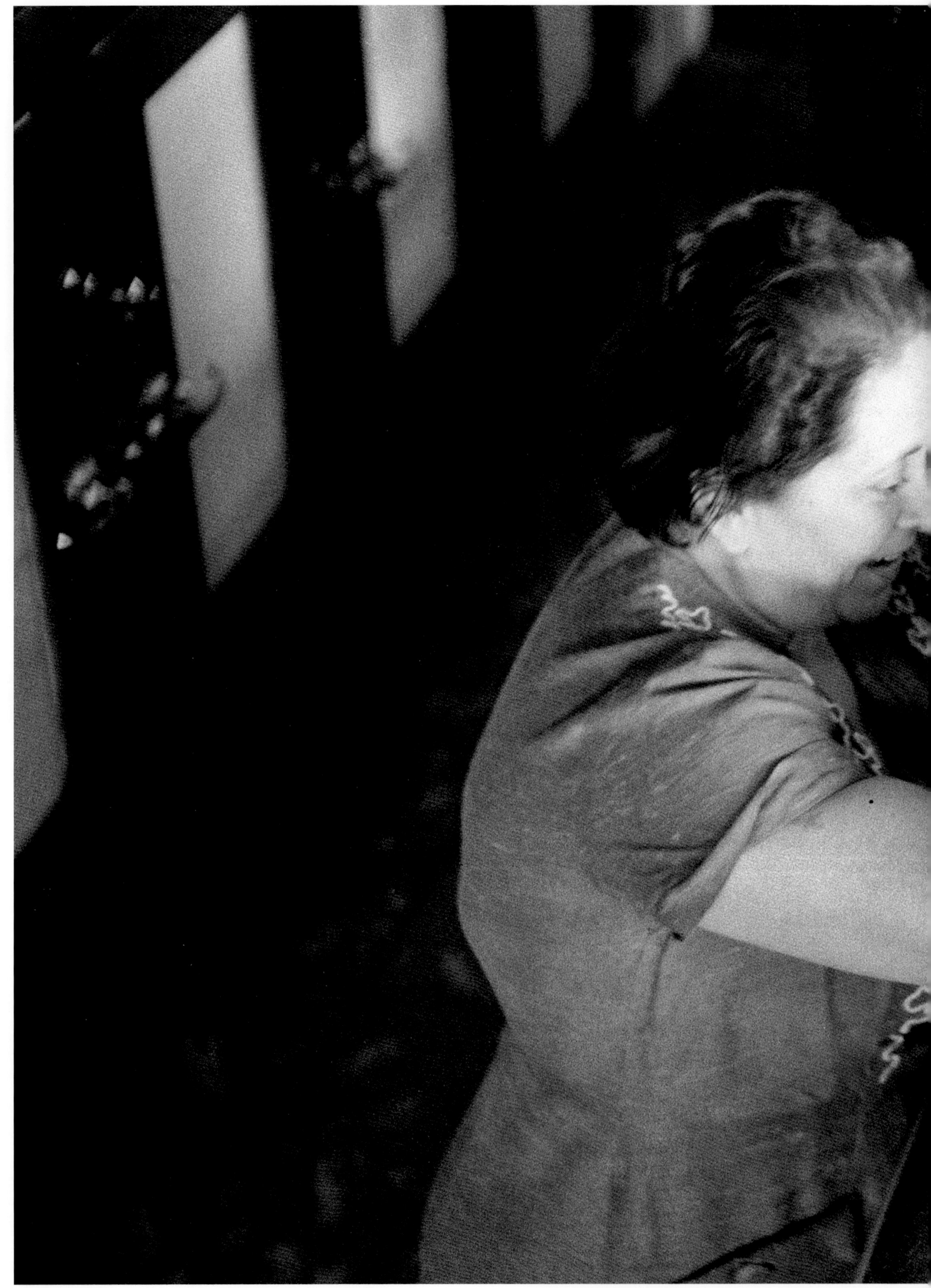

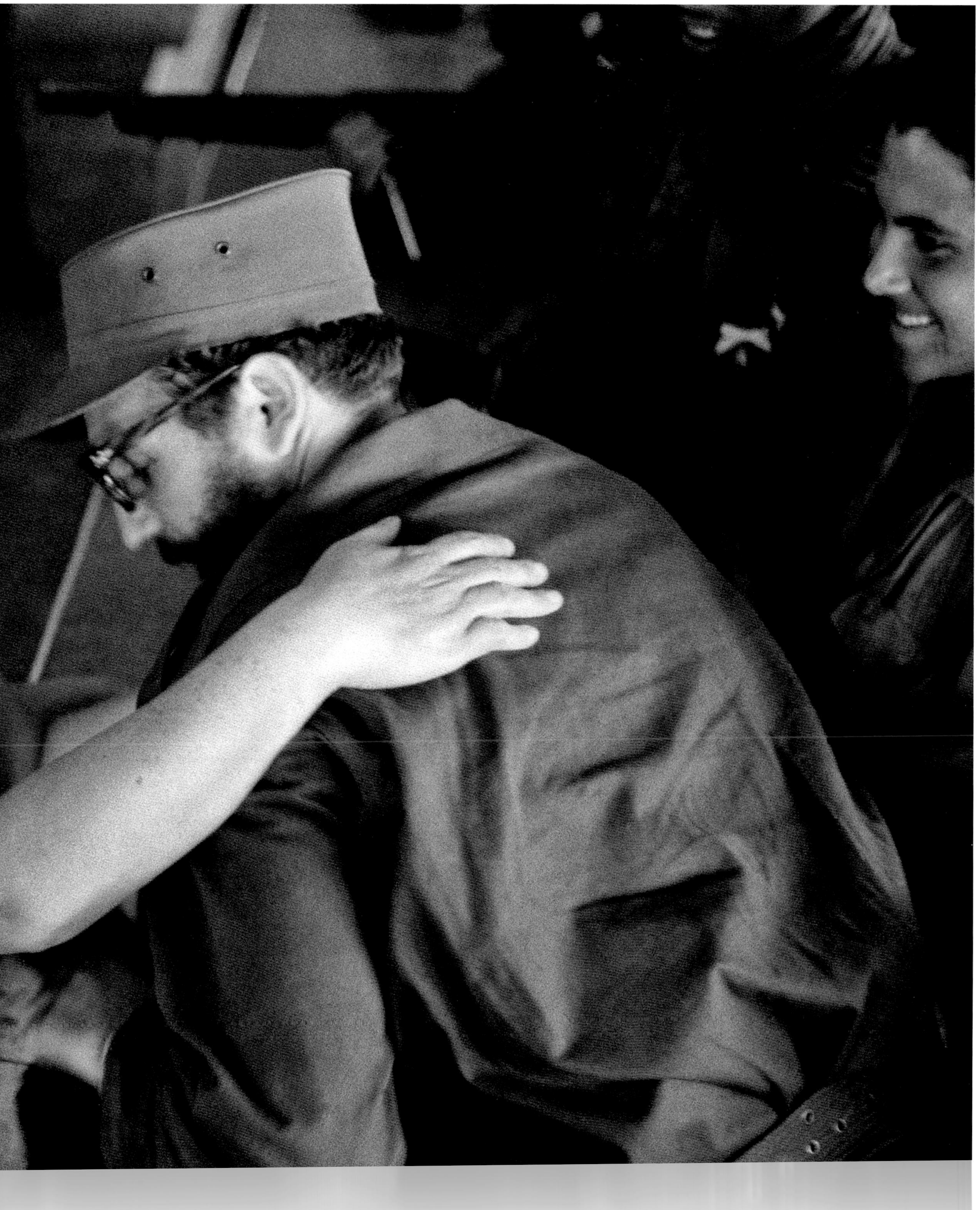

Fidel stops to give some money to the nuns who run an orphanage near Matanza.

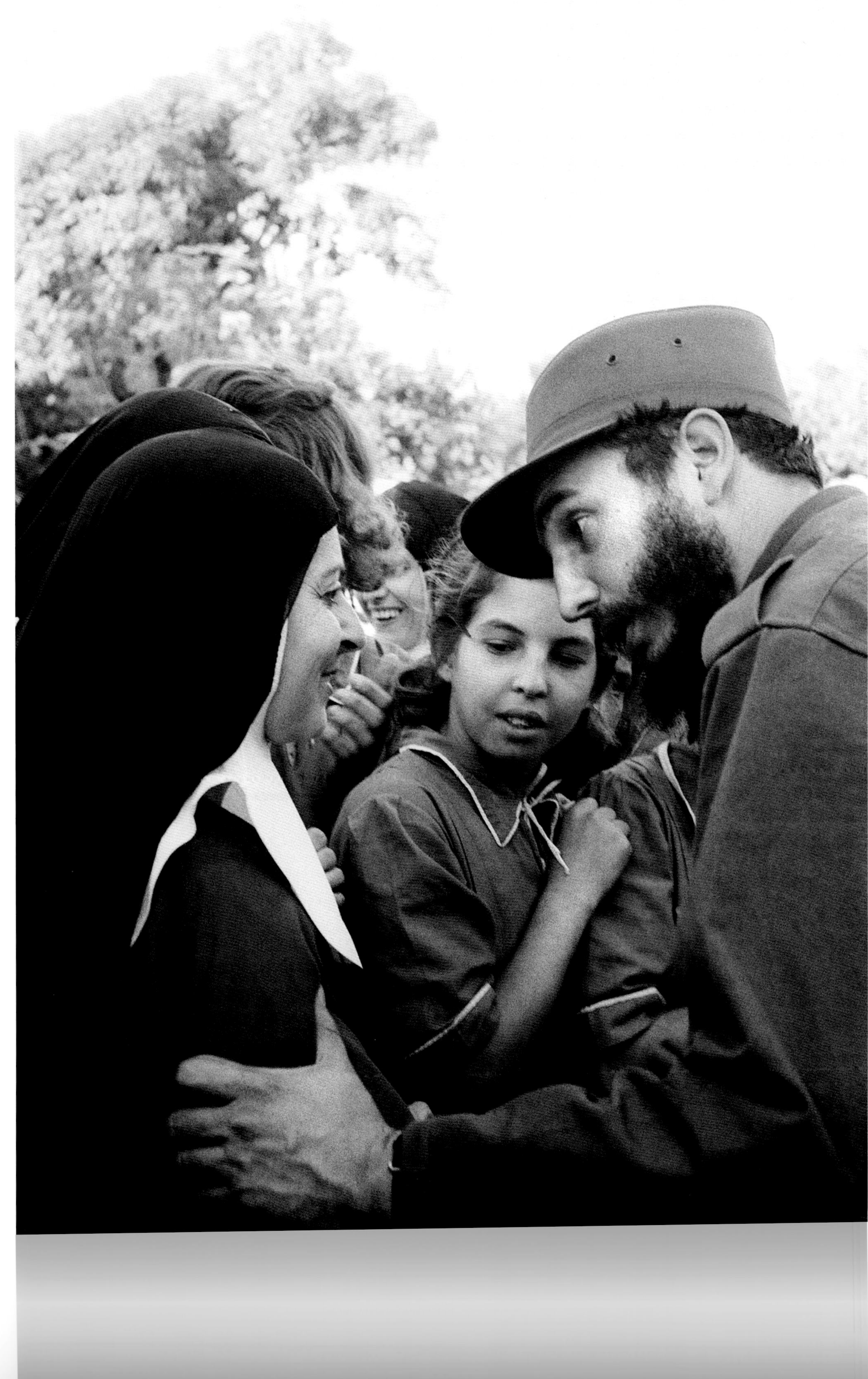

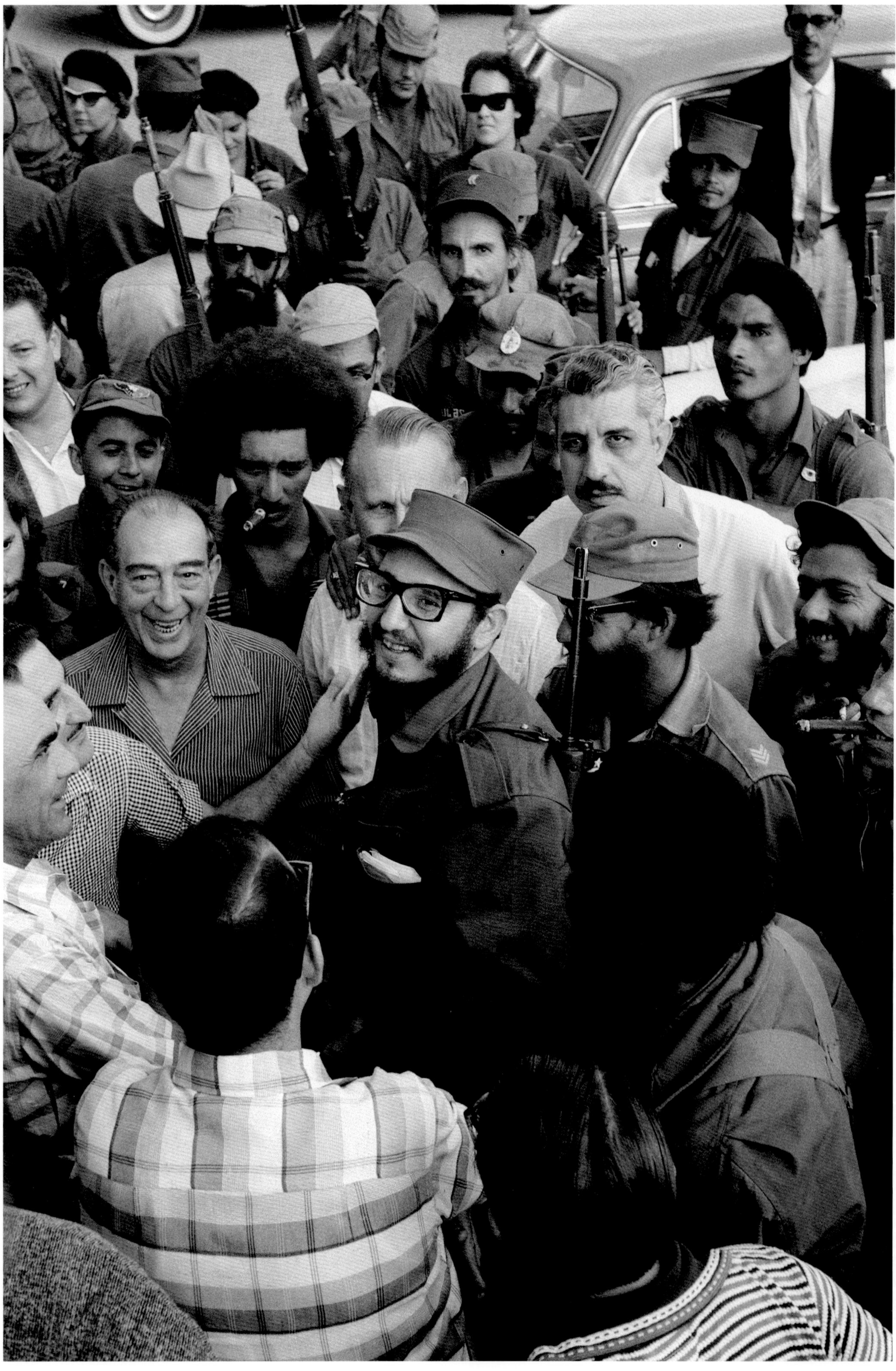

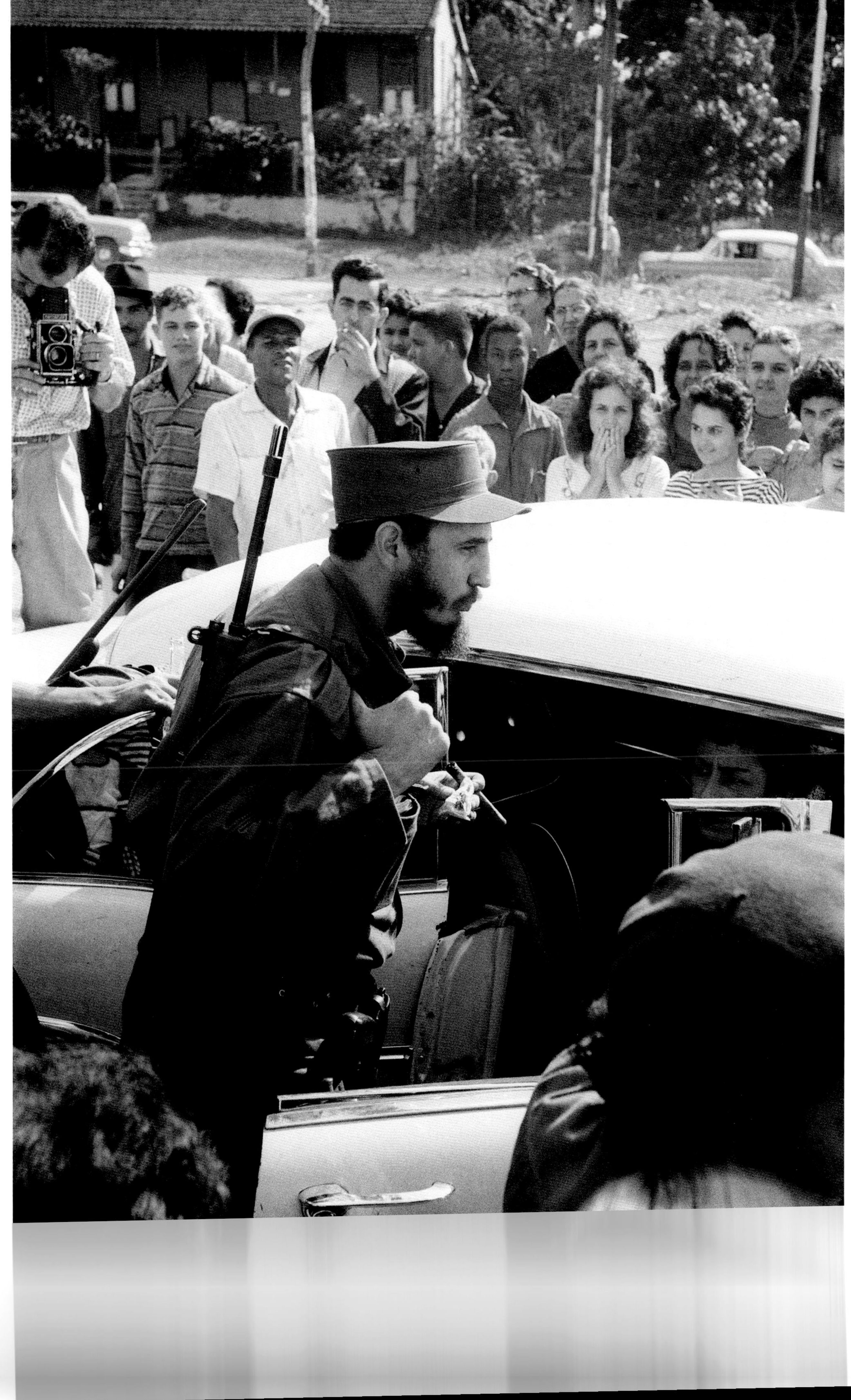

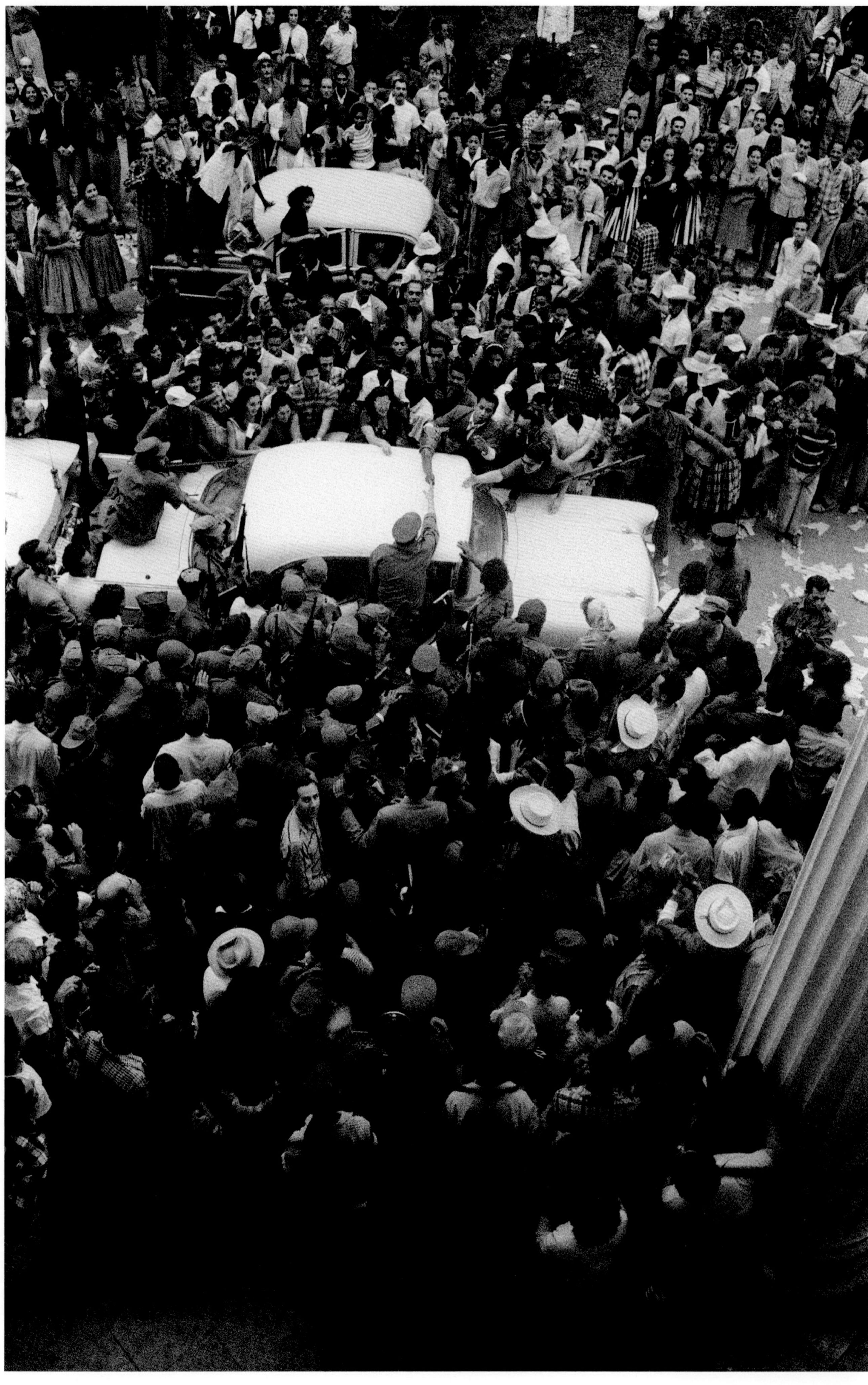

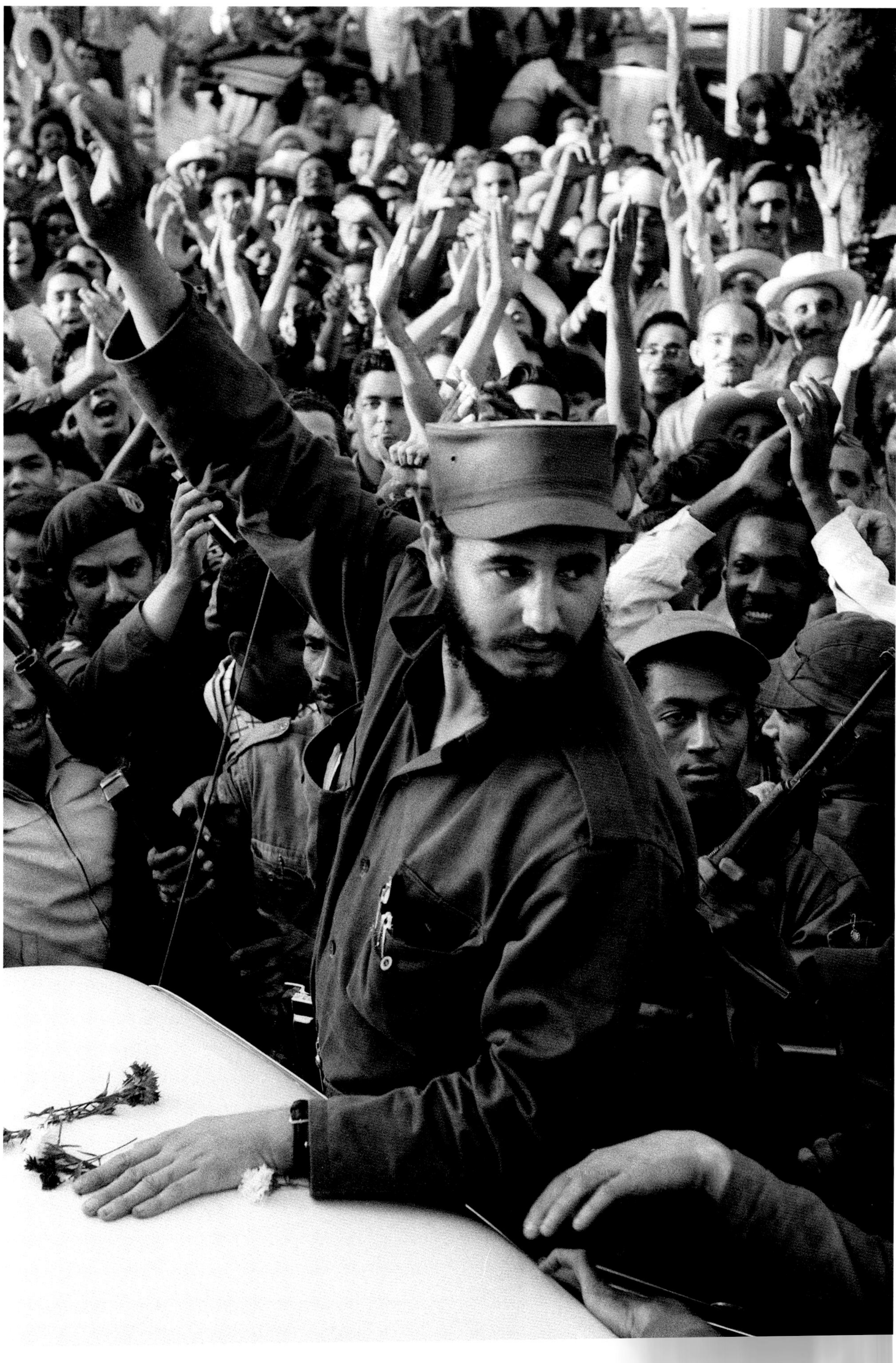

Fidel on top of a tank on the parade entering Havana. The young boy with him is his 8-year-old son, who was flown to Havana from New York to meet his father. He lives with his mother who is divorced—a divorce not recognized by Castro who is a devout Catholic. The mother has remarried a Batista supporter and member of the Batista government.

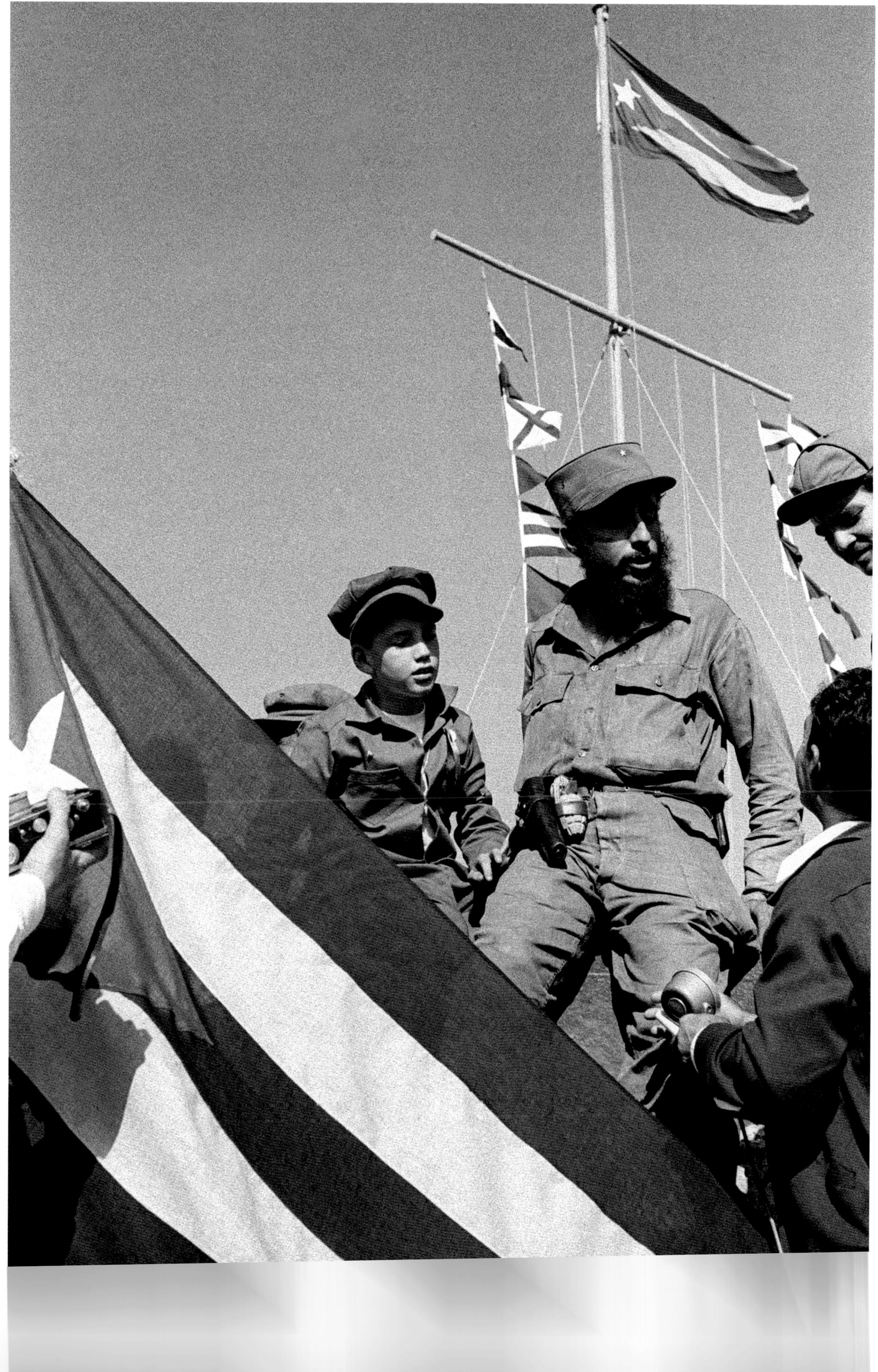

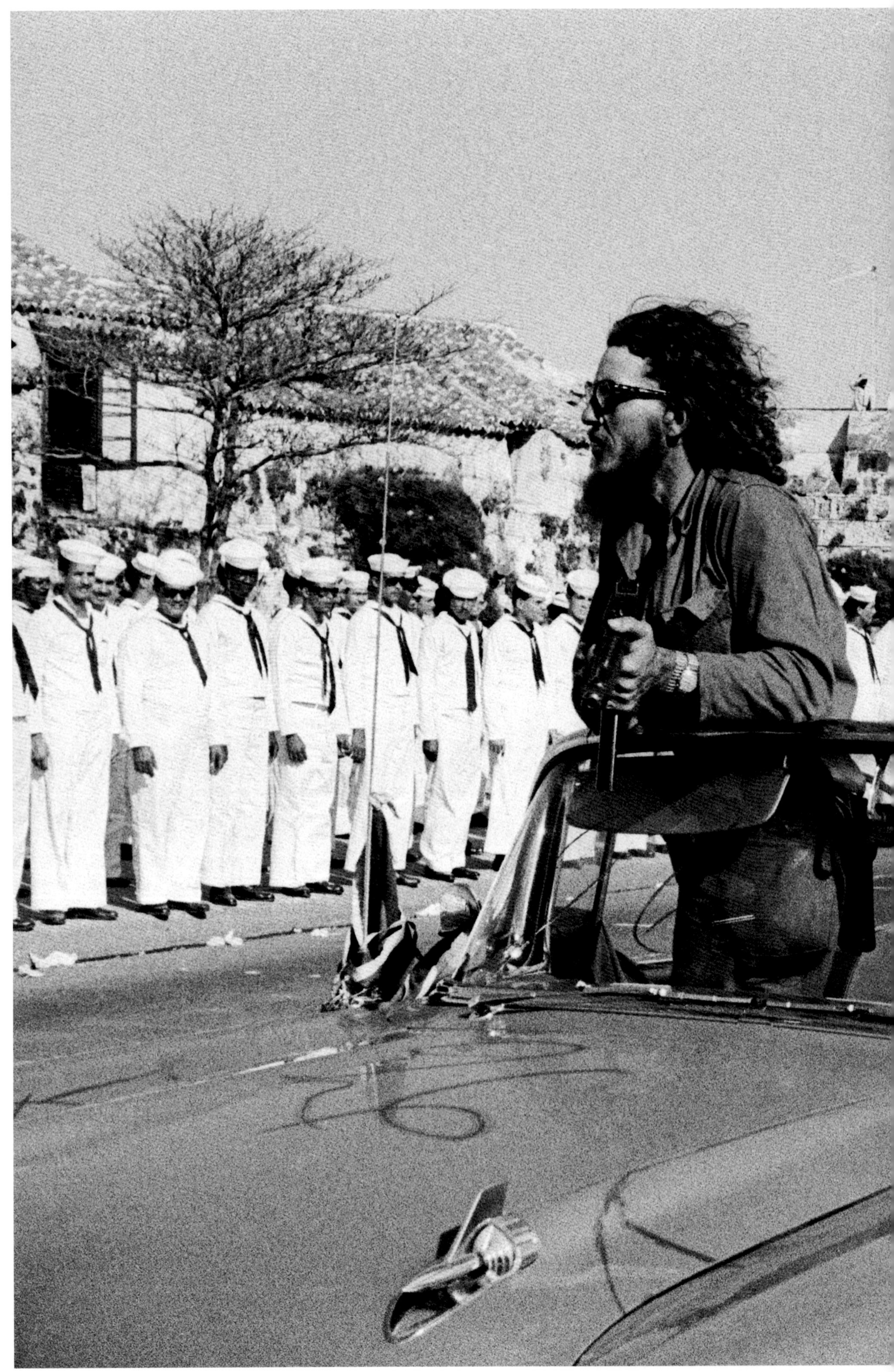

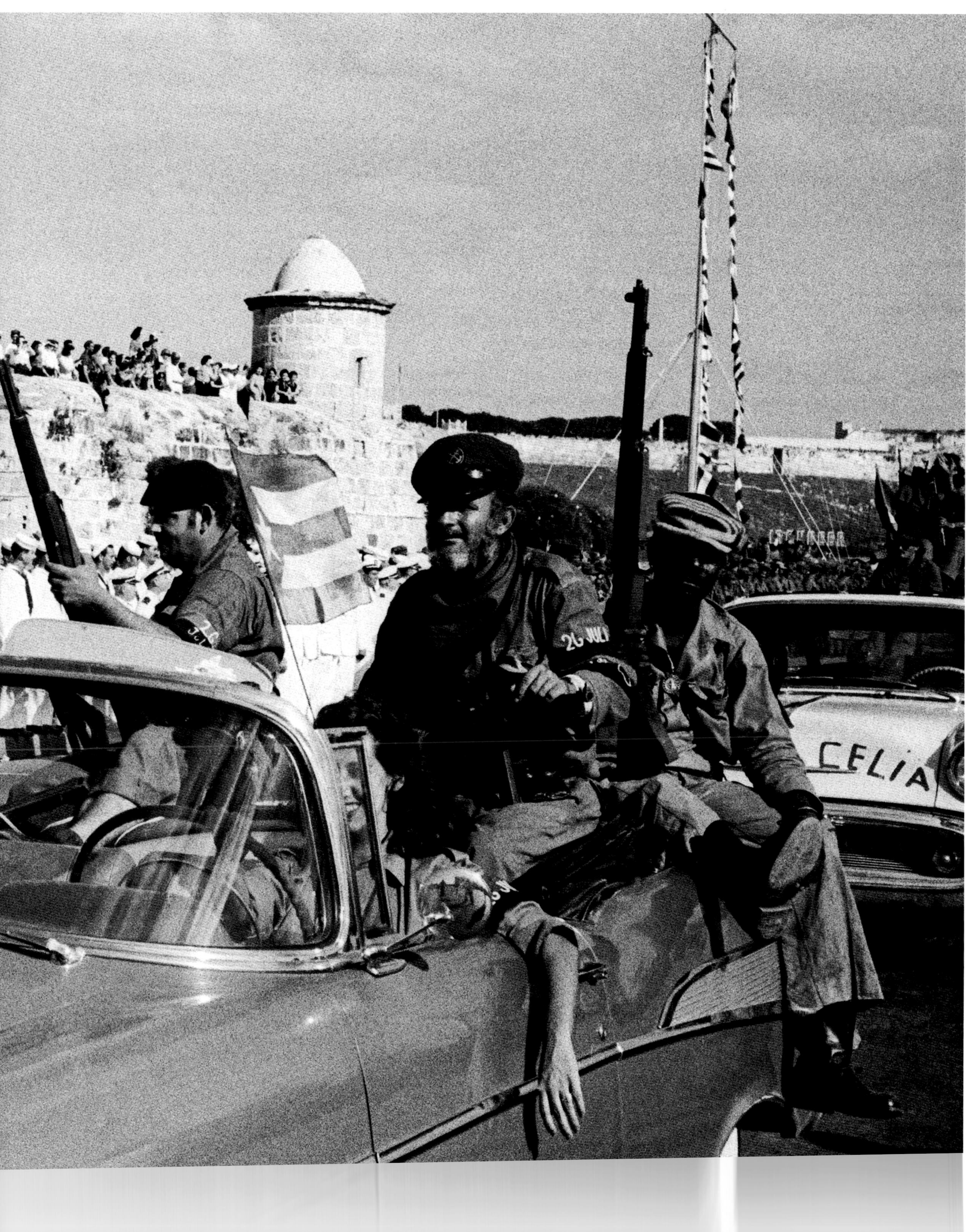
CELIA

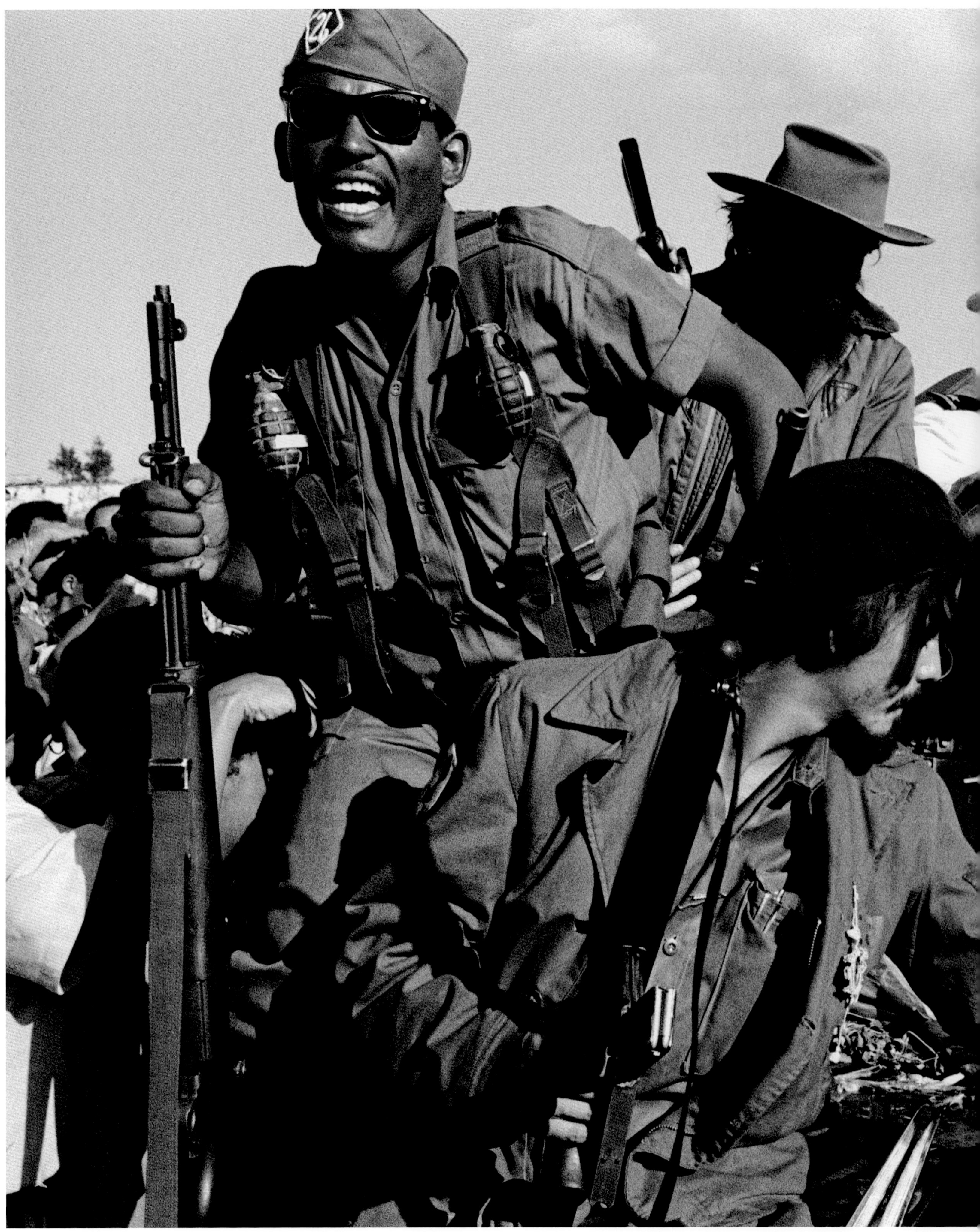

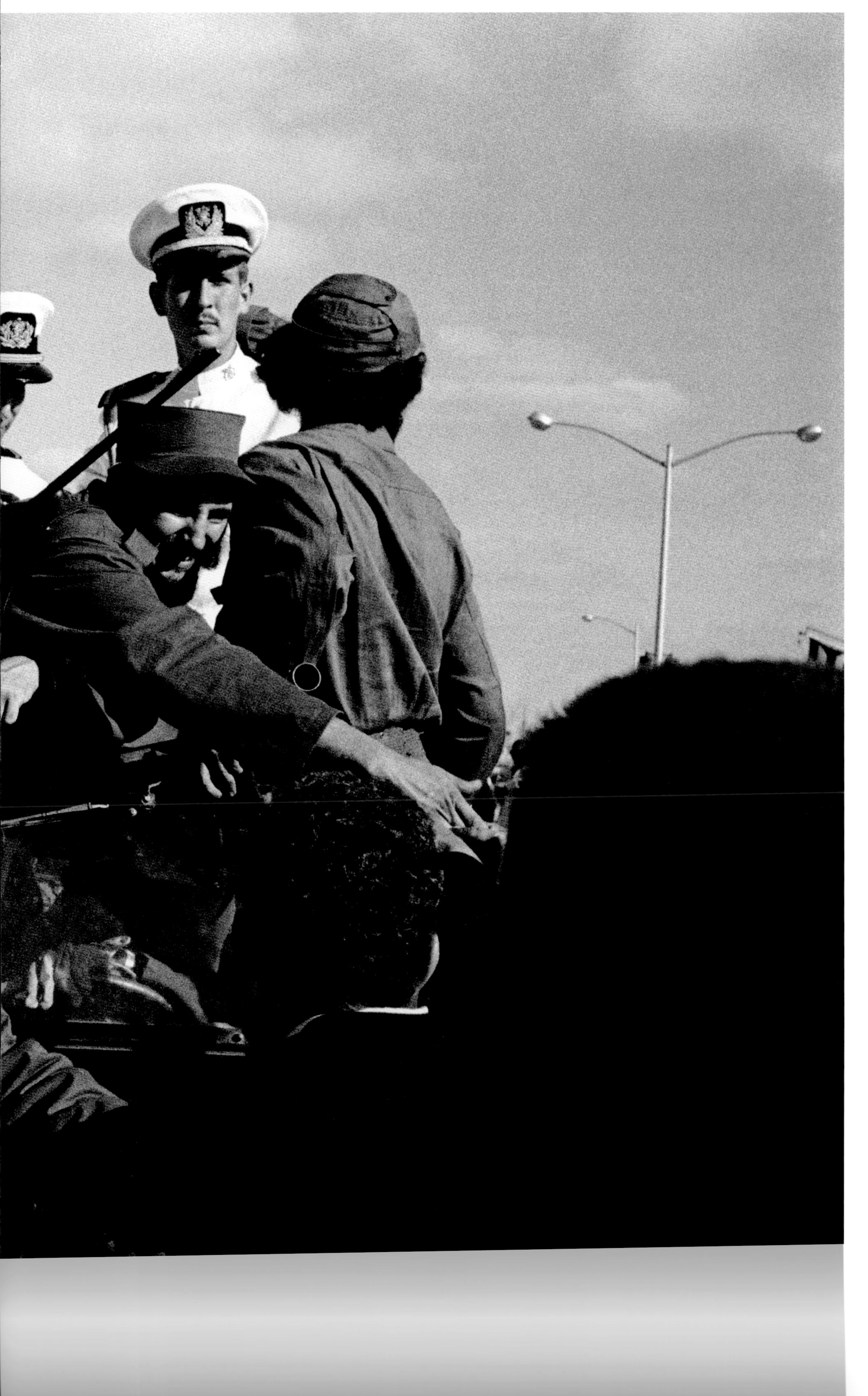

During Castro's arrival into Havana, I waded through mobs and mobs of people pushing towards the palace for a thousand yards. The crush was so great that I lost a camera and my shoes while taking pictures.

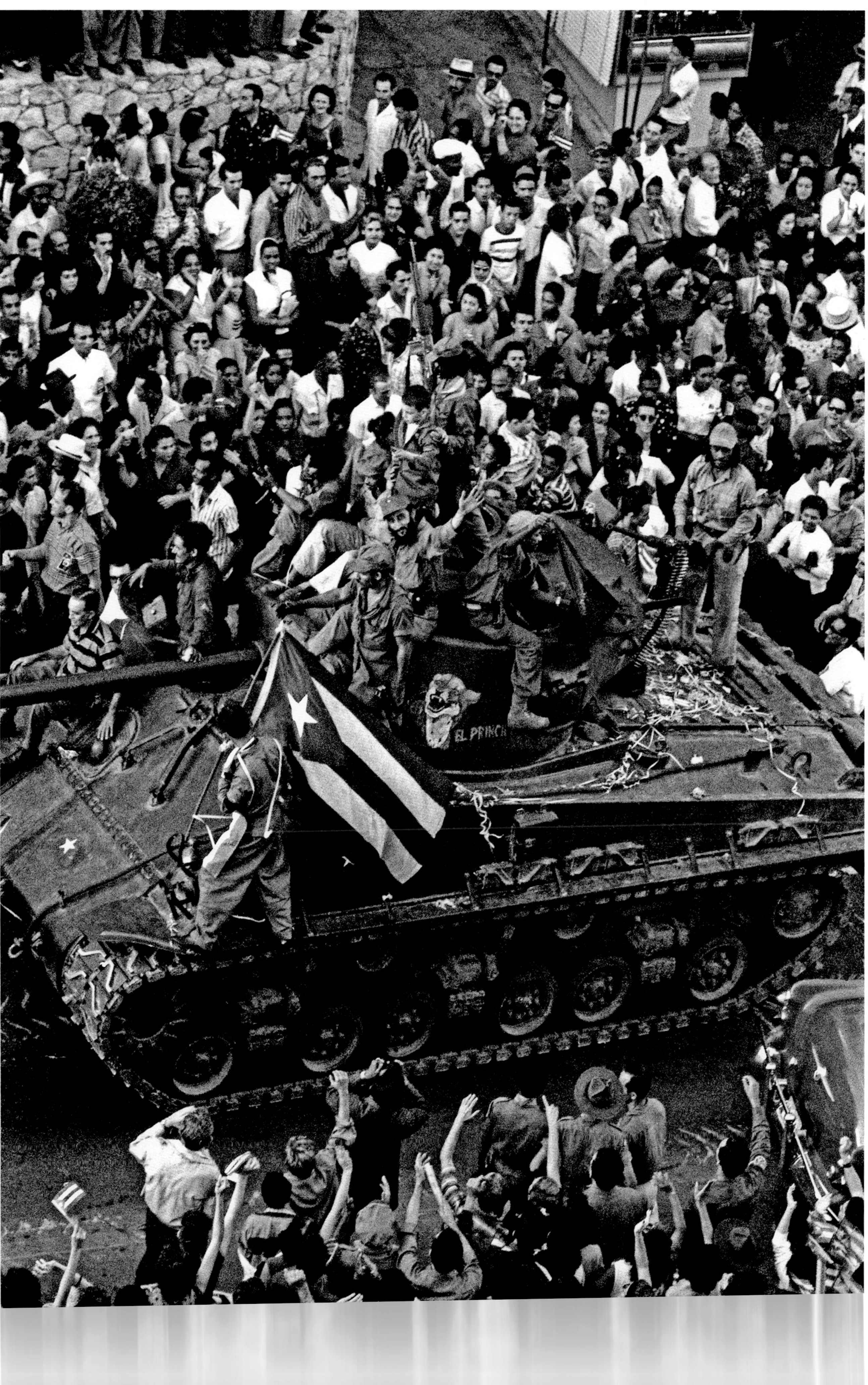

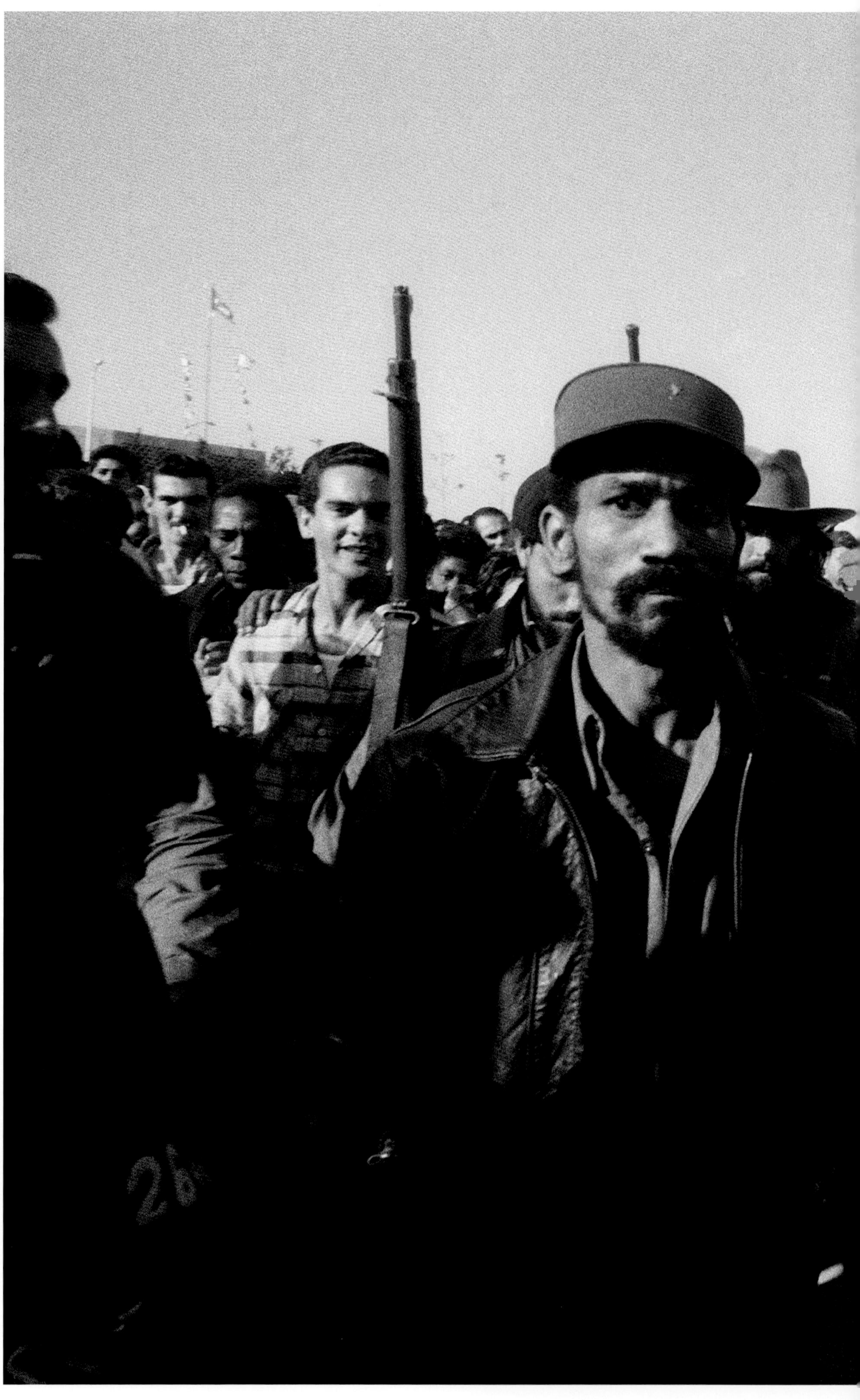
26

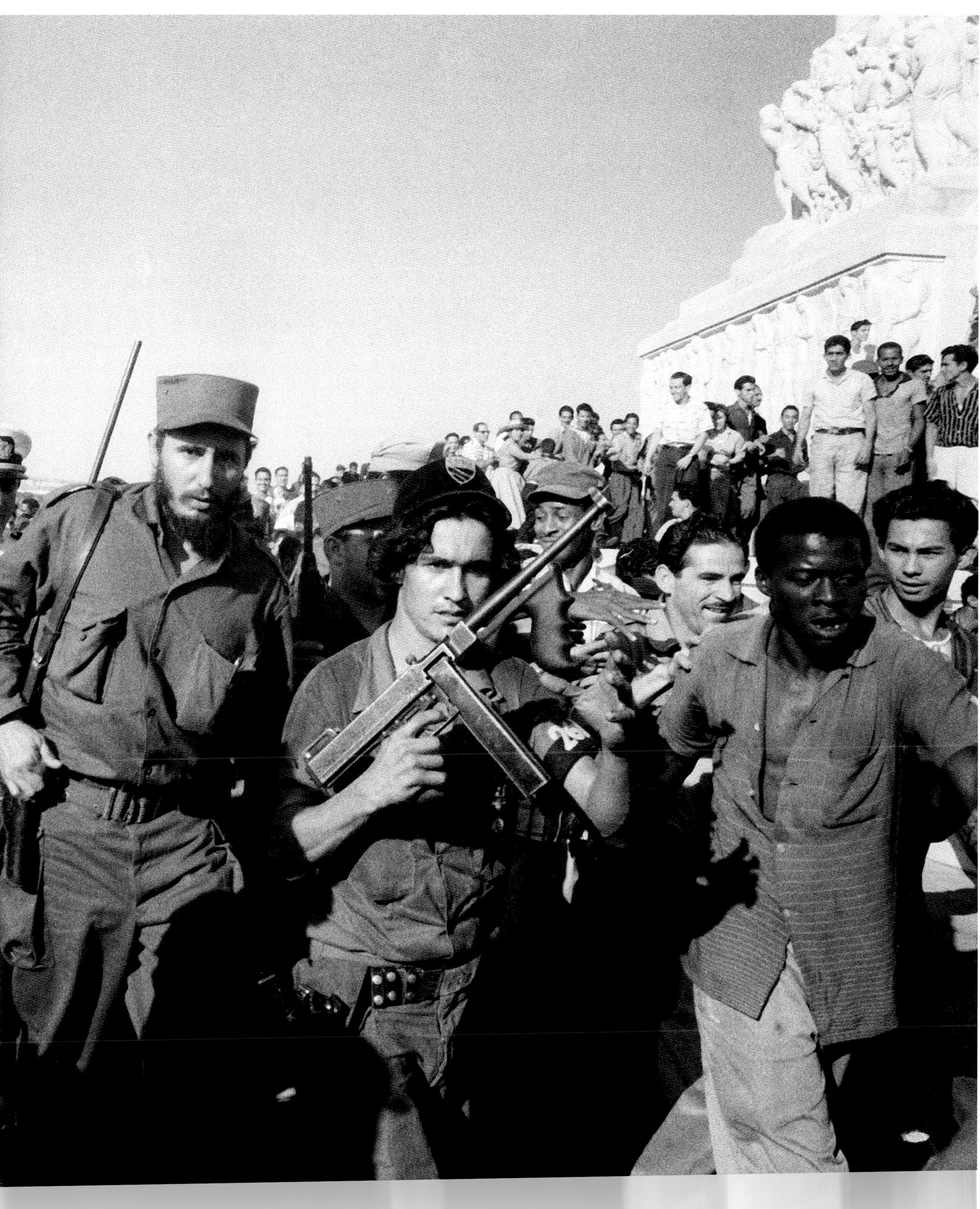

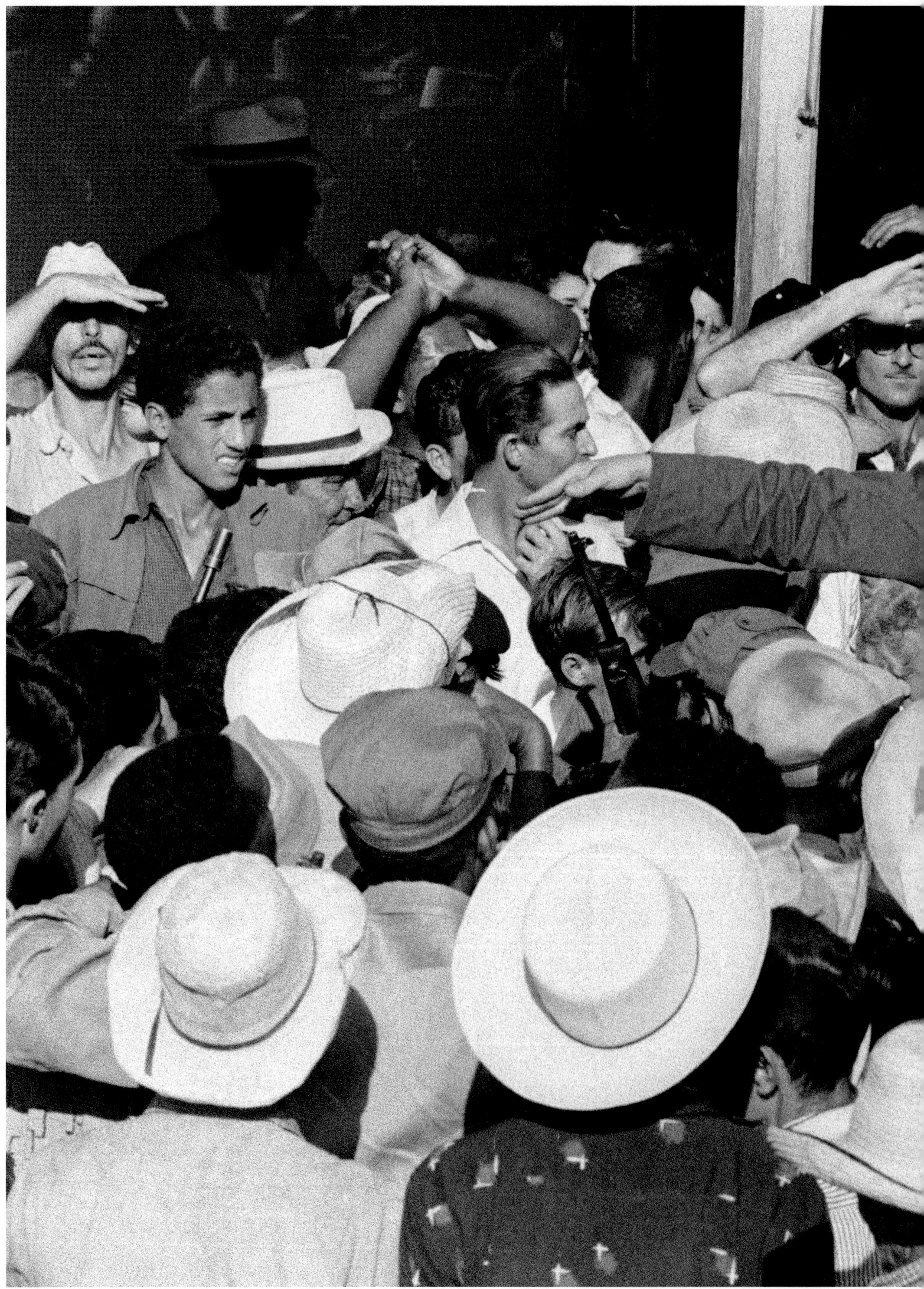

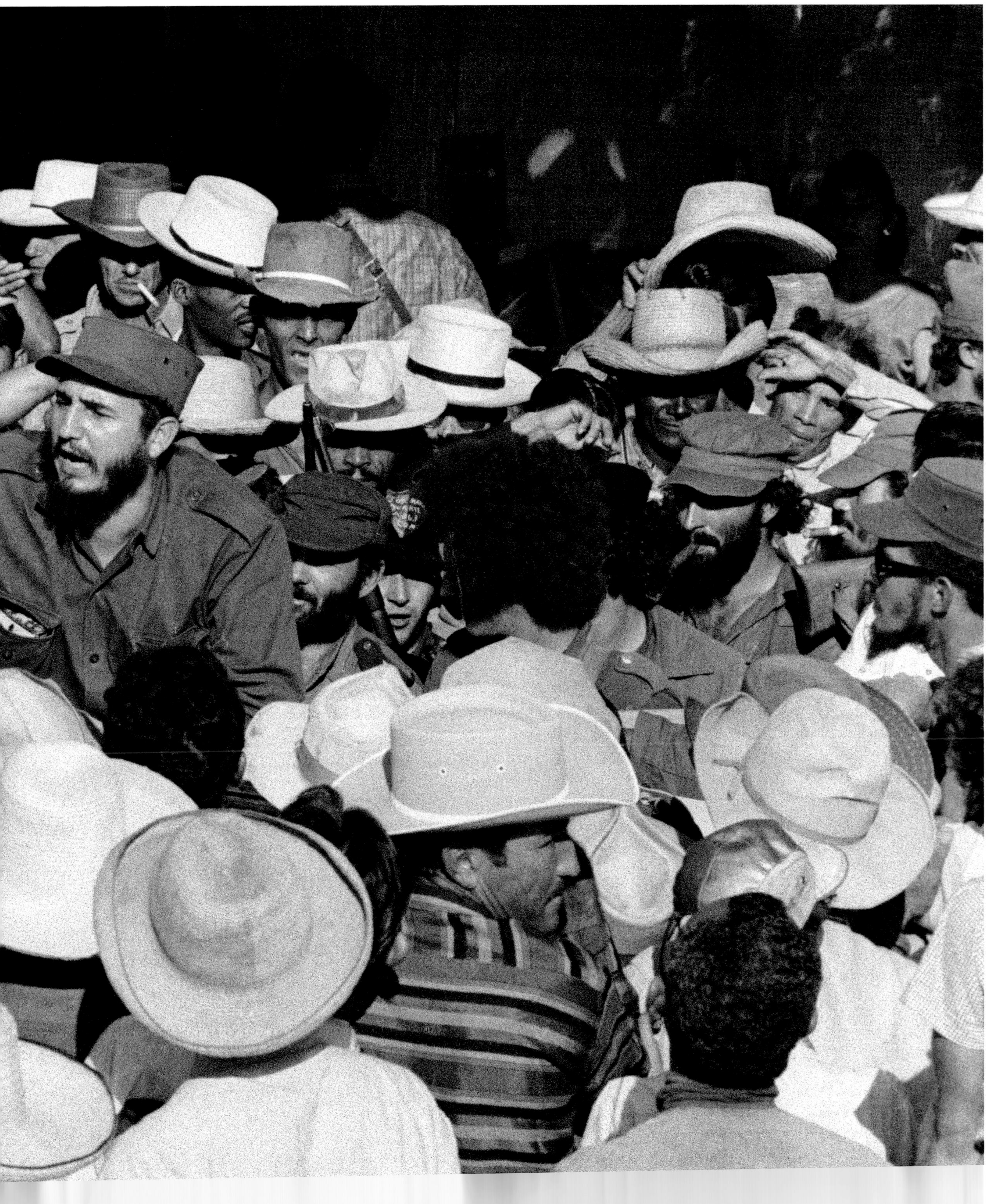

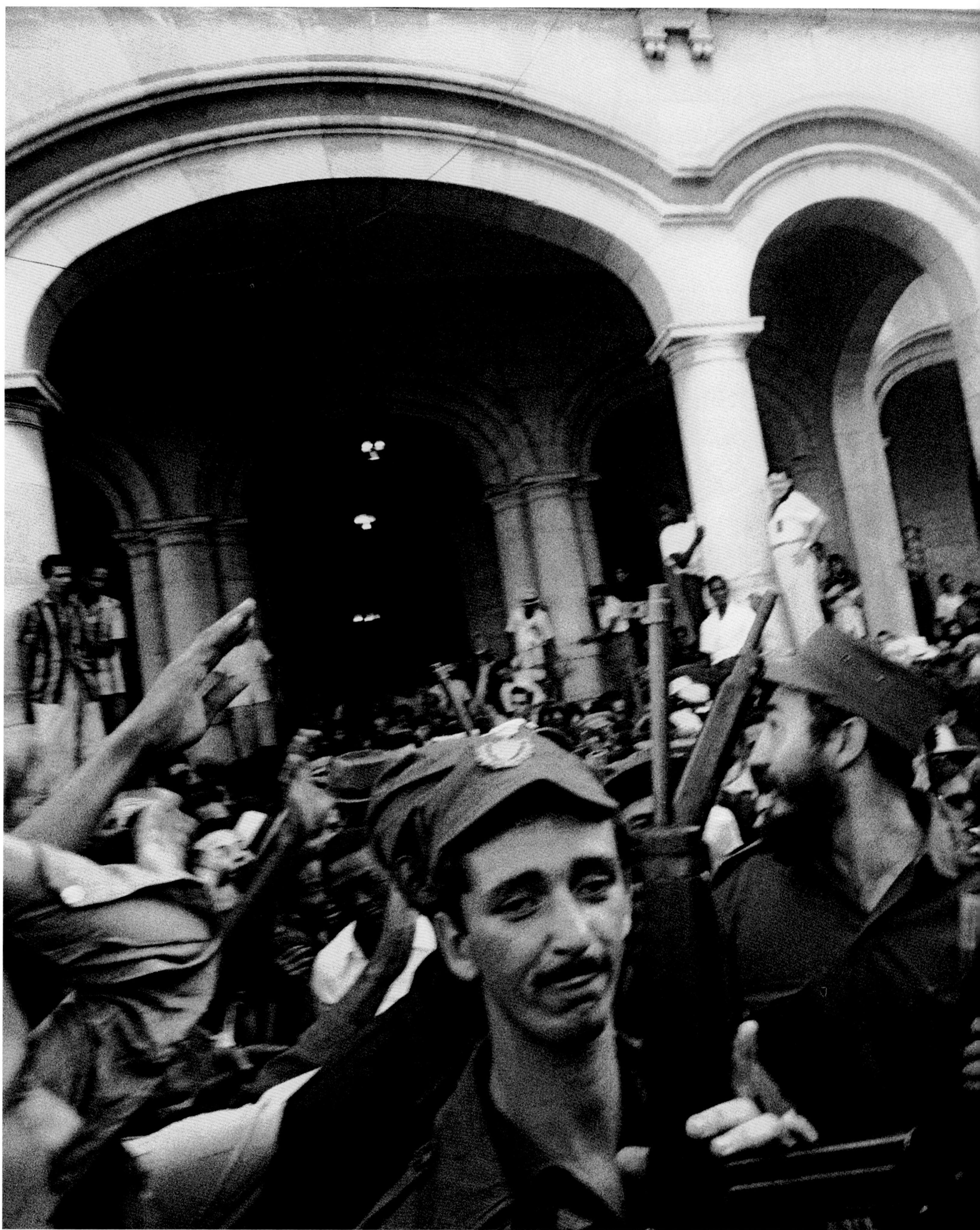

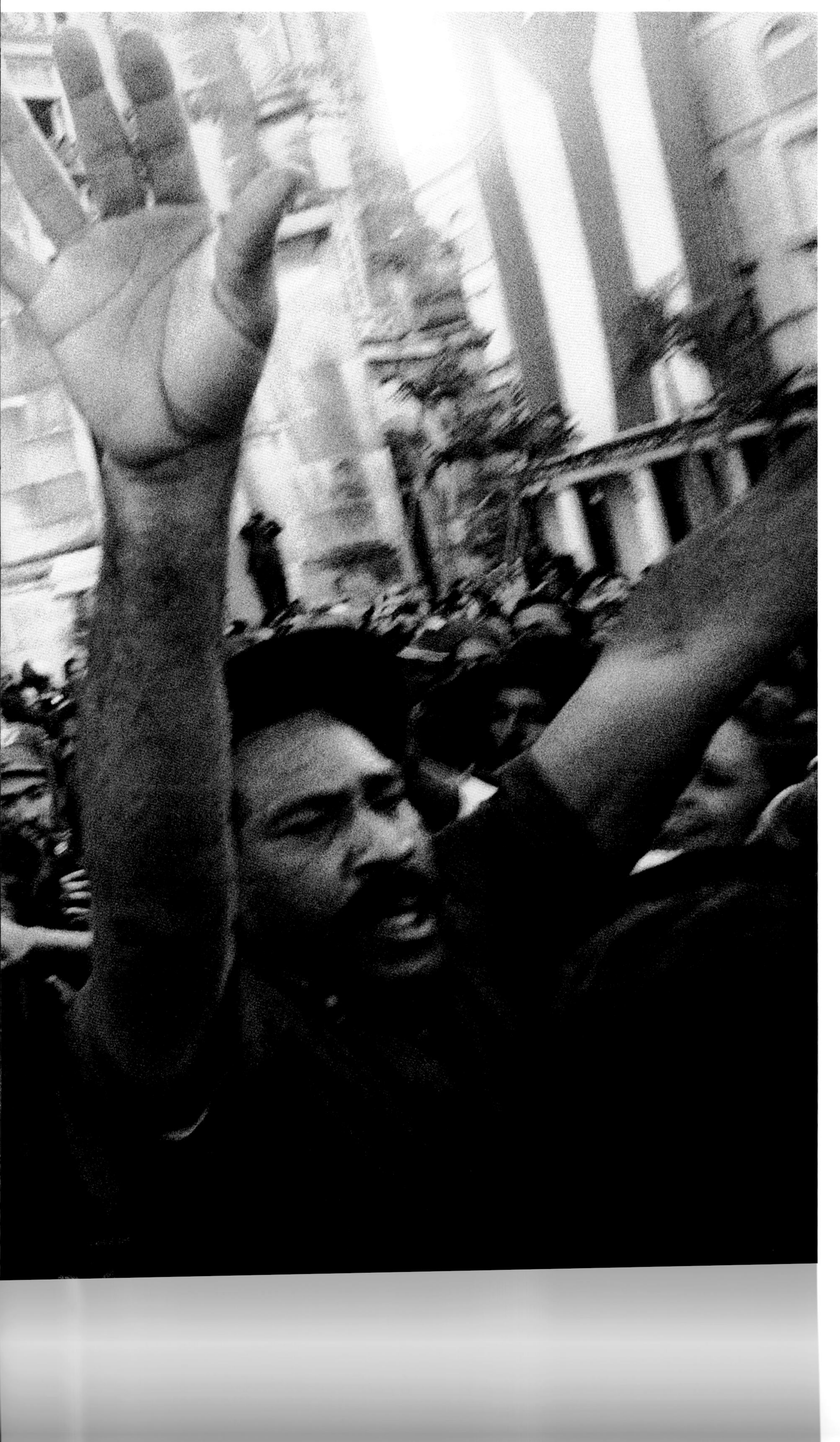

At thirty-two, Castro is not old enough to be elected president of Cuba, so Doctor Manuel Urrutia—a Cuban exile in New York—is nominated Batista's replacement.

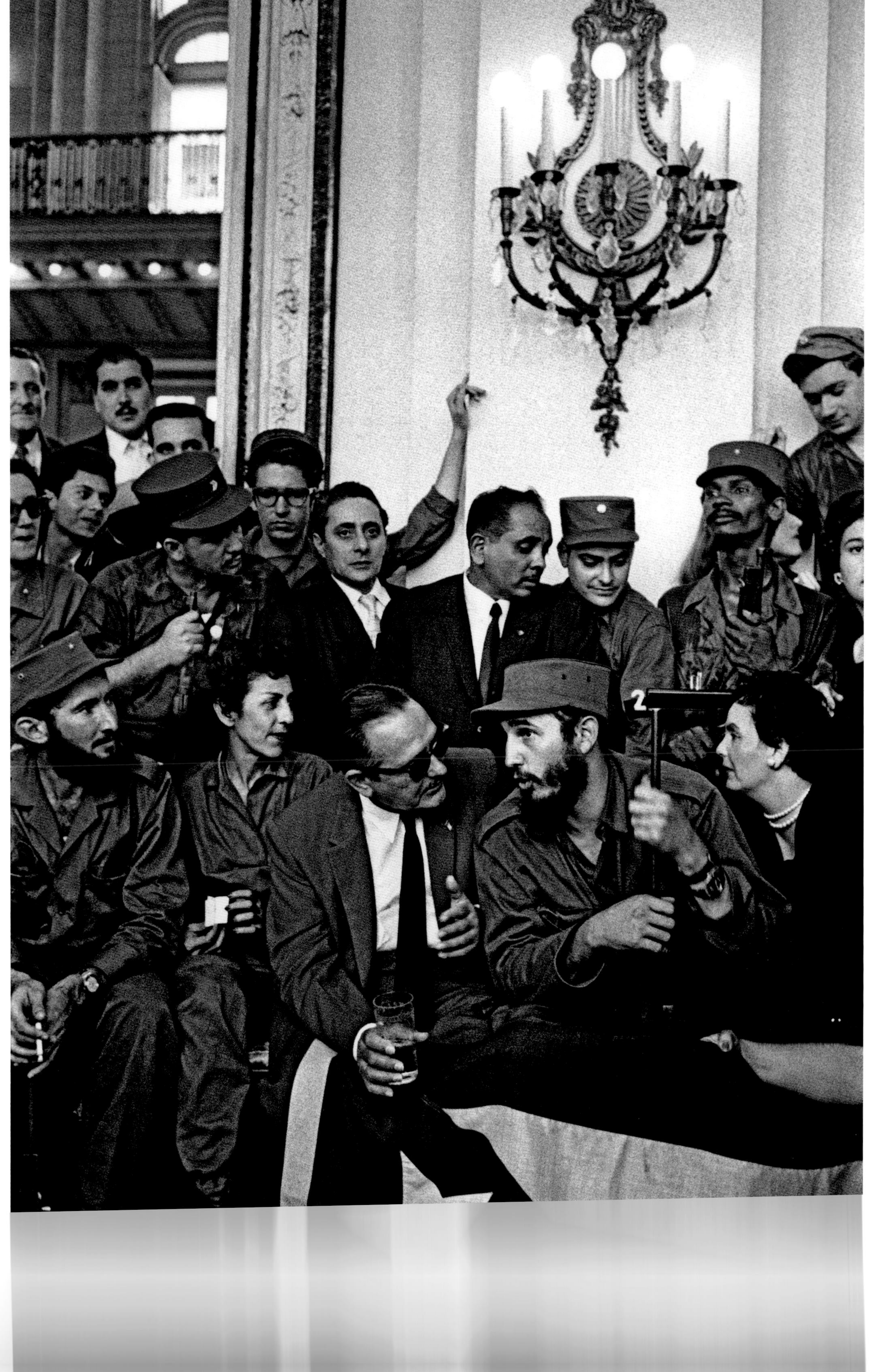

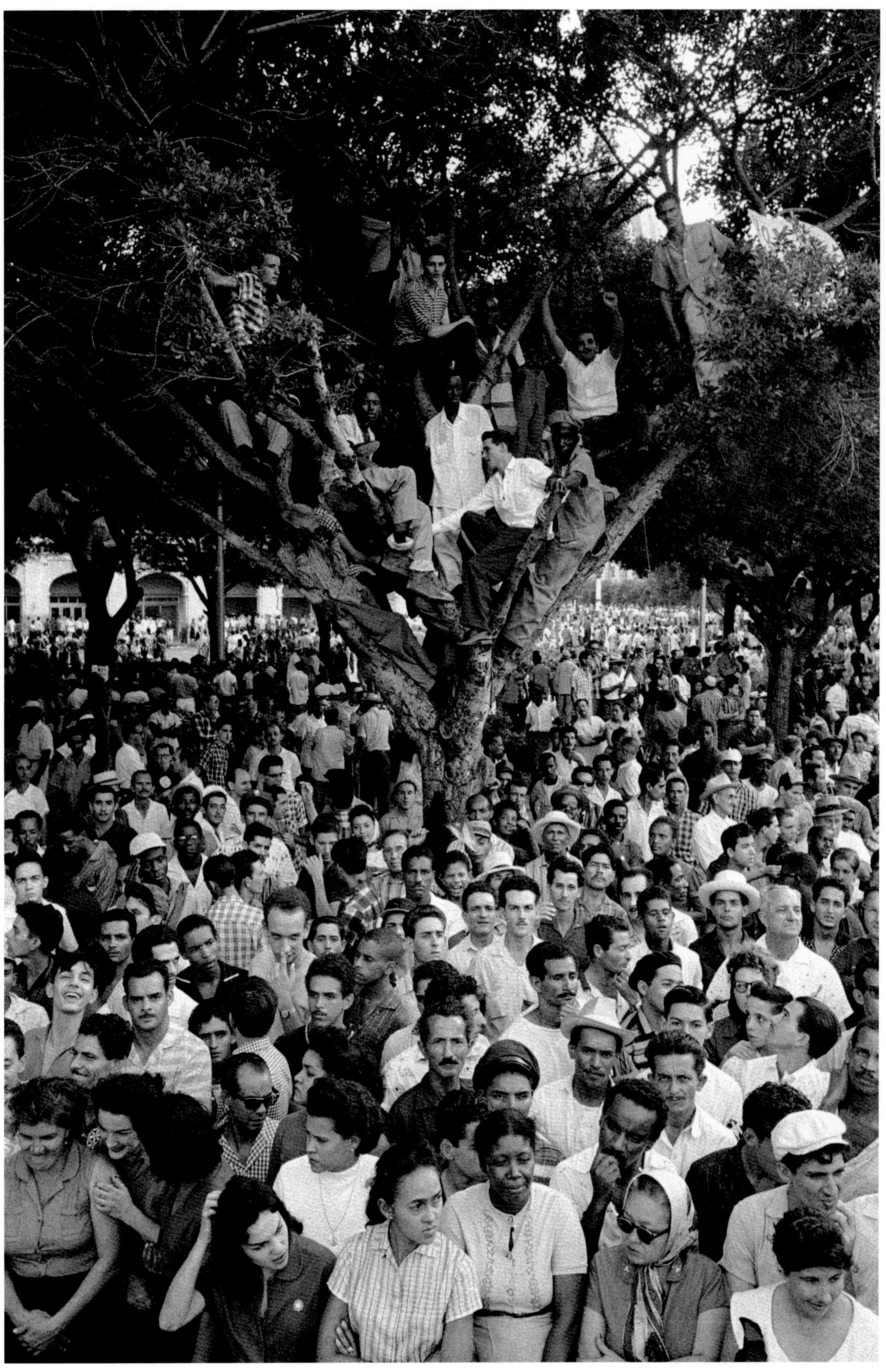

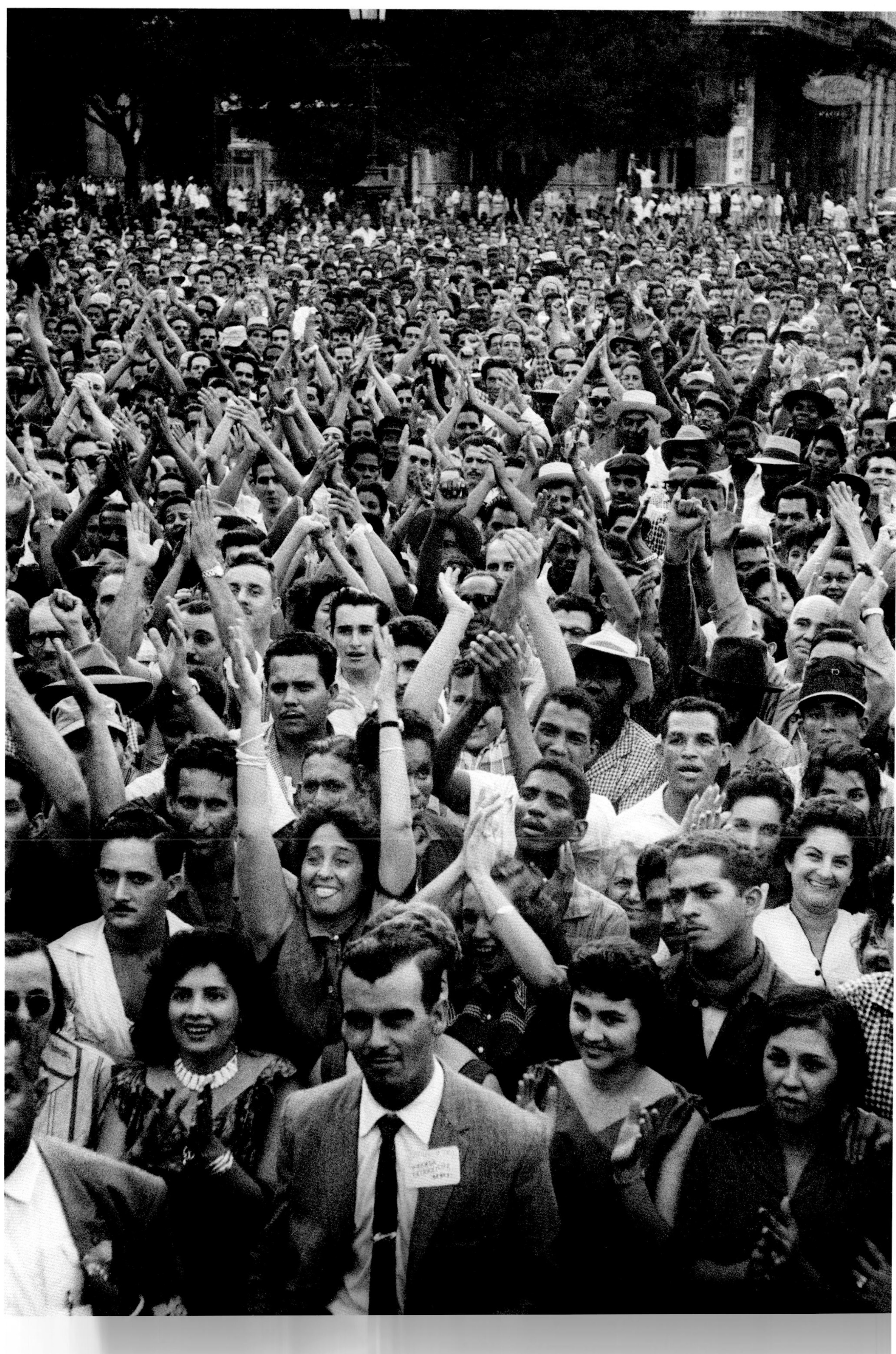

Castro and Urrutia address a delirious crowd from the balcony of the presidential palace.

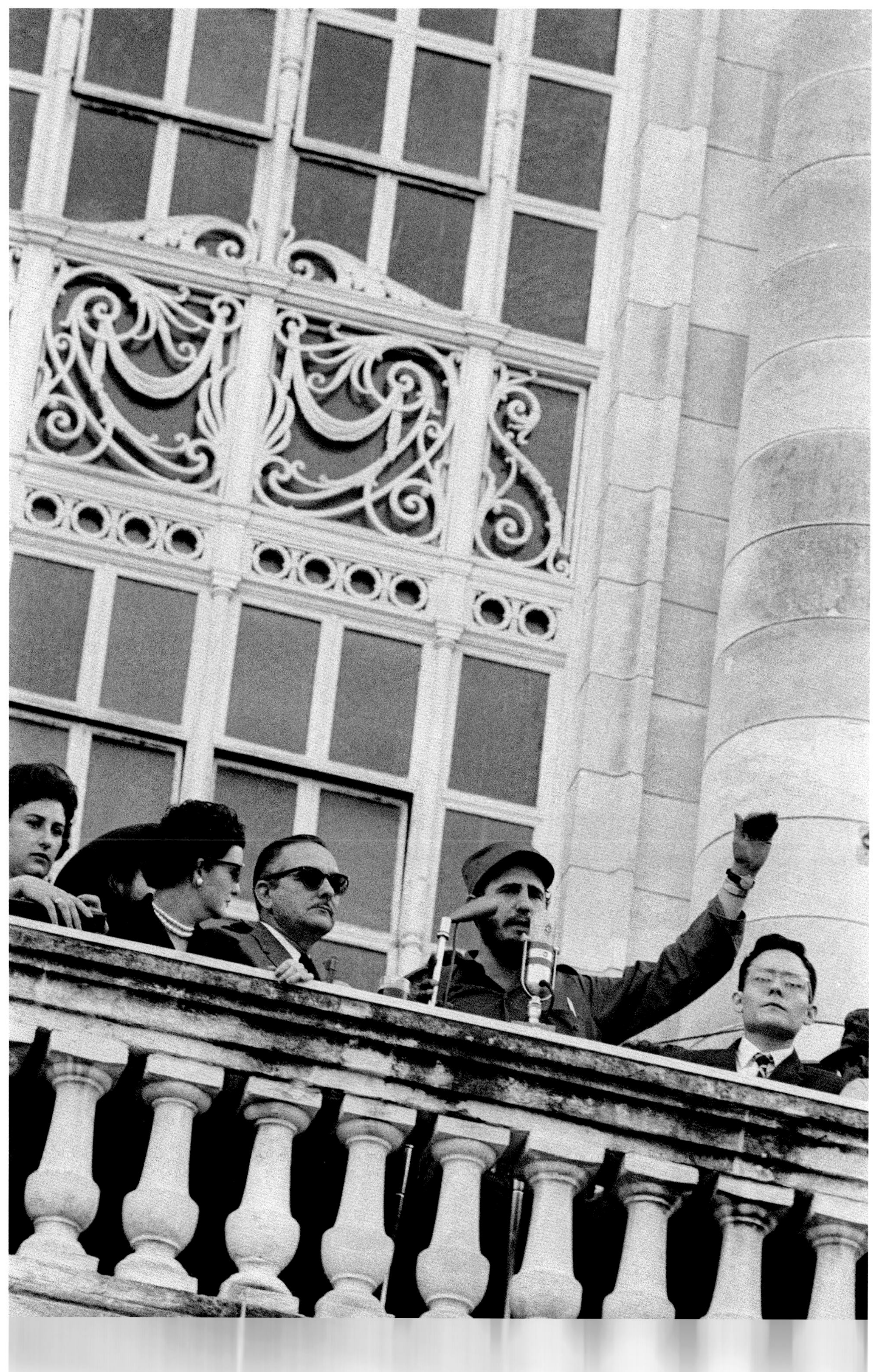

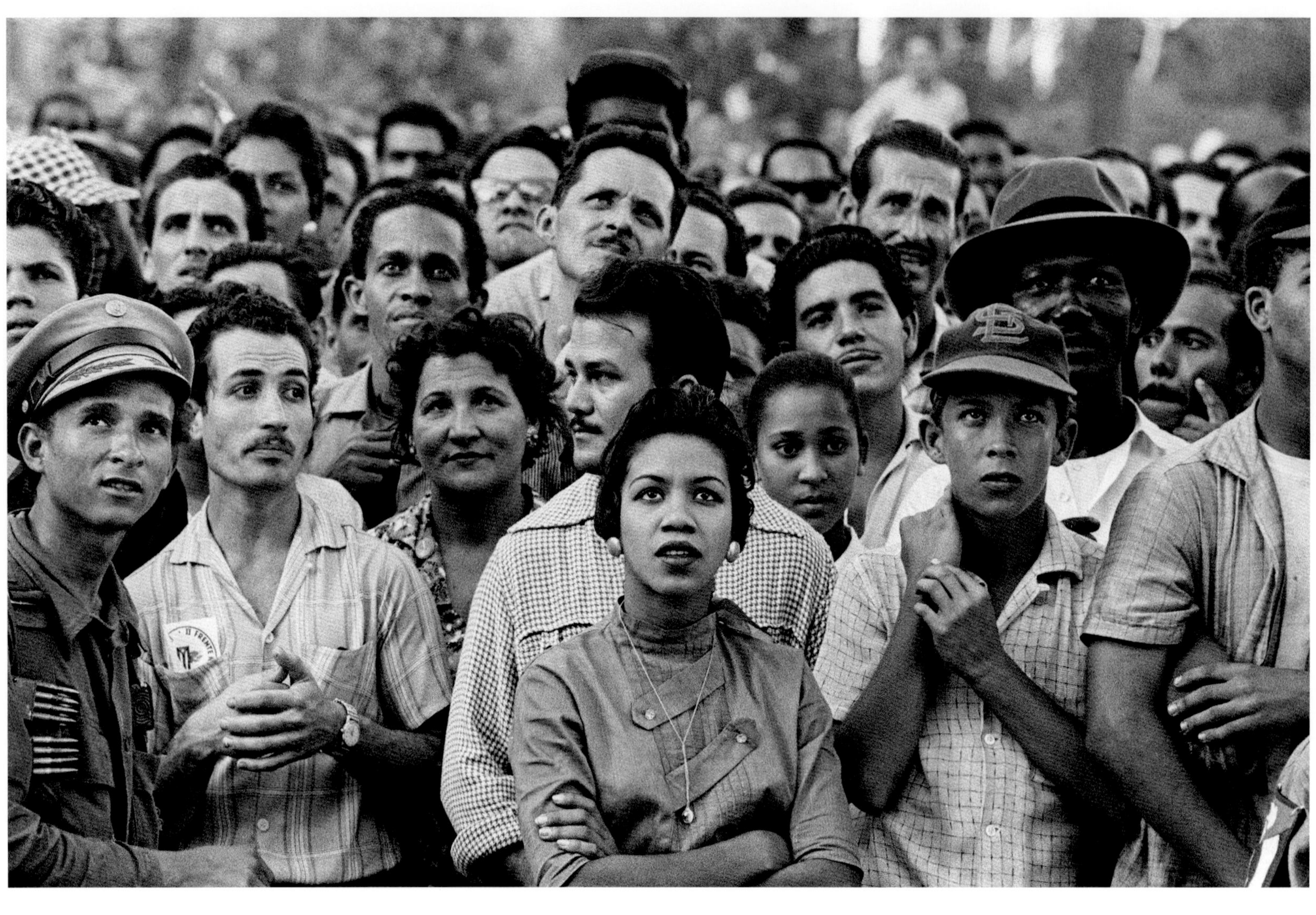

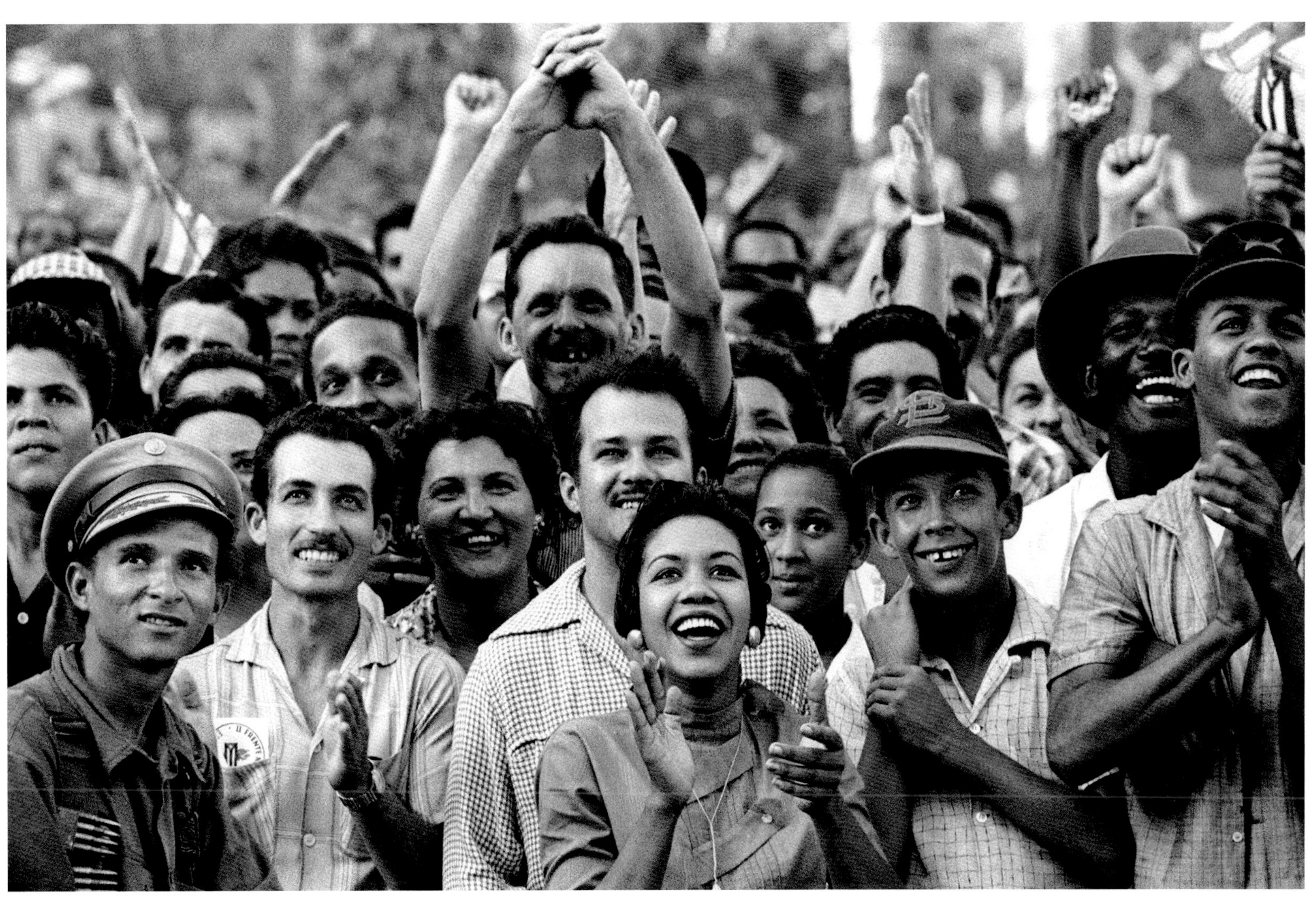

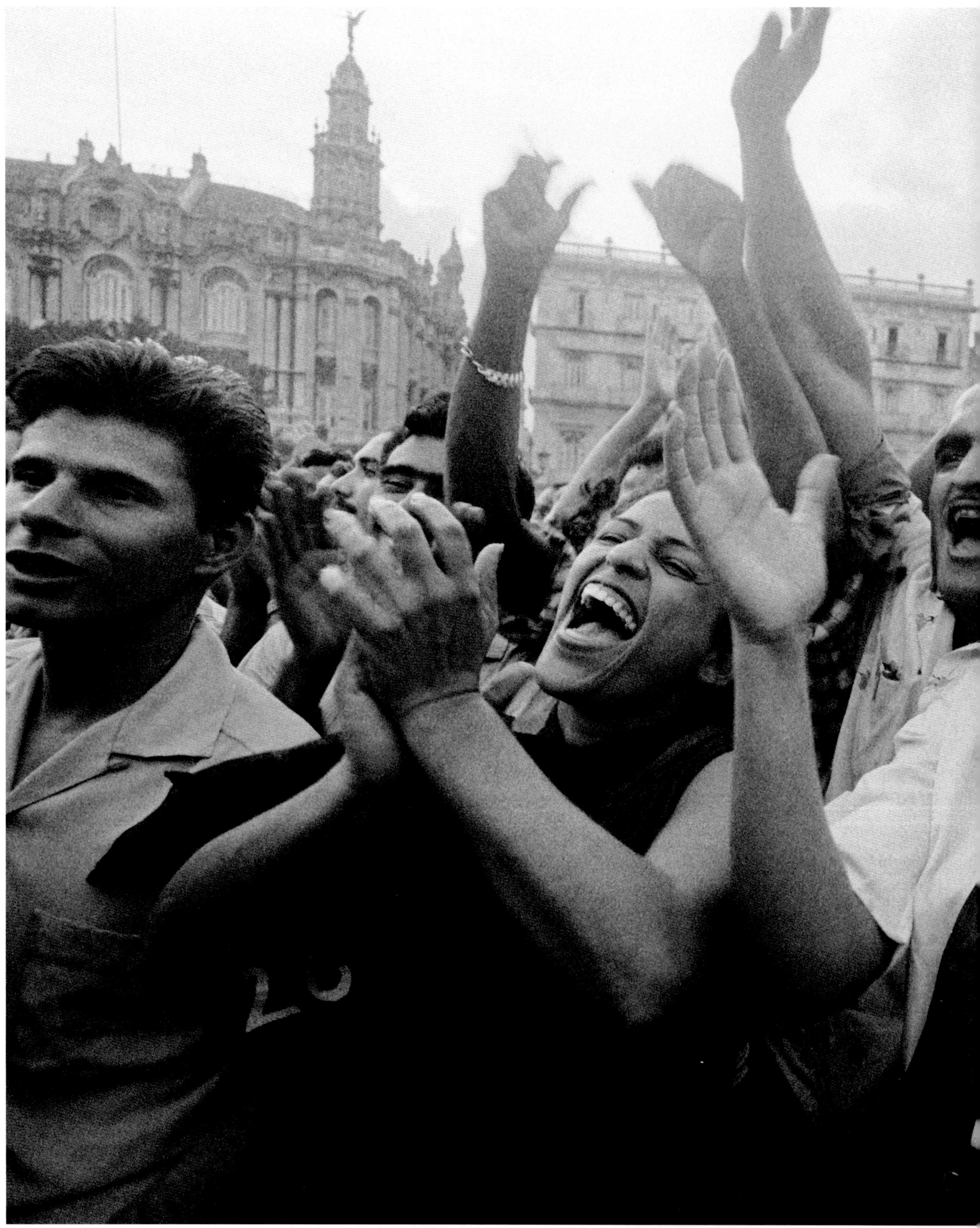

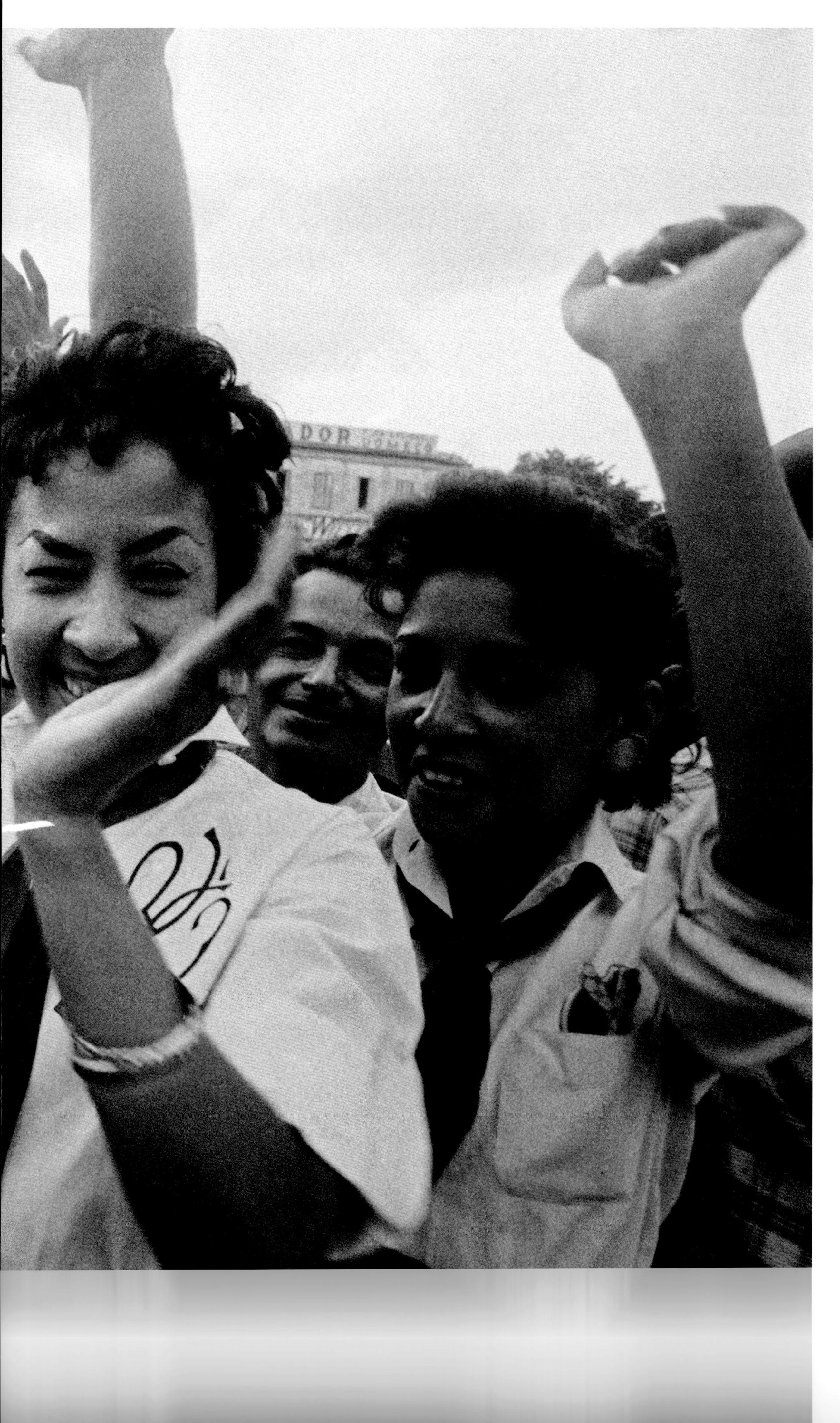

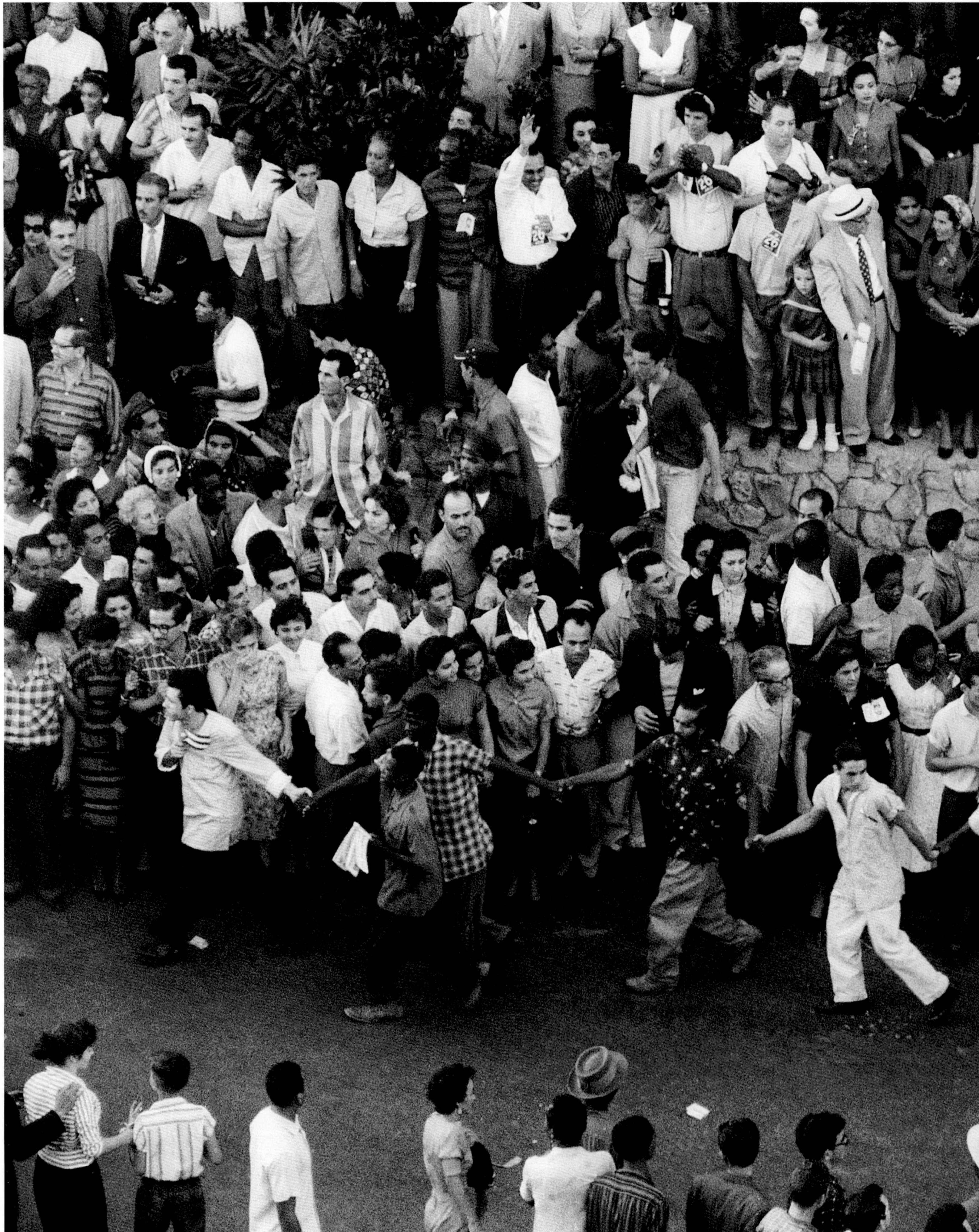

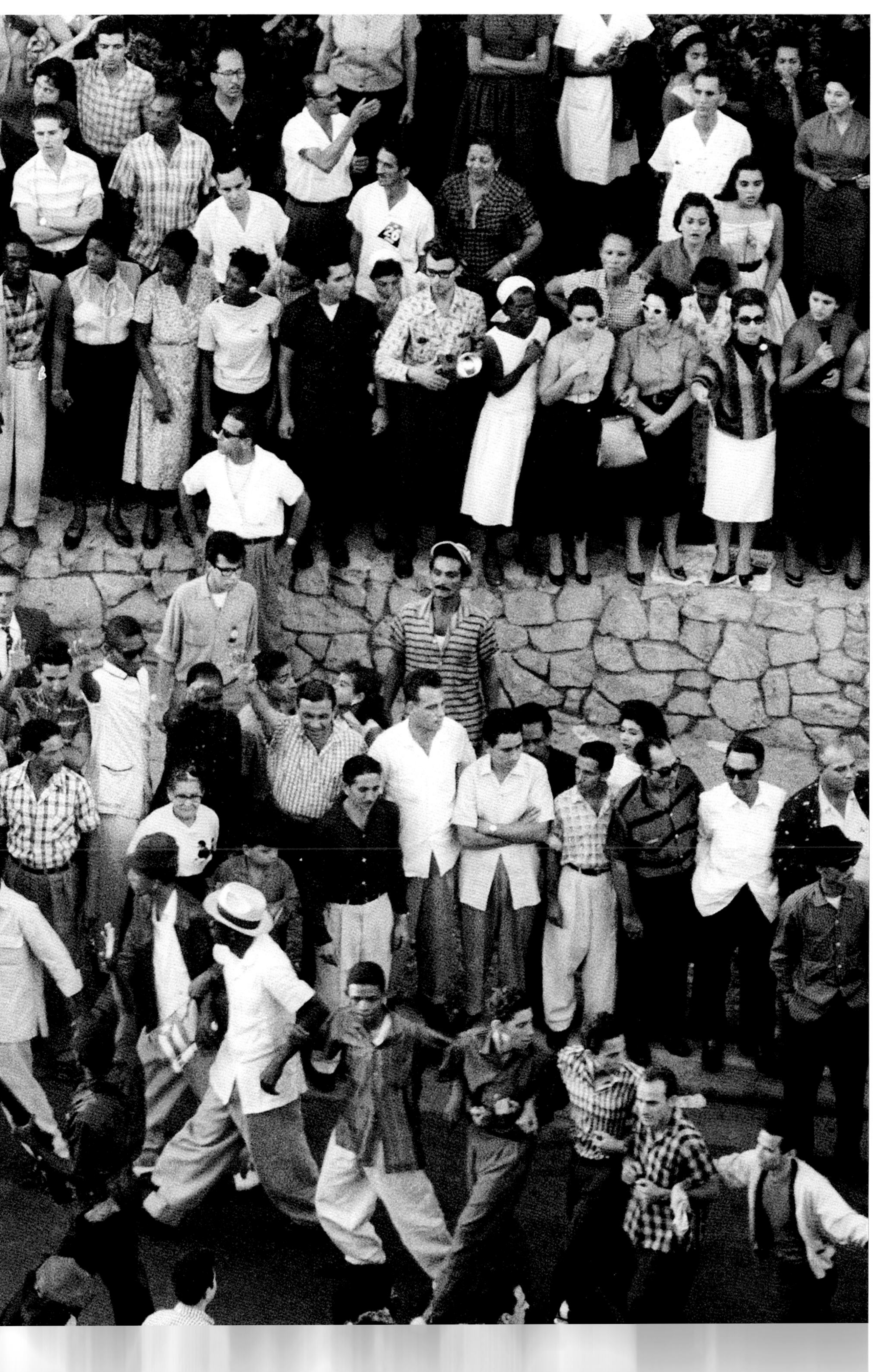

Fidel Castro, January 10, 1959

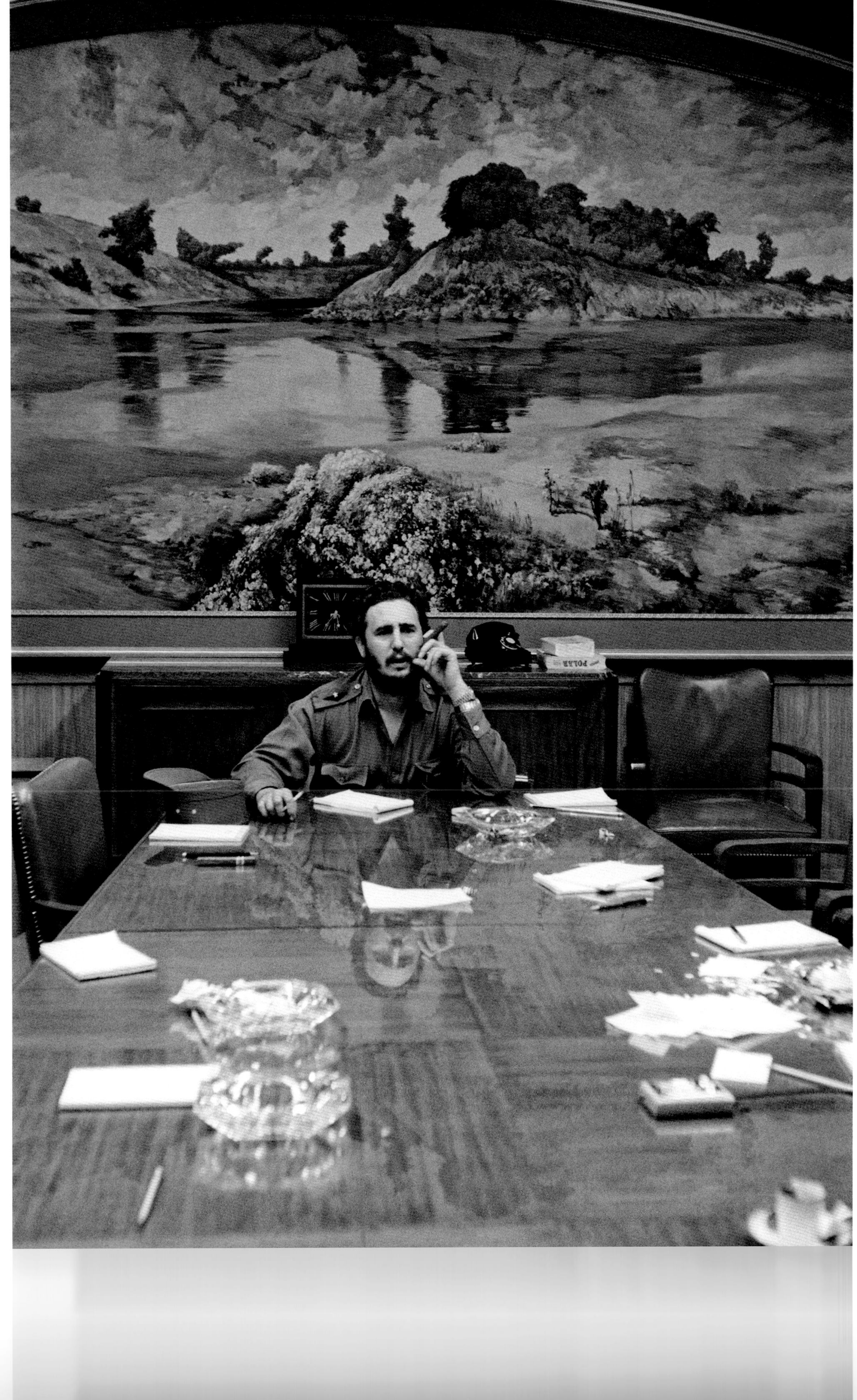

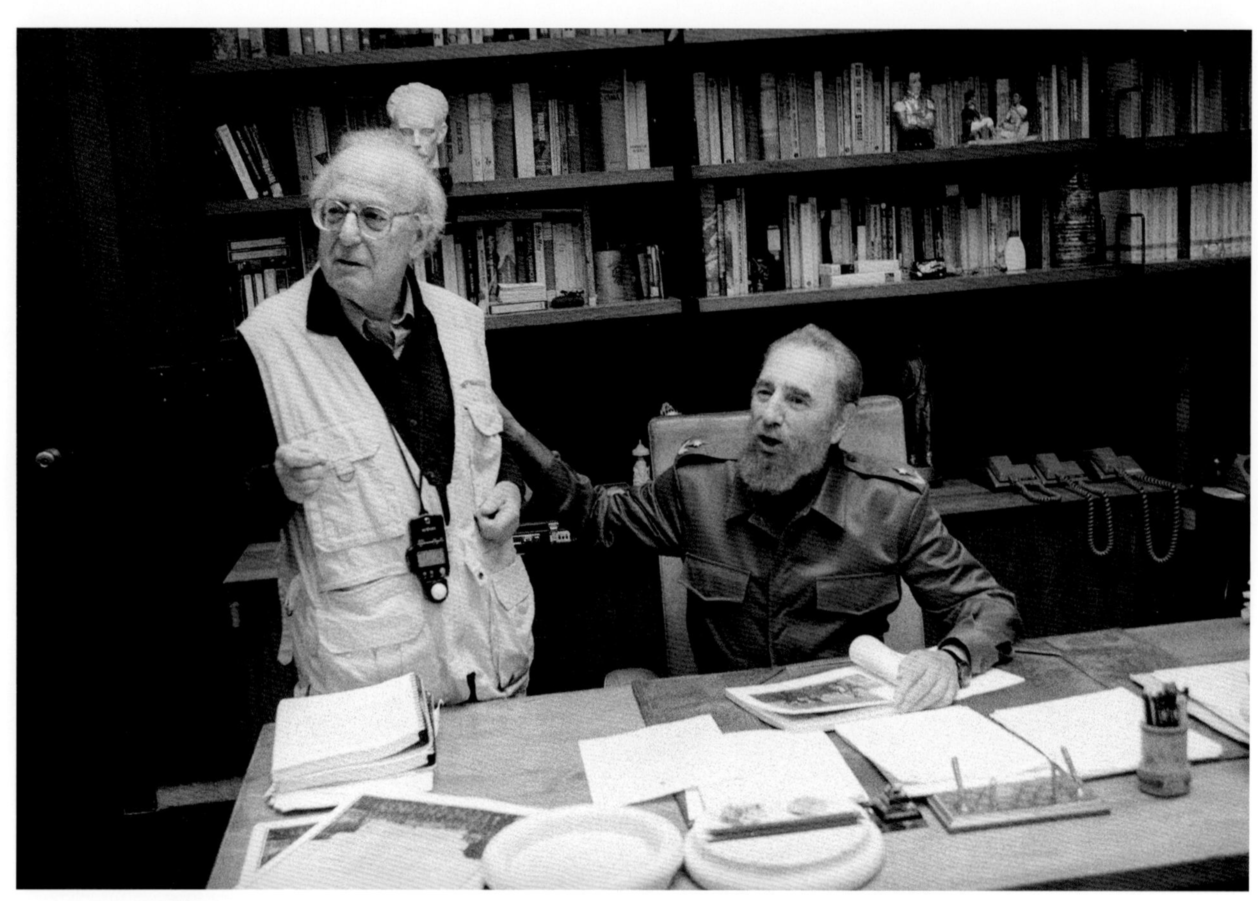

Burt's wife, Elena Prohaska Glinn, remembers when Burt journeyed to Havana to photograph Fidel and Gorbachev: "He called me on a lousy Cuba to New York connection and reported to me how Fidel looked so old. There was a long pause and I asked, 'and how did he think you looked?'"

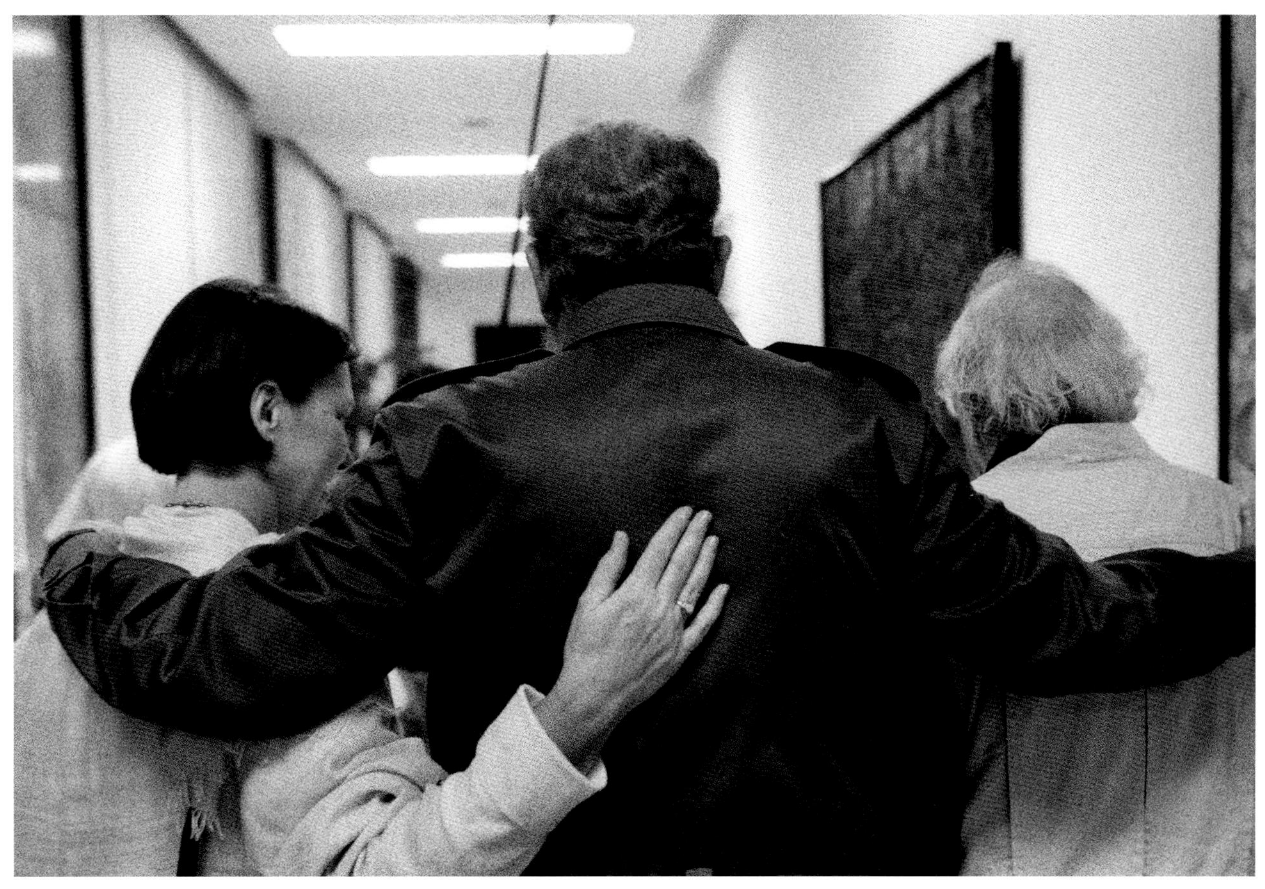

"This book is dedicated to our son Sam Glinn, who learned from Burt that a photo taken from the back view is often better than from the front."

Elena Prohaska Glinn

Edited by Michael Shulman and Tony Nourmand
Art Direction and Design by Joakim Olsson
Project Co-ordination and Text Edited by Alison Elangasinghe
Production Assistance by Rory Bruton
Pre-Press by HR Digital Solutions

First published 2015 by Reel Art Press, an imprint of Rare Art Press Ltd., London, UK.

www.reelartpress.com

First Edition
10 9 8 7 6 5 4 3 2 1

ISBN: 978-1-909526-31-0

The Day Havana Fell by Burt Glinn, originally published in *Havana: The Revolutionary Moment* (2002).
Rebel Victory in Cuba essay written in early 1960 by Barbara Miller, a Magnum employee (first in New York, later in Paris).

Printed by Graphius, Gent.